HOW WE GOT TO THE
MOON

The People, Technology, and Daring Feats of Science Behind Humanity's Greatest Adventure

JOHN ROCCO

CROWN BOOKS FOR YOUNG READERS
NEW YORK

This book,

from launch to splashdown,

is for Hayley.

Copyright © 2020 by John Rocco

All rights reserved. Published in the United States by Crown Books for Young Readers,
an imprint of Random House Children's Books, a division of Penguin Random House LLC, New York.

Crown and the colophon are registered trademarks of Penguin Random House LLC.

Visit us on the Web! rhcbooks.com

Educators and librarians, for a variety of teaching tools, visit us at RHTeachersLibrarians.com

Note: All measurements in this book are quoted in Imperial units, rather than
metric units, just as they were used during the time of Apollo. Many acronyms
are introduced throughout, as that was the shorthand language of the engineers.
This text conforms to the NASA Style Guide for NASA History Authors
and Editors, with some adaptations for use with young readers.

All art is created by John Rocco except for pp. 24, 141, and 217.
The following illustrations are exact replicas of historic documents. The author has chosen to correct any errors the
originals contained, setting off the corrections in brackets for clarity—p. 24: letter courtesy of the John F. Kennedy
Presidential Library; p. 141: astronaut menu courtesy of NASA; p. 217: Jack Garman's notes courtesy of NASA.

Library of Congress Cataloging-in-Publication Data
Names: Rocco, John, author.
Title: How we got to the moon : the people, technology, and daring feats of science
behind humanity's greatest adventure / John Rocco.
Description: First edition. | New York : Crown Books for Young Readers, [2020] | Includes bibliographical references
and index. | Audience: Ages 10 and up | Audience: Grades 4 and up | Summary: "This beautifully illustrated oversized
guide to the people and technology of the Moon landing by award-winning author/illustrator John Rocco is a must-
have for space fans, classrooms, and tech geeks." —Provided by publisher.
Identifiers: LCCN 2019040738 (print) | LCCN 2019040739 (ebook) | ISBN 978-0-525-64741-6 (hardcover) |
ISBN 978-0-525-64742-3 (library binding) | ISBN 978-0-525-64743-0 (epub)
Subjects: LCSH: Project Apollo (U.S.)—Juvenile literature. | Space flight to the moon—Juvenile literature.
Classification: LCC TL789.8.U6 A5811459 2020 (print) | LCC TL789.8.U6 (ebook) | DDC 629.45/4—dc23

The text of this book is set in 11-point Adobe Caslon Pro.
The illustrations in this book were created using pencil, watercolor, and digital painting.

MANUFACTURED IN CHINA
10 9 8 7 6 5 4 3 2
First Edition

CONTENTS

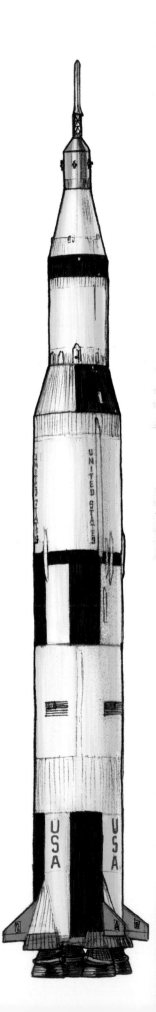

PART 1

A Race to the Moon   7

PART 2

Designing a Moon Rocket   27

PART 3

Building a Launch Vehicle   59

PART 4

Building a Spacecraft   93

PART 5

Staying Alive in Space   131

PART 6

Support on the Ground   155

PART 7

We Choose to Go to the Moon   193

Epilogue   241
Apollo Piloted Missions   242
A Note About Research   244
Acknowledgments   246
Sources   247
For Further Reading   249
Commonly Used Acronyms During Apollo   250
Index   251

"It's not a miracle. We just decided to go."
—Jim Lovell, astronaut

Between 1968 and 1972, we sent men in giant rocket ships to go to and explore the Moon. This project was called Apollo. For the first time in humankind's history, we left our planet and traveled to another celestial body. This effort is considered one of the greatest technological achievements of the human race. We didn't have cell phones, microcomputers, or the internet. What we did have was a goal: to put a man on the Moon and bring him back safely.

Pressing a foot into the lunar dust became the finish line in a race between two superpowers—the United States and the Soviet Union. Four hundred thousand people, in companies spread all over the United States, worked around the clock to help achieve this goal. To the men and women working on Apollo, it was more than an exploration of this new frontier called space; it was a race for survival. The American way of life was at stake.

The pages that follow attempt to explain how we did it, the challenges we faced along the way, and the ingenious solutions we came up with to get it done. The engineering of the Apollo missions may seem impossibly complex, but I assure you, every bit can be boiled down to the basic building blocks of science and mathematics.

Along the way, you will meet many people, though they represent only the tiniest fraction of the Apollo workforce. Some of them are well known while others are not, but each was an important contributor in this grand adventure.

This is the story of how we got to the Moon.

"Children, inspired by the excitement of spaceflight, have come to appreciate the wonder of science, the beauty of mathematics, and the precision of engineering. Young minds in our country and around the world now believe they can do great things. And they can, if they apply themselves as intensely as the Apollo workforce did four decades ago."

—Neil Armstrong, Apollo 11 commander,
on the 40th anniversary of the first Moon landing

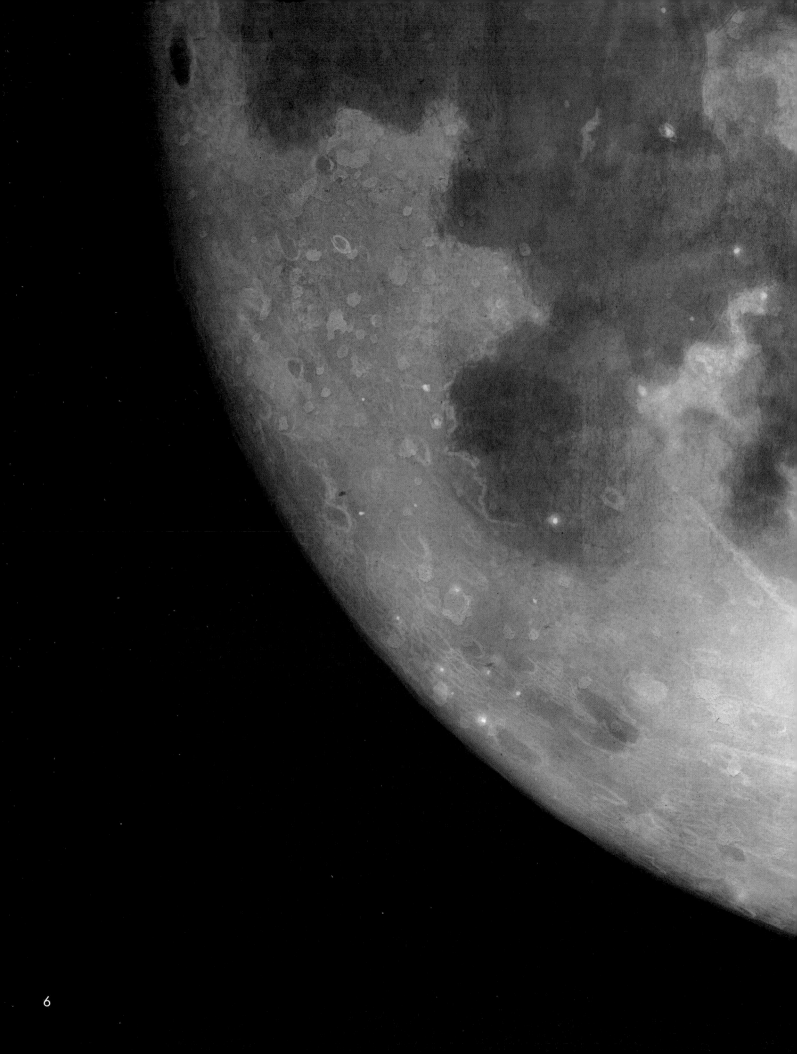

PART 1

A Race to the Moon

*"We choose to go to the Moon in this decade and do the other things,
not because they are easy, but because they are hard. . . ."*

—PRESIDENT JOHN F. KENNEDY,
SPEECH AT RICE UNIVERSITY, HOUSTON, TX, 1962

To understand how we got to the Moon and why we decided to go there, we must first travel back in time: This story begins in the year 1957, a dozen years after the end of World War II. Two superpowers have emerged—the communist Soviet Union and the democratic United States—both trying to prove to potential allies and the world that their ideas, politics, military, and way of life are superior.

Both sides possess nuclear bombs that could level entire cities, and they know using these bombs could devastate all of humanity—but they also know having these bombs gives them power, so each side continues to develop bigger and more terrible weapons. The two countries fight not on the battlefield, in a hot war, but with threats and technological achievements in what comes to be known as the Cold War.

As part of this effort, both countries are developing powerful new rockets. These rockets—born from the minds of German scientists—can be used to carry weapons higher, faster, and farther.

It becomes a race to prove technological superiority and global domination. Its pace is dazzling and frightening, and it will all come together, all its promise and threat, in a metal sphere about the size of a beach ball.

It all starts with a beep . . . beep . . . beep. People all over the world pick up the faint signal on shortwave radios, and Americans are listening with both fascination and terror.

The sound is coming from a silver orb less than two feet in diameter. It is the first artificial satellite, and the Russians launched it into the new frontier of space. They call it Sputnik, the Russian word for "fellow traveler"—in this case meaning "Earth's companion"—and it will circle the planet about every 90 minutes for weeks. The Soviet Union suddenly has a rocket capable of putting something into space, and the United States does not. Americans panic that the Russians will begin to put other things into space, like spy satellites or even atomic bombs.

SEMYORKA AND SPUTNIK

The Semyorka rocket, originally designed to carry nuclear warheads, was used to launch Sputnik into orbit. The two-stage rocket was 110 feet tall, with four engines on the outside and a single engine in the middle.

Sputnik was a hollow metal sphere 22.8 inches across, weighing 184 pounds. Its four long antennas sent out signals from the radio transmitter nestled inside. After Sputnik was in orbit for three weeks, the batteries ran out, but the satellite continued to silently orbit for another nine weeks before gradually falling back toward Earth and burning up in the atmosphere.

The First Rocket to Reach Space

During World War II, German scientists under the leadership of Wernher von Braun had developed a rocket called the A4, which was so powerful it could reach space. German army leaders realized that the A4 could carry bombs hundreds of miles to land on their enemies, and they immediately ordered the manufacture of thousands of them. They renamed the rocket the V-2 (V for "vengeance").

The scientists designing these rockets had different ideas about how they should be used; instead of carrying bombs, they could carry humans into outer space, and someday even to the Moon.

The Soviet Union and the United States each desperately wanted this rocket technology for its own military. When it was clear that Germany was going to lose the war, both countries took steps to acquire the technology and the scientists who created it.

A V-2 rocket on its mobile Meillerwagen launchpad

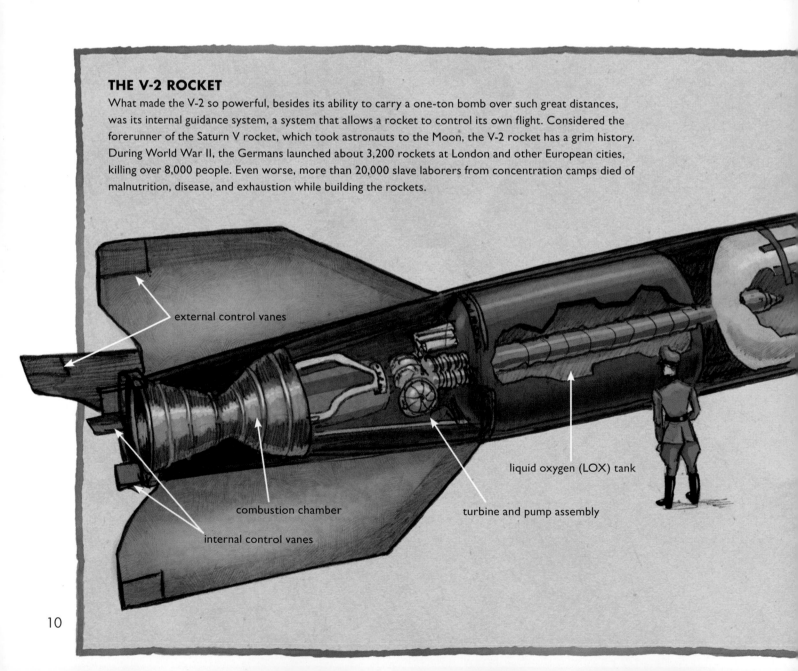

THE V-2 ROCKET

What made the V-2 so powerful, besides its ability to carry a one-ton bomb over such great distances, was its internal guidance system, a system that allows a rocket to control its own flight. Considered the forerunner of the Saturn V rocket, which took astronauts to the Moon, the V-2 rocket has a grim history. During World War II, the Germans launched about 3,200 rockets at London and other European cities, killing over 8,000 people. Even worse, more than 20,000 slave laborers from concentration camps died of malnutrition, disease, and exhaustion while building the rockets.

external control vanes

combustion chamber

internal control vanes

liquid oxygen (LOX) tank

turbine and pump assembly

German rocket scientists Hermann Oberth (third from right) and Wernher von Braun (second from right) in Berlin in 1930

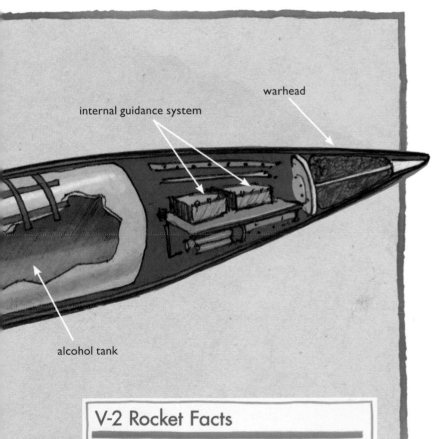

internal guidance system

warhead

alcohol tank

V-2 Rocket Facts

Length	45 ft. 11 in.
Diameter	5 ft. 5 in.
Weight	27,600 lb.
Payload	2,200 lb.
Maximum Altitude	128 mi.
Maximum Distance	200 mi.
Maximum Speed	3,580 mph

In a mission called Operation Paperclip, the United States managed to secure Wernher von Braun, the mastermind behind the V-2, along with over a hundred other German scientists. They were brought back to the United States to advance rocket technologies for the military. Von Braun again pushed for the rockets to be used for space exploration, but just as in Germany, military leaders were not interested. He and the rest of the scientists were eventually stationed in the small town of Huntsville, Alabama, where they continued to build weapons for the military, waiting for their chance to create rockets that would carry humans into space.

Meanwhile, the Soviet Union also had a rocket mastermind: Sergei Korolev. Like von Braun, Korolev was most interested in using rockets for space exploration, but was tasked with creating rockets to carry bombs. After years of research and design, Korolev persuaded Russian leaders to let him put a small satellite into Earth orbit as a demonstration of the Soviet Union's superior technology. That satellite was Sputnik—the starter gun in the race for space.

Wernher von Braun (1912–1977)

Pioneer of Space Travel

As a young boy, Wernher von Braun was fascinated with the idea of space exploration, which was fueled by reading the science-fiction novel *From the Earth to the Moon* by Jules Verne. Soon after, he discovered the book *The Rocket into Planetary Space* by physicist Hermann Oberth, which inspired him to study calculus and trigonometry in order to master the physics of spaceflight.

At 18 von Braun joined the German Society for Space Travel, and in order to further his ambition, he went to work for the German army to develop liquid-fueled rockets. By the time he was 30 years old, von Braun's rocket team had developed the A4 rocket (renamed the V-2 by the German army).

Carrying a one-ton warhead, the first V-2 was launched toward England in September 1944, and after hearing of its success, von Braun said, "The rocket worked perfectly, except for landing on the wrong planet."

On May 2, 1945, von Braun and his team of scientists and engineers surrendered to the Americans, because they believed coming to the United States would allow them to work on rockets with the goal of space travel.

Once in the United States, von Braun began publishing his ideas and concepts in popular magazines. He even collaborated with Walt Disney on a series of films in which he explained his ideas for traveling to the Moon and Mars.

Von Braun later became the director of NASA's Marshall Space Flight Center and the chief architect of the Saturn V launch vehicle.

The Space Race

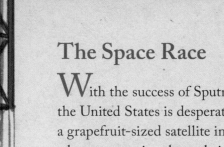

Wﬁith the success of Sputnik, the Russians have clearly made a statement to the world, and the United States is desperate to respond. On December 6, 1957, the US Navy is about to send a grapefruit-sized satellite into space aboard a rocket called Vanguard. Unlike the Russians, who are secretive about their operations, the Americans televise their launch for all to see. Viewers watch with awe and anticipation as the countdown begins. Finally, the United States is going to get off the starting block.

The powerful rocket comes to life, spewing clouds of smoke and fire as it begins its liftoff. But after rising only four feet off the ground, it falls back to the launchpad in a fireball that underscores the American failure. Newspapers call it "Flopnik" and "Stayputnik."

After the second Vanguard rocket explodes less than a minute into its flight, it seems the United States will never get off the ground. Then, finally, on January 31, 1958, a Redstone rocket built by von Braun's team successfully launches the orbital satellite Explorer 1. However, the victory is short-lived: the Soviet Union announces that two months earlier, they put a dog, named Laika, into orbit aboard Sputnik 2.

EXPLORER 1

The first US satellite, Explorer 1, launched in 1958, was also the first orbiting object to provide scientific data about space. Built by physicist William H. Pickering and his team at the Jet Propulsion Laboratory (JPL) in California, it carried with it several experiments to measure radiation, temperature, and micrometeorites. It sent back data continually for nearly four months and remained in Earth orbit until 1970.

Explorer 1 Facts

Length	80 in.
Diameter	6 in.
Weight	31 lb.

antenna wire

external temperature gauge

high-power transmitter

cosmic-ray and meteorite package

NASA Is Born

1958

The American people are anxious and angry that the United States is so far behind the Soviet Union in the space race. President Dwight D. Eisenhower has to do something. He believes that the United States' efforts toward space activity need to be unified into one agency. So on July 29, 1958, Congress creates the National Aeronautics and Space Administration. NASA will include all the different organizations that are working on spaceflight technology, including Wernher von Braun and his team in Huntsville.

Eisenhower also believes that in order to win this race, we will need more brainpower. On September 2, 1958, he signs the National Defense Education Act (NDEA), which provides funding for American schools, increasing the amounts of science and mathematics taught in classrooms.

Project Mercury
1958–1963

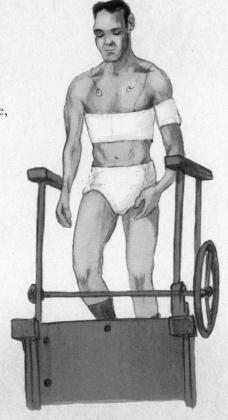

The United States knows that the Russians are planning to put a man into space, so NASA's first priority is to find American candidates suitable for spaceflight. This project is named Mercury, and its goal is to put a man into Earth orbit and return him safely. But what kind of person will have the right capabilities? Mountain climbers, deep-sea divers, race-car drivers, even circus performers and those in many other professions are considered. Finally, it's determined that military test pilots will be the best candidates, because of their experience with advanced airplanes and risky situations with unsure outcomes. The size of the space capsule means that they cannot be taller than five feet 11 inches. They also have to be under 40 years old and in peak physical condition.

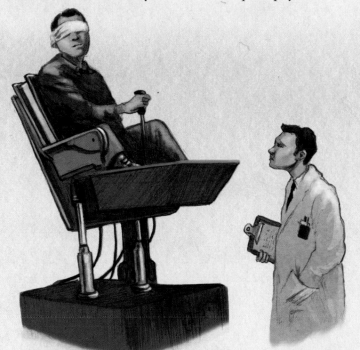

From the 508 military test pilots screened, 36 are invited to the Lovelace Clinic in Albuquerque, New Mexico, for an extensive series of grueling mental and physical exams. Of the 18 candidates who complete the exams and score the highest, only seven are chosen.

William R. "Randy" Lovelace II (1907–1965)
Physician

Randy Lovelace spent years working with the Army Air Corps studying the effects of extreme altitudes on pilots, many times using himself as a test subject. In 1958, he was hired by NASA to help select potential astronauts for Project Mercury. In 1964, Lovelace was appointed NASA's director of space medicine, but less than a year later he and his wife died in a private plane crash near Aspen, Colorado.

The Mercury 7

At a press conference on April 9, 1959, NASA introduces the Mercury 7 to the world. They're called astronauts, from the Greek words *astron*, meaning "star," and *nautes*, meaning "sailor" or "voyager." These seven "star voyagers" are put on the cover of *Life* magazine and immediately become national heroes, even though it will be another two years before the first one will ride into space. In the meantime, each will be involved in specific aspects of the design and planning of Project Mercury.

Over the next several months, the Mercury program gets under way with the testing of various rockets. Even though several of the rockets blow up, each astronaut is eager to be the first American in space. Much to their dismay, on January 31, 1961, it is a chimpanzee named Ham who takes the first trip.

The Mercury 7: Front row (left to right): Walter M. "Wally" Schirra Jr., Donald K. "Deke" Slayton, John H. Glenn Jr., and M. Scott Carpenter. Back row: Alan B. Shepard Jr., Virgil I. "Gus" Grissom, and L. Gordon "Gordo" Cooper Jr.

Ham (1957–1983)

First Chimpanzee in Space

NASA wasn't sure if a human could perform tasks while in space, so it sent a chimpanzee as a test. During Ham's 16-minute flight, he was tasked to push a lever every time he saw a blue light illuminate. If he did it correctly, he received a banana pellet. If he did it wrong, he got a mild electric shock to his foot. Although terrified, Ham performed well and survived the flight into space with only some minor bruising on his nose.

After the flight, Ham retired from NASA to live at the National Zoo in Washington, DC. He died in January 1983 and is buried at the New Mexico Museum of Space History.

German rocket scientist Guenter Wendt holds Ham prior to his flight.

Female pilot Geraldyn "Jerrie" Cobb takes a turn in the gimbal rig, used to train astronauts to control a tumbling spacecraft.

Lovelace's Woman in Space Program

Randy Lovelace, who designed the series of exams used to select the Mercury 7, thinks that women should also get the opportunity to be astronauts. He feels so strongly that he develops a privately funded initiative—the Woman in Space Program—that runs from 1960 to 1962. Nineteen experienced female pilots endure all the exact same tests as the men. Of this group, 13 women not only pass the tests, but many of them score higher than their male counterparts. Lovelace takes the results to NASA, but the women are denied the opportunity to become part of its space program. NASA states that all candidates are required to be military test pilots, and women are not allowed to be military pilots at this time. It will be another 16 years before NASA hires women to be astronauts.

Soviet Firsts

While the Mercury 7 astronauts watched NASA rockets blow up on the launchpad time after time, the Russians continue to lead the space race.

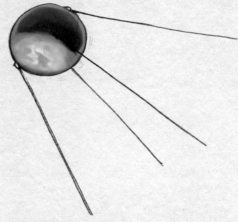

October 4, 1957: The first artificial satellite (Sputnik) is launched.

November 7, 1957: A dog named Laika becomes the first animal to travel in space. (Laika died from heat-related stress before reentry.)

September 14, 1959: The Luna 2 probe lands on the Moon, becoming the first spacecraft to reach the lunar surface.

August 19, 1960: Two dogs, named Belka and Strelka (along with a rabbit, 42 mice, and two rats), orbit Earth for 24 hours. All the animals survive the flight.

April 12, 1961: Yuri Gagarin becomes the first human in space.

First in Space

Yuri Gagarin (1934–1968)

"Orbiting Earth in the spaceship, I saw how beautiful our planet is. People, let us preserve and increase this beauty, not destroy it!"

Yuri Gagarin had dreamed of flying airplanes ever since he was a boy. On April 12, 1961, as a cosmonaut (the Russian term for *astronaut*), he became the first human being to travel into space. His spacecraft, Vostok 1, orbited Earth in a little under two hours. The Vostok was not designed to land safely, so it required that Gagarin eject from the spacecraft four miles above Earth and parachute down the rest of the way. Upon landing in a large field, Gagarin was met by a surprised woman and child who thought he had come from outer space. They were right!

Valentina Tereshkova (b. 1937)

"A bird cannot fly with one wing only. Human spaceflight cannot develop any further without the active participation of women."

Twenty-six-year-old Valentina Tereshkova boarded the Vostok 6 spacecraft on June 16, 1963, and flew into the history books. She became the first woman in space, as well as the first civilian in space and the only woman in history to have been on a solo space mission. Tereshkova orbited Earth 48 times during her three-day mission and spent more time in space than all the American astronauts combined up to that point. It would be another 20 years before NASA put a woman in space: Sally Ride, on the Space Shuttle Challenger. In 2013, Tereshkova offered to go on a one-way trip to Mars if the opportunity arose.

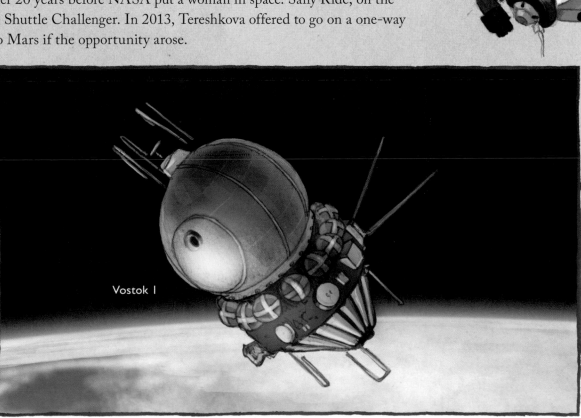

Vostok 1

Alan B. Shepard Jr. (1923–1998)

First American in Space

Alan Shepard was the Mercury astronaut chosen for the first US piloted space mission. Compared with Yuri Gagarin's flight, which orbited Earth, Shepard's flight would be a simple one: go up into space and come back down.

At 5:15 a.m. on May 5, 1961, Shepard crammed himself into the tiny Mercury capsule he had named Freedom 7. Cloud cover and technical difficulties kept delaying the flight as Shepard waited, lying on his back, for over three hours. And then another problem arose: Shepard had to pee. The launch crew was not expecting this. The whole flight was supposed to last only 20 minutes, so they hadn't equipped the capsule with a urine collection device. To pull Shepard out of the capsule so he could go to the bathroom would delay the launch even further. They finally all agreed that he should just go in his spacesuit.

After Shepard relieved himself, the launch proceeded, at 9:34 a.m. An estimated 45 million people in the United States watched it live on television. Although it took place three weeks after Gagarin's flight, it was the United States' first space success, and Shepard became an American hero.

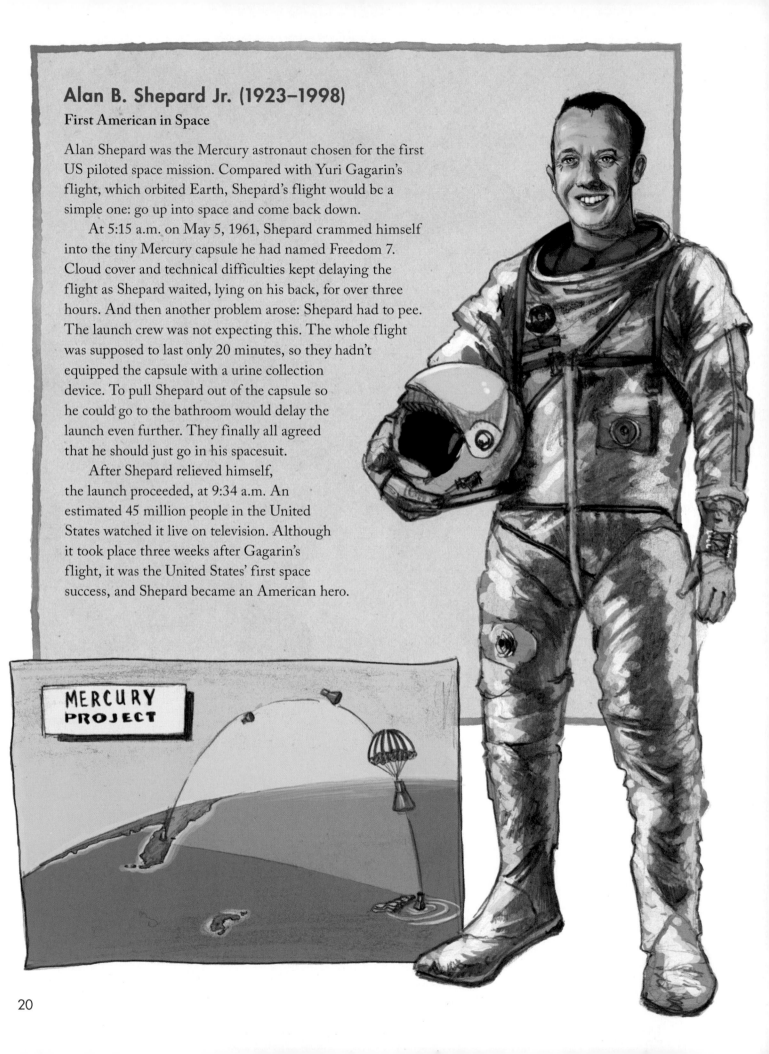

MERCURY PROJECT

Mercury Missions

Riding in tiny capsules on top of modified military missiles, the other Mercury astronauts continue with daring flights into space over the next two years. Although the Americans meet with success, they have yet to surpass the achievements of the Russians in human spaceflight.

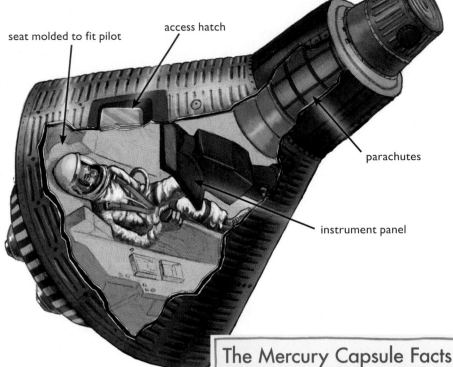

seat molded to fit pilot

access hatch

parachutes

instrument panel

The Mercury Capsule Facts

Height	6 ft. **10** in.
Diameter	6 ft. **2.5** in.
Weight	**3,000** lb.

Liberty Bell 7 • July 21, 1961
Astronaut: Virgil I. "Gus" Grissom
Mission Purpose: A second suborbital flight
Flight Duration: 15 minutes, 37 seconds
Problem: The capsule sinks in the ocean during recovery.

Friendship 7 • February 20, 1962
Astronaut: John H. Glenn Jr.
Mission Purpose: Putting the first American into Earth orbit
Flight Duration: 4 hours, 55 minutes, 23 seconds
Problem: A false warning indicating that the heat shield had come loose causes the mission to be cut short after three orbits.

Aurora 7 • May 24, 1962
Astronaut: M. Scott Carpenter
Mission Purpose: Duplicating John Glenn's flight
Flight Duration: 4 hours, 56 minutes, 5 seconds
Problem: A communication error causes Carpenter to land 250 miles from the recovery area, forcing a delay in the rescue effort.

Sigma 7 • October 3, 1962
Astronaut: Walter M. "Wally" Schirra Jr.
Mission Purpose: A six-orbit engineering test flight
Flight Duration: 9 hours, 13 minutes, 11 seconds

Faith 7 • May 15, 1963
Astronaut: L. Gordon "Gordo" Cooper Jr.
Mission Purpose: Evaluating the effects of one full day in space
Flight Duration: 34 hours, 19 minutes, 49 seconds

The seventh Mercury 7 astronaut, **Donald K. "Deke" Slayton,** is grounded before his flight in 1962 due to a heart condition. Instead of leaving the astronaut corps, he moves to flight crew operations and in 1966 becomes its director. His new responsibilities include selecting the crews for future spaceflights. His flight status will be restored in 1971, allowing him to fly into space on the Apollo-Soyuz mission in 1975.

Where Space Begins

It's difficult to say where "space" begins, because there is no definable point where the atmosphere of Earth stops. Our atmosphere gradually gets thinner and thinner the farther you get from the ground. You can even find traces of Earth's atmosphere as far away as the Moon.

That said, the Kármán Line, as defined by the International Aeronautical Federation, is officially where space starts. It is 62.1 miles above sea level. The engineer and physicist Theodore von Kármán was the first person to calculate the point where the atmosphere was too thin to give an airplane lift (see p. 30).

ATMOSPHERIC LAYERS

thermosphere 53–621 mi.

mesosphere 31–53 mi.

stratosphere 6–31 mi.

ozone layer

troposphere 0–6 mi.

International Space Station • 254 mi.

Alan Shepard in Freedom 7 • 116 mi.

Kármán Line • 62.1 mi.

airplanes • 6 mi.

Theodore von Kármán (1881–1963)

Aerospace Engineer

Born in Budapest, Hungary, Theodore von Kármán immigrated to the United States in 1930. He developed many important aeronautical technologies, and in 1944, while working at the California Institute of Technology (Caltech), he cofounded the Jet Propulsion Laboratory.

Hubble Space Telescope • 336 mi.

Yuri Gagarin in Vostok 1 • 203 mi.

Sputnik • 134 mi.

John Glenn on Friendship 7 • 154 mi.

A Bold Step

Only four months into his presidency, John F. Kennedy has some big decisions to make. Just days after Yuri Gagarin becomes the first human in space, Kennedy asks Vice President Lyndon B. Johnson what the United States and the three-year-old NASA organization can do to overtake the Soviet Union. In a memo, he writes:

THE WHITE HOUSE

WASHINGTON

April 20, 1961

MEMORANDUM FOR

VICE PRESIDENT

In accordance with our conversation I would like for you as Chairman of the Space Council to be in charge of making an overall survey of where we stand in space.

1. Do we have a chance of beating the Soviets by putting a laboratory in space, or by a trip around the moon, or by a rocket to land on the moon, or by a rocket to go to the moon and back with a man. Is there any other space program which promises dramatic results in which we could win?

2. How much additional would it cost?

3. Are we working 24 hours a day on existing programs. If not, why not? If not, will you make recommendations to me as to how work can be speeded up.

4. In building large boosters should we put [our] emphasis on nuclear, chemical or liquid fuel, or a combination of these three?

5. Are we making maximum effort? Are we achieving necessary results?

I have asked Jim Webb, Dr. Weisner, Secretary McNamara and other responsible officials to cooperate with you fully. I would appreciate a report on this at the earliest possible moment.

Johnson meets with Wernher von Braun and top officials at NASA, the army, and the navy, and has answers for Kennedy by the following week, but nothing is definitive.

May 6, 1961

In the parking lot behind the Old Executive Office Building in Washington, DC, the head of NASA, James Webb, asks his associate administrator, Robert Seamans Jr., if he thinks we can land a man on the Moon by the end of the decade. Seamans considers it for a minute and then replies, "Yes."

May 25, 1961

Kennedy makes a speech to Congress

"I believe that this nation should commit itself to achieving the goal, before this decade is out, of landing a man on the Moon and returning him safely to the Earth. No single space project in this period will be more impressive to mankind, or more important for the long-range exploration of space; and none will be so difficult or expensive to accomplish."

In one fell swoop, John F. Kennedy moves the finish line of this space race. It's no longer about occupying space in low-Earth orbit or building a space station, or anything else the Russians are clearly capable of winning—Kennedy wants the United States to land a man on the Moon and return him safely to Earth before December 31, 1969. NASA has eight and a half years to get it done.

And with that, the Apollo program is born.

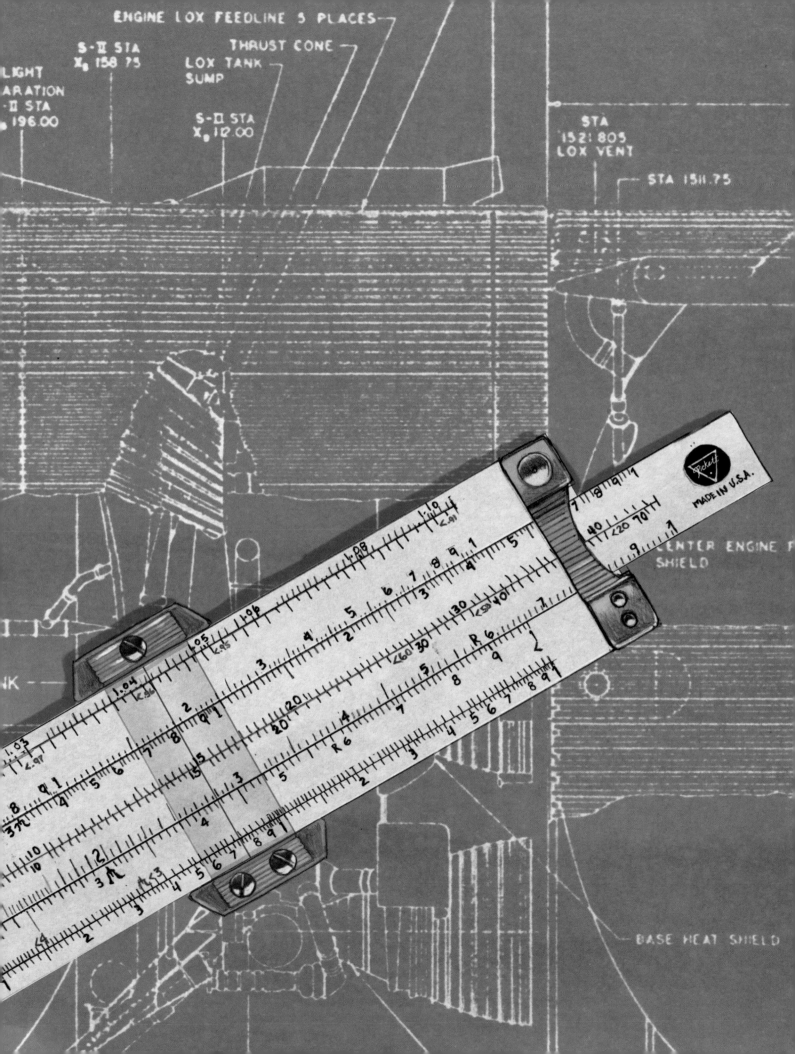

GOX LINE

PART 2

Designing a Moon Rocket

"The dream of yesterday is the hope of today and the reality of tomorrow."

—ROBERT H. GODDARD, ROCKETRY PIONEER

The goal has been set. The deadline has been given. Now we just have to figure out how to do it.

People have been thinking about the Moon since at least the beginning of recorded history. Some people, like Jules Verne (1828–1905), wrote stories about traveling there and landing on it. Scientists like Wernher von Braun and Sergei Korolev read those stories and spent most of their lives thinking about how to do it.

It is not a simple thing to send a man to the Moon. There is so much to think about, so much to calculate, so much to do to make it safe. We will need to invent things that don't exist, try things that have never been done, and make sure everything works . . . perfectly.

NASA Gets a Mission

The leaders at NASA are thrilled! What a challenge. They are tasked with figuring out a way to send a human being 240,000 miles away, land him on the Moon, and get him back safely. What kind of spaceship will they need? What kind of rocket will go that far, and how will it work? Will an astronaut be able to survive in space that long? The questions keep piling up, and NASA has little time to work out the answers. The clock is ticking, and the stakes are unimaginably high.

If we don't get to the Moon first, the Russians will.

A problem this wide-ranging and complex can be solved only by an extraordinary number of minds working together. NASA starts hiring engineers by the busload. Most of them are fresh out of college. They have no idea how to get a man on the Moon, but they all understand Newton's laws of motion, which are the foundation of how rockets work.

NEWTON'S LAWS OF MOTION

Isaac Newton described the three laws of motion that are the basis for modern physics in *Principia Mathematica*, published in 1687.

First Law of Motion

Every object is in a state of rest or motion and does not change unless acted upon by a force.

If a marble is rolling along and isn't slowed down by the friction of the ground or another force, it will continue rolling forever. This can be changed only if an outside force does something to the marble.

Second Law of Motion

Force is mass times acceleration.

Mass is the amount of matter in an object, commonly measured by how much it weighs. If you exert the same force on two objects of a different mass, you will get different accelerations. The smaller mass will exhibit greater acceleration. Shooting a marble with your thumb will give the marble a strong acceleration across the floor. Shooting a bowling ball with your thumb will result in much less acceleration because of its larger mass.

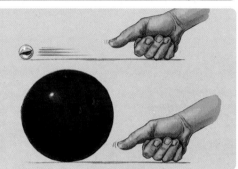

Third Law of Motion

For every action, there is an equal and opposite reaction.

When a cannonball is shot out of a cannon with a particular amount of force, it will exert the exact same amount of force on the cannon, sending the cannon in the opposite direction. The cannon doesn't move nearly as far as the cannonball, though, because it has a much greater mass.

HERO'S REACTION ENGINE

About 2,000 years ago, the engineer and mathematician Hero of Alexandria invented a machine that used the same laws of physics that rockets do today. His machine, called an aeolipile, was quite simple. Water in a sealed kettle was heated to boiling over a fire. As the steam expanded, it traveled up two tubes into a sphere, which had two L-shaped openings. The steam would force its way out of the openings, causing the sphere to spin. Although the machine demonstrated basic mechanical principles, it had no useful purpose and was more of a curiosity or an entertaining toy.

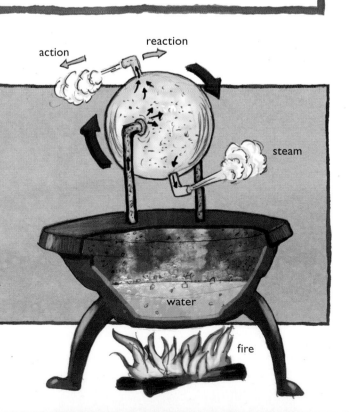

How an Airplane Flies

In 1958, most of the experienced engineers in the new NASA organization had worked at companies that built airplanes. The astronauts were former pilots. Both groups know about the forces that affect how things fly in our atmosphere.

In an airplane, the wing is designed to create lift to overcome the airplane's weight. The engine is designed to produce thrust to overcome drag and move the airplane forward.

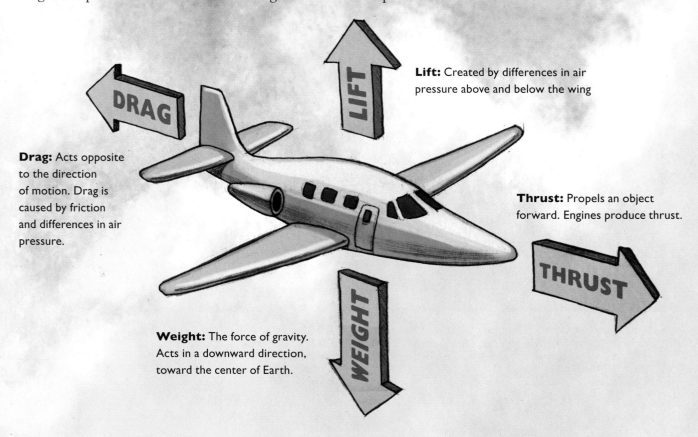

Lift: Created by differences in air pressure above and below the wing

Drag: Acts opposite to the direction of motion. Drag is caused by friction and differences in air pressure.

Thrust: Propels an object forward. Engines produce thrust.

Weight: The force of gravity. Acts in a downward direction, toward the center of Earth.

HOW A WING CREATES LIFT

A wing is shaped and tilted so the air moving over it moves faster than the air moving under it. This creates a lower air pressure above the wing and a higher air pressure below it. The result is an upward push on the wing.

You may have felt this when sticking your hand out the window of a moving car. If you tilt your hand, you will feel a force pushing your hand upward. That is lift.

HOW A JET ENGINE CREATES THRUST

Jet engines take cold air and compress it while adding combustible fuel. This causes the highly compressed gases to expand quickly out the backs of the engines, creating forward thrust.

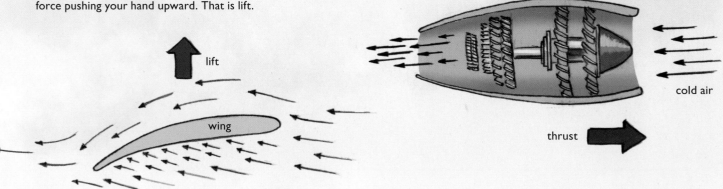

How a Rocket Flies

NASA's engineers have to recalibrate their thinking in order to design a rocket that will fly in the vacuum of space. There is no air in space, so there will be no lift, causing wings to be useless. The only drag a rocket will encounter is during the first few minutes of flight, until it leaves the atmosphere. The engineers are left with two variables: weight and thrust.

Both jets and rockets use combustion engines to create thrust. In order to create combustion, an engine needs fuel and oxygen. Jet engines use the oxygen present in the atmosphere in combination with jet fuel to create combustion. A rocket will need to bring its own source of oxygen with it in order to create combustion in the vacuum of space.

WEIGHT

THRUST

The dartlike shape of a rocket is an aerodynamic design, creating the least amount of drag during its travel through the atmosphere on the way to space.

The fins on a rocket are designed to stabilize the rocket's flight through the atmosphere and are unnecessary once it reaches space.

THRUST TO WEIGHT

Thrust is the force that a rocket engine produces. It is measured in pounds. A one-pound rocket will need to create one pound of thrust in order to equalize the amount of gravity pulling it toward Earth. In order to fly away from Earth, the rocket must create more pounds of thrust than the overall weight of the rocket. In this example, as the fuel burns, the weight of the rocket decreases and the acceleration increases.

This is Newton's second law of motion at work: force = mass × acceleration ($F = ma$)

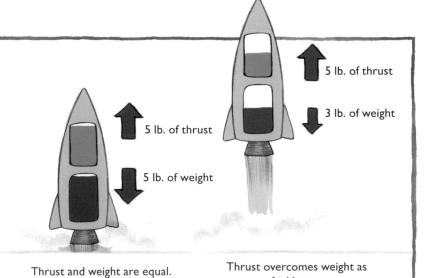

5 lb. of thrust

3 lb. of weight

5 lb. of thrust

5 lb. of weight

Thrust and weight are equal.

Thrust overcomes weight as fuel burns.

Robert H. Goddard (1882–1945)

Father of Modern Rocketry

Robert Goddard was 17 years old when he had the vision that would define his life's work. He was up in a cherry tree doing some pruning, thinking about the book he'd been reading by H. G. Wells, *The War of the Worlds*. All of a sudden, an idea shot into his brain: what if he could invent a device that could fly to Mars?

"As I looked toward the fields at the east," he later wrote, "I imagined how wonderful it would be to make some device which had even the possibility of ascending to Mars, and how it would look on a small scale if sent up from the meadow at my feet. . . . I was a different boy when I descended the tree from when I ascended, for existence at last seemed very purposive."

Goddard went on to study math and physics, and pursued his ideas for making a rocket that could fly into space. In 1919, after years of research and experimentation, Goddard published one of the most important papers on rocketry, called "A Method of Reaching Extreme Altitudes."

An editorial in *The New York Times* heavily criticized Goddard and his work, saying that a rocket couldn't work in the vacuum of space because it would have nothing to push against. It said Goddard lacked the knowledge that was taught daily in high schools.

The comments hurt Goddard, but he chose to ignore them and press on with his research. To prove them wrong, he rigged a pistol loaded with a blank cartridge to a spindle inside a sealed bell jar and pumped out all the air, creating a vacuum. Using electricity, he fired the pistol, which spun around the spindle. This proved beyond a doubt that a propulsion engine could work in the vacuum of space.

Then on a cold March day in 1926, standing in the snow at his aunt Effie's farm in Auburn, Massachusetts, Goddard launched the first liquid-fueled rocket. It flew for a brief 2.5 seconds and reached a height of only 41 feet, but it changed rocketry forever.

As Apollo 11 headed for the Moon, *The New York Times* issued an apology: "Further investigation and experimentation have confirmed the findings of Isaac Newton in the 17th Century and it is now definitely established that a rocket can function in a vacuum as well as in the atmosphere. *The Times* regrets the error."

action

reaction

Sealed bell jar simulating the vacuum of space. The firing of the gun causes it to move in the opposite direction, rotating it on the spindle.

How Rocket Engines Work

For every action there is an equal and opposite reaction.
Newton's third law of motion is the fundamental principle behind rockets. Heat burns the rocket's fuel, which causes gases to expand and rush out the open end, the nozzle, of the rocket at great speeds, creating thrust. This causes the rocket to move in the opposite direction.

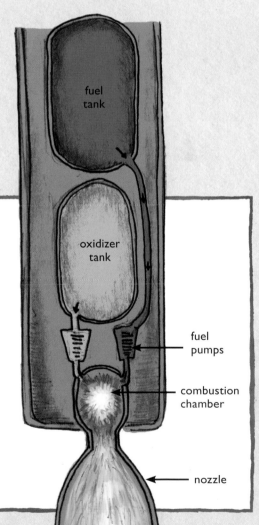

propellant

fuse

guide stick

FIREWORK ROCKETS

Around the year 1000, the Chinese discovered that if one end of a lit firework rocket was left open, the firework would fly off in the opposite direction from the flame. They later added a guide stick in order to control the firework's flight. These were the first true rockets.

These rockets work by igniting a substance called a propellant that has been packed inside a tube, leaving a hollow area in the center. The hot gases created from the burning propellant shoot out the open end.

SOLID-FUEL ROCKETS

Solid-fuel rockets work on the same principle as firework rockets, but the hollowed-out core, or channel, acts as the combustion chamber. If the rocket needs to be more powerful, the channel can be molded into a star shape, thereby creating a larger surface area to burn. As with firework rockets, once solid-fuel rockets are lit they cannot be shut down, and will burn until all the propellant is gone.

cross section
with star-shaped
channel

fuel
tank

oxidizer
tank

fuel
pumps

combustion
chamber

nozzle

LIQUID-FUELED ROCKETS

For liquid-fueled rockets, fuel pumps send two propellants into a combustion chamber, where they ignite and expand, sending a blast out through the nozzle, which creates thrust. The larger the rocket engine, the greater the amount of thrust it can create.

Unlike firework rockets and solid-fuel rockets, liquid-fueled rockets *can* be shut down, by simply cutting off the fuel.

The Slide Rule: The Tool That Got Us to the Moon

A whole lot of calculations. That is what the engineers at NASA are faced with as they try to figure out how to send a spacecraft to the Moon. How much fuel is needed? How much does it weigh? How do these measures change over time? Mass, thrust, Earth's gravity, and the Moon's gravity all have to be taken into consideration. The calculations become even more complex when you consider that not only is Earth rotating, but the target (the Moon) is orbiting around Earth. Hundreds of thousands of calculations will have to be made to figure out how to hit that target.

Desktop computers, which could solve these equations in seconds, are decades away from being invented. Even the pocket calculator won't be introduced until 1972.

What the engineers do have is a slide rule, or "slipstick"— a mechanical analog computer. It looks like a complicated ruler made from three strips of wood or plastic. The middle strip slides back and forth and has a cursor that can be positioned to help find corresponding numbers. With this tool, a scientist or engineer can quickly multiply and divide, and compute complex equations.

HOW A SLIDE RULE WORKS

Figure A. On the left-hand side of the slide rule, you will see several letters indicating the scales. There is also a sliding piece of clear plastic with a line down the middle, called the cursor.

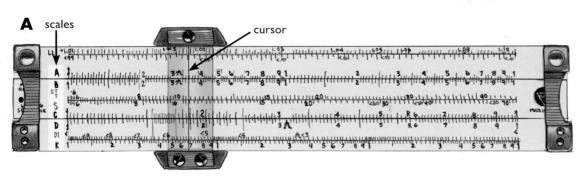

Figure B. Here's an example of how to use the slide rule to find the answer to a fairly simple math problem: What is 3 × 2.5? You line up the number 1 on the C scale with the number 3 on the D scale. Then, with the sliding cursor, find 2.5 on the C scale, and the answer (7.5) is revealed on the corresponding line on the D scale.

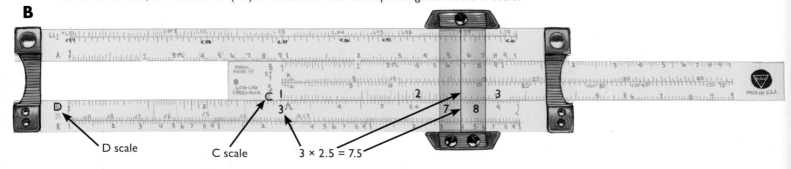

You might consider this an extremely elaborate approach, but with practice and patience, the slide rule helped engineers accurately calculate the complex equations necessary to get us to the Moon.

Today, calculators and computers have replaced the slide rule, but it was a common tool before 1972.

The Human Computers

Walking the halls of the NASA offices in the early 1960s, you will often overhear an engineer ask for a computer. He isn't asking for a machine. He is actually asking for an employee. And not just any employee, but one of the many hundreds of brilliant women NASA employs to do the tedious but critical work of computing the large and complex mathematical equations that are necessary for space exploration.

Langley Research Center, now part of NASA, has been hiring female mathematicians since before World War II. But because of the gender inequality of the times, it is next to impossible for women to study engineering with an eye toward a career. Instead, they take jobs as computers, even though many of them are more qualified than the male engineers. The computers work with pencils, slide rules, and primitive calculators that are the size of small suitcases.

African American computers, given the derogatory name "Colored Computers," have it worst of all. They are segregated from the white computers, and opportunities for advancement are almost nonexistent. However, a few of these women, like Katherine Johnson (see p. 36), will prove themselves so invaluable to the program that they are able to break out of the group and take on some of the most important work done at NASA, including helping to calculate the trajectories for the launching and landing of the Apollo 11 mission to the Moon.

THE FRIDEN STW-10 CALCULATING MACHINE

This electromechanical calculator assisted the human computers with complex arithmetic during the Apollo program. This type of machine had been in use since the 1930s. Unlike the slide rule, which could help solve only one problem at a time, the STW-10 could keep a running tally of multiple calculations. Also unlike the slide rule, it weighed 40 pounds and could not fit in a pocket.

Katherine Johnson (1918–2020)

NASA Mathematician

"I don't have a feeling of inferiority. Never had. I'm as good as anybody, but no better."

On February 20, 1962, astronaut John Glenn was going to climb into a capsule strapped to the top of a ballistic missile. If his mission went as planned, he would be the first American to orbit Earth. All the preparations had been made. A new, nonhuman computer, made by IBM, had calculated his trajectory and landing numbers. Glenn was ready to put his life at stake, but he had one important request in the weeks leading up to the mission. He wanted Katherine Johnson to run the numbers by hand to make sure they were right. It took her almost two days to do the calculations—but when she had completed them, Glenn had the final confirmation he needed.

Katherine Johnson was born in West Virginia, and even as a young girl, she loved numbers and saw the beauty in mathematics. She would count the steps to school, the steps to church, the dishes in the sink. . . . "Anything that could be counted, I did," she later said. After graduating from college at 18, Johnson worked as a schoolteacher. Then in 1953, a rare opportunity opened up at the National Advisory Committee for Aeronautics (NACA) in Hampton, Virginia. NACA was hiring African American women as computers for space research. Johnson jumped at the chance.

Her work was outstanding—so swift and accurate that, after NACA had become NASA, she was assigned to work in the Space Task Group. Her calculations enabled Alan Shepard to become the first American in space, and she worked on many Mercury, Gemini, and Apollo missions, including Apollo 11.

Johnson continued to work for NASA until 1986. She was awarded the Presidential Medal of Freedom by President Barack Obama in 2015, and in 2017, when she was 99, NASA dedicated a research facility in her name.

Katherine Johnson's love of mathematics, and her own sheer grit, helped her rise above the segregation and sexism of the time in a profession dominated by white men. Her numbers helped get us to the Moon.

The Thing About Gravity

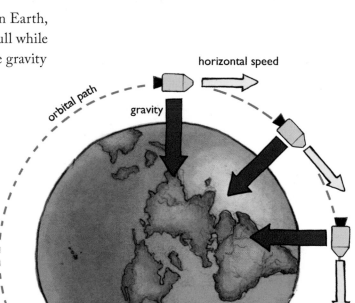

The force of gravity is everywhere. You cannot escape it.

Gravity is the mutual attraction between two objects. The greater the mass of an object, the greater its gravitational pull. Earth keeps the Moon in orbit using gravity, just as the Sun keeps Earth in orbit with its gravitational pull. Earth has a gravitational pull on you, too. That is what keeps you from simply floating away.

Because the Moon has a much smaller mass than Earth, you will not feel the same amount of gravitational pull while standing on its surface. The Moon has one-sixth the gravity of Earth. For example, if you weigh 120 pounds on Earth, you would weigh only about 20 pounds on the Moon.

Astronauts in low-Earth orbit, or in an expanded orbit while heading to the Moon, may have the illusion of zero gravity, a term meaning "weightlessness," but what they're really experiencing is a constant sensation of falling. After all, that's what they're doing. A spacecraft in orbit has enough speed that it is perfectly balanced between horizontal motion and falling back to Earth.

WEIGHTLESSNESS

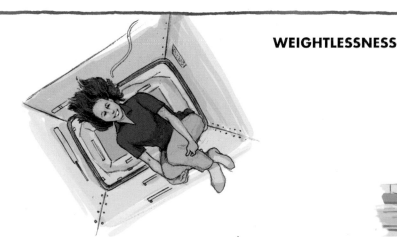

The International Space Station flies at roughly 17,500 miles per hour around Earth. It's in a continuous state of free fall, which gives the astronauts the sensation of being in zero gravity.

It's the same feeling you get when you suddenly drop down in a roller coaster or jump off a diving board. For a brief second, you feel weightless.

Earth

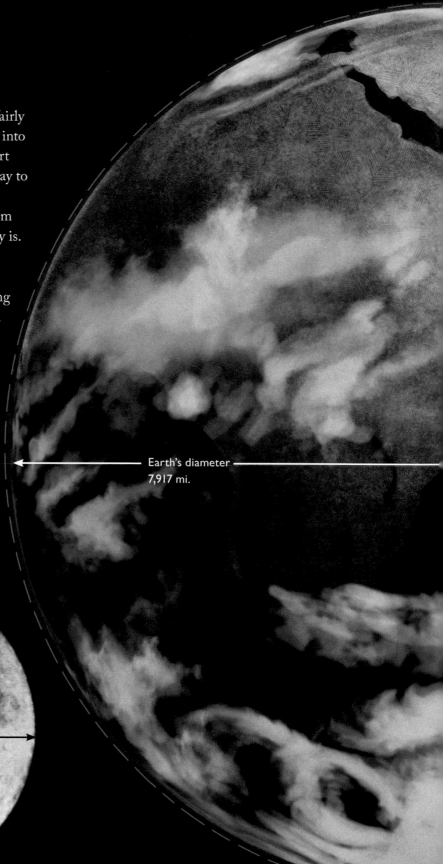

Average distance between Earth and the Moon (238,500 miles)

How Far Away Is the Moon?

After Project Mercury, NASA's engineers feel fairly confident that they know how to put an astronaut into orbit around Earth. Now it is time for them to start thinking about how to send an astronaut all the way to the Moon.

To get a grasp of the complexity of this problem we have to look at how far away the Moon actually is.

The Mercury flights traveled about 125 miles from Earth. If you were to drive that distance in a car, it would take you a little over two hours. Going the 238,500 miles from Earth to the Moon would take almost six months of nonstop driving.

We're used to seeing diagrams in books of Earth and the Moon very close to each other, but what we often overlook is that they're not to scale. Most diagrams of the Earth-Moon system or the solar system can't be shown to scale, because the planets are so far apart that it would be impossible to put them on one page and have any detail at all.

Earth's diameter
7,917 mi.

Moon's diameter
2,159 mi.

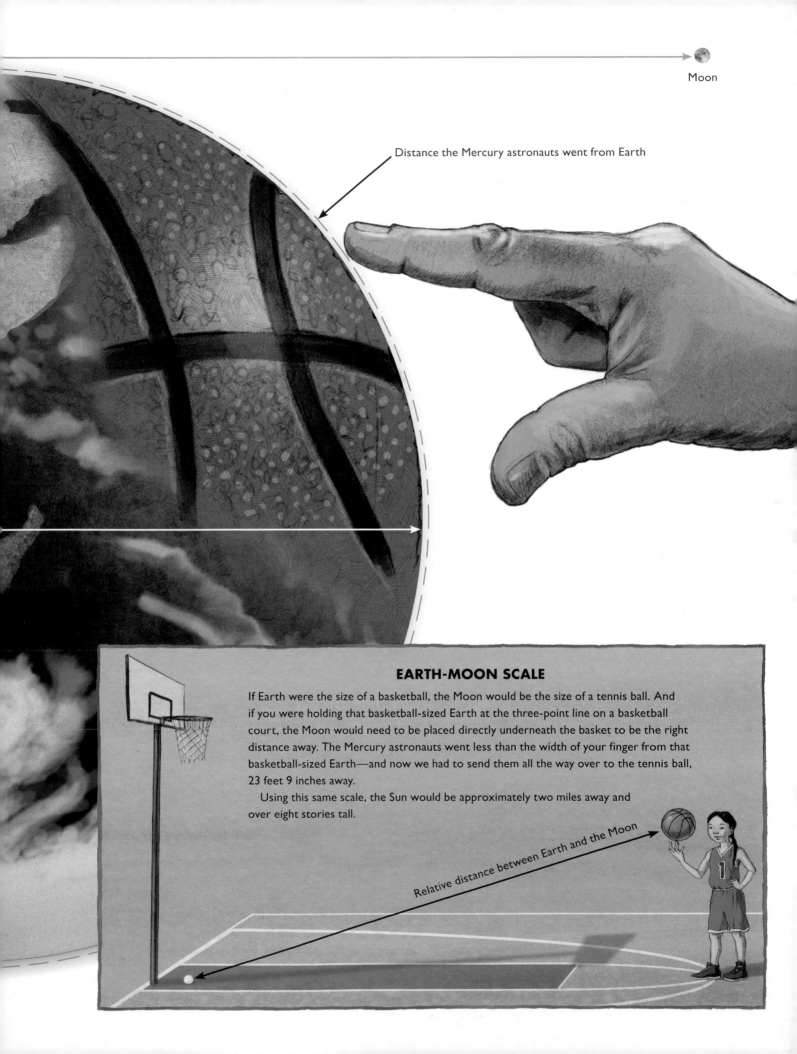

Moon

Distance the Mercury astronauts went from Earth

EARTH-MOON SCALE

If Earth were the size of a basketball, the Moon would be the size of a tennis ball. And if you were holding that basketball-sized Earth at the three-point line on a basketball court, the Moon would need to be placed directly underneath the basket to be the right distance away. The Mercury astronauts went less than the width of your finger from that basketball-sized Earth—and now we had to send them all the way over to the tennis ball, 23 feet 9 inches away.

Using this same scale, the Sun would be approximately two miles away and over eight stories tall.

Relative distance between Earth and the Moon

Getting into Orbit and Heading to the Moon

Now the NASA engineers have the problem of sending a piloted, completely outfitted spacecraft on a journey beyond orbit, all the way out to the Moon and back.

Earth Orbital Velocity

The human computers calculate that a rocket must travel 4.9 miles per second (about 17,500 miles per hour) to get into orbit around Earth. At this speed, known as orbital velocity, the rocket will overcome Earth's gravity enough to be perfectly balanced between falling back to Earth and heading out to space. This balance creates an orbital path around Earth (see p. 37). Anything less than 4.9 miles per second, and the rocket will fall back to Earth.

Earth Escape Velocity

In order to break free of its orbit, the spacecraft will need to either slow down or speed up. If the spacecraft slows down by firing its engines in the direction of its movement, Earth's gravity will eventually pull it back to the ground. But if the spacecraft speeds up by firing its engines in the opposite direction of its movement, its orbit will extend outward. The lowest point of the orbit is called the perigee, and its highest point is called its apogee.

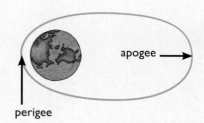

perigee   apogee

If the spacecraft increases its speed to seven miles per second (25,200 miles per hour) at the exact right moment, it will extend its apogee so far out that lunar gravity will begin to pull it toward the Moon. This is called escape velocity. By the time the spacecraft reaches the Moon, this velocity will cause it to whip around the Moon and begin a long fall back to Earth.

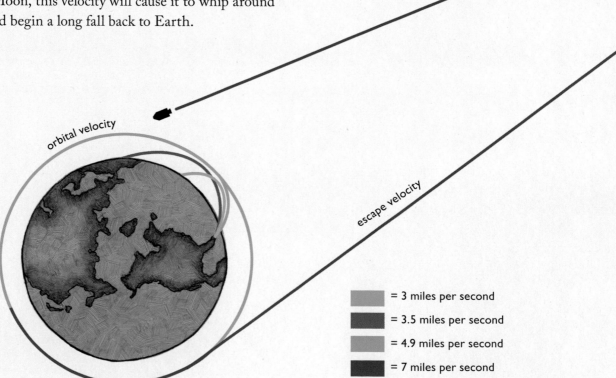

orbital velocity

escape velocity

■ = 3 miles per second

■ = 3.5 miles per second

■ = 4.9 miles per second

■ = 7 miles per second

Lunar Orbital Velocity

However, the engineers calculate that if the spacecraft slows down to one mile per second (3,600 miles per hour) as it goes around the far side of the Moon, it will fall into a lunar orbit. This can be accomplished by burning the spacecraft's engines in the direction of its movement. They call this Lunar Orbit Insertion (LOI).

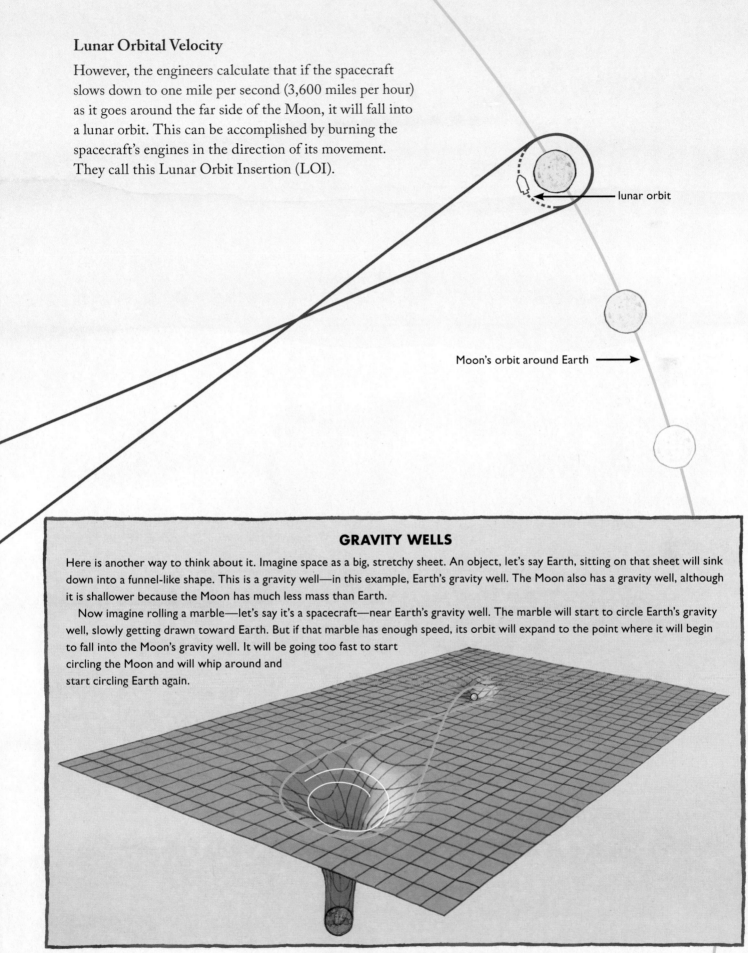

lunar orbit

Moon's orbit around Earth

GRAVITY WELLS

Here is another way to think about it. Imagine space as a big, stretchy sheet. An object, let's say Earth, sitting on that sheet will sink down into a funnel-like shape. This is a gravity well—in this example, Earth's gravity well. The Moon also has a gravity well, although it is shallower because the Moon has much less mass than Earth.

Now imagine rolling a marble—let's say it's a spacecraft—near Earth's gravity well. The marble will start to circle Earth's gravity well, slowly getting drawn toward Earth. But if that marble has enough speed, its orbit will expand to the point where it will begin to fall into the Moon's gravity well. It will be going too fast to start circling the Moon and will whip around and start circling Earth again.

Questions, Questions, and More Questions

NASA's engineers need to know more about the Moon before they can build a spacecraft to land on it. There are countless unknowns. Are there so many rocks and craters that it will be impossible to land? Will the spacecraft's engines ignite the surface like gunpowder? What is the Moon's gravity like? Thomas Gold, an Austrian-born scientist and NASA consultant, predicts that the Moon is covered in a thick layer of dust. NASA interprets this to mean that the spacecraft will sink out of sight.

Answers won't come from staring at the Moon through a telescope and guessing. We need to send objects to the Moon—objects that can take pictures, objects that can land and probe the surface and send back information.

NASA's Jet Propulsion Laboratory builds several different robotic spacecraft to help gather information to answer these questions.

Close-Up Photos of the Moon

The Ranger Program (1961–1965)
The Rangers are designed to send back close-up images of the lunar surface. The first six Rangers blow up on the launchpad, miss the Moon entirely, or have equipment malfunctions. Finally, in July 1964, Ranger 7 sends back over 4,000 pictures, allowing engineers to get close-up views of the lunar surface. Rangers 8 and 9 send back even more information.

Studying the Surface of the Moon

The Surveyor Program (1966–1968)
The robotic spacecraft known as Surveyors are designed to see if it is possible to make a soft landing, instead of a crash landing, on the surface of the Moon. Five out of the seven Surveyors successfully land.

Photographs a Surveyor takes of its footpads and its robotic shovels convince engineers that the lunar surface will be more than suitable for a piloted Apollo landing.

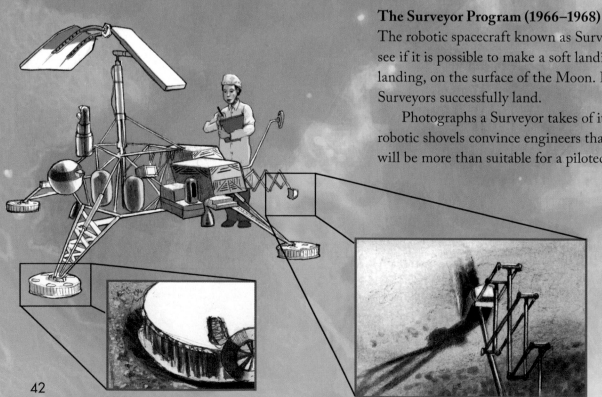

Picking a Landing Site

The Lunar Orbiter Program (1966–1967)

Five Lunar Orbiters successfully take nearly 2,000 photographs of the lunar surface as they circle the Moon. We discover that the Moon is littered with boulders the size of cars, craters twice as deep as the Grand Canyon, and mountains taller than any in the continental United States. These pictures allow geologist Farouk El-Baz to assist NASA in selecting the landing site. It is critical to find a flat, safe place for the astronauts to land.

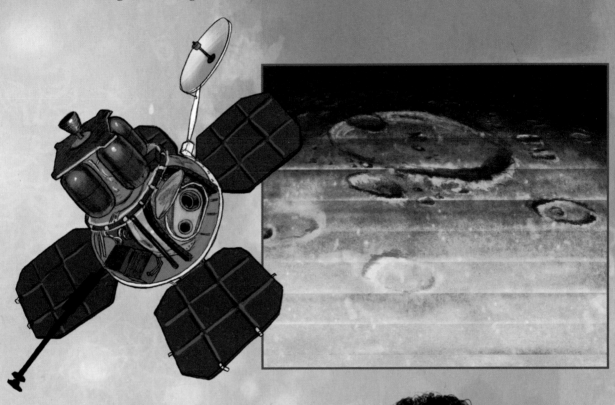

Farouk El-Baz (b. 1938)
Geologist

After studying every last mountain, crater, boulder, and rock depicted in thousands of photographs, no one knew the Moon better than Farouk El-Baz. Born and raised in Egypt, he discovered his love for geology on Boy Scout camping trips east of Cairo. In 1967, while working for Bellcomm Inc., a division of AT&T, El-Baz not only helped identify where the astronauts should land on the Moon, he also trained them in observation and photography. El-Baz even had a spacecraft named after him on the popular television series *Star Trek: The Next Generation*, which aired from 1987 to 1994.

The Gemini Program
1961–1966

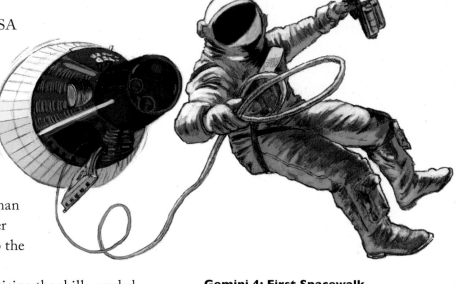

As the Mercury program nears its end, NASA keeps working to catch up with and beat the Soviet Union. Wernher von Braun and his team have been working on a huge rocket called the Saturn, which will have the capabilities to send a piloted spacecraft to the Moon, but it's not ready yet and won't be for years to come.

While work on the Saturn continues, NASA develops the Gemini program—two-man missions in low-Earth orbit—to work out other challenges they must master for the mission to the Moon to succeed.

The Gemini missions are focused on practicing the skills needed to spacewalk, to rendezvous two spacecraft in orbit, and to dock two spacecraft together.

Over the course of 10 piloted missions, we not only are able to accomplish these goals, but also manage to beat the Russians to a few milestones, including a new record for the longest-duration mission in space and the first docking of two spacecraft.

Gemini 4: First Spacewalk
Launch Date: June 3, 1965
Command Pilot: James A. McDivitt
Pilot: Edward H. "Ed" White
Duration: 4 days, 1 hour, 56 minutes
Ed White becomes the first American to do a spacewalk. He says returning to the space capsule was the saddest moment of his life.

Gemini 6A: First Rendezvous
Launch Date: December 15, 1965
Command Pilot: Walter M. "Wally" Schirra Jr.
Pilot: Thomas P. "Tom" Stafford
Duration: 1 day, 1 hour, 51 minutes
Gemini 6A completes the first piloted rendezvous with another spacecraft (Gemini 7). The two spacecraft come within 12 inches of each other while both are traveling at over 17,500 miles per hour.

Gemini 7: Longest-Duration Mission
Launch Date: December 4, 1965
Command Pilot: Frank Borman
Pilot: James A. "Jim" Lovell Jr.
Duration: 13 days, 18 hours, 35 minutes
Gemini 7 proves that men can operate in space for two weeks. Having two people in such a cramped space for over 330 hours isn't easy, but the mission leads to design changes that improve the Apollo Command Module.

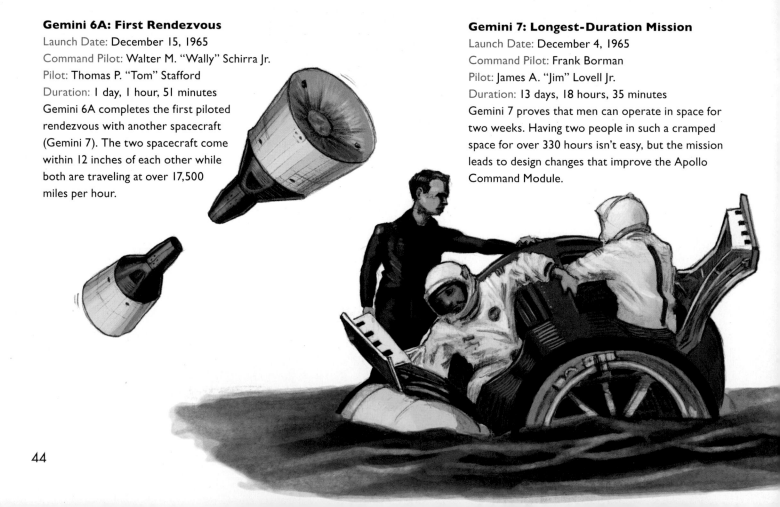

Gemini 8: First Successful Docking
Launch Date: March 16, 1966
Command Pilot: Neil A. Armstrong
Pilot: David R. Scott
Duration: 10 hours, 41 minutes
Gemini 8 executes the first successful docking between two spacecraft. But a thruster malfunction causes a deadly situation, in which the spacecraft starts tumbling out of control at a rate of one revolution a second. Armstrong is able to correct the problem seconds before passing out from the force of gravity, called g-force, caused by the spinning. If he hadn't acted fast, he and Scott both would have died.

Gemini 12: Completion of All Program Objectives
Launch Date: November 11, 1966
Command Pilot: James A. "Jim" Lovell Jr.
Pilot: Edwin E. "Buzz" Aldrin
Duration: 3 days, 22 hours, 34 minutes
Gemini 12 successfully completes all the program objectives with a rendezvous, a docking, and a spacewalk record of 5 hours and 30 minutes.

Astronaut Buzz Aldrin snaps a photo of himself outside the spacecraft. The first selfie in space!

Approaches to a Moon Landing

While the Gemini missions are working on rendezvous, docking, and extravehicular activities (EVAs), another term for spacewalks, there is still a lot of debate about how we will actually get to, and land on, the Moon. The design of the Apollo spacecraft depends entirely upon the approach we take, and with the "end of the decade" deadline drawing near, we need to decide quickly.

Direct Ascent

Our first idea is to send a giant rocket filled with enough fuel to go directly from Earth to the Moon and land tailfirst. Then, after the astronauts climb out and explore the surface, they would fire the rocket engines again to come back home. This is called direct ascent. Authors, artists, and scientists have been exploring this approach for hundreds of years, and the idea seems sound . . . until the engineers do the math.

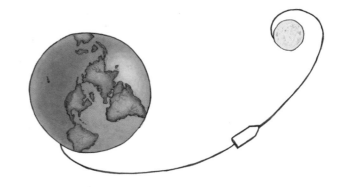

The problem is that a rocket with enough fuel to escape Earth's gravity, fly to the Moon, land, and then return would have to be enormous. Once the engineers calculate how much fuel would be necessary to complete the task, they realize the rocket will need to be over 60 feet tall. Landing such a large rocket on the Moon tailfirst and then having the astronauts climb down to the surface would be much too difficult.

*Image based on the work of space-artist Chesley Bonestell (1888–1986)

Earth Orbit Rendezvous

The second idea, championed by Wernher von Braun, is called Earth Orbit Rendezvous (EOR). We would send two or more rockets up into Earth orbit with the parts to build a spacecraft that would go to the Moon. The idea makes sense on paper, because this "Moon spacecraft" would not need to carry all the fuel necessary to escape Earth's gravity, which would mean it could be much smaller.

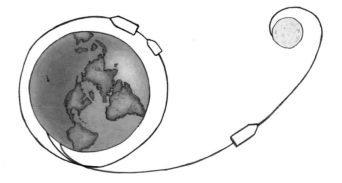

The problem with EOR is that it would take many launches into Earth orbit to build the spacecraft. Not only would this be expensive, but the spacecraft would have to be large enough to carry all the fuel that would allow it to return to Earth.

A Third Option

NASA has ongoing debates about direct ascent versus EOR. Both options would require a large vehicle to land on the Moon with enough fuel on board to be able to take off from the surface and get back to Earth. The engineers and NASA management have other concepts, but those ideas are so risky no one considers them realistic—for example, sending the astronauts to the Moon and having them wait there until we figure out a way to get them home!

Tom Dolan, an engineer at Vought Astronautics, starts thinking about the problem in a different way. He comes up with an idea to use two connected spacecraft: one to get the astronauts to the Moon and into orbit around it, and another, smaller craft that would detach itself and fly down to the surface separately. When the astronauts are done exploring the lunar surface, they would fly back up to meet with the main spacecraft. The smaller spacecraft could be light and disposable, saving a lot of weight. Dolan calls this concept Manned Lunar Landing and Return (MALLAR).

When Dolan presents his idea to leaders of the space program, it is immediately dismissed. "Too risky!" they say. This is because NASA hasn't yet perfected an Earth Orbit Rendezvous—so the idea of a two-spacecraft rendezvous *nearly a quarter of a million miles away* seems impossible, not to mention incredibly dangerous.

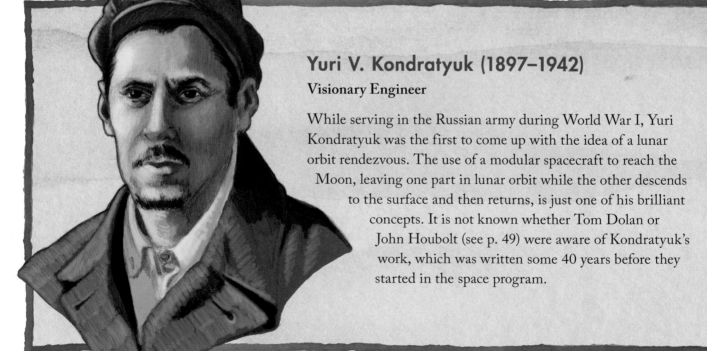

Yuri V. Kondratyuk (1897–1942)
Visionary Engineer

While serving in the Russian army during World War I, Yuri Kondratyuk was the first to come up with the idea of a lunar orbit rendezvous. The use of a modular spacecraft to reach the Moon, leaving one part in lunar orbit while the other descends to the surface and then returns, is just one of his brilliant concepts. It is not known whether Tom Dolan or John Houbolt (see p. 49) were aware of Kondratyuk's work, which was written some 40 years before they started in the space program.

A demoralized Dolan gives up on MALLAR. The idea is mostly forgotten until it lands on the desk of a quiet, somewhat reserved NASA engineer by the name of John C. Houbolt, who is intrigued. He does the calculations, the simulations, and the analysis, and becomes convinced that not only is it the best way to get man to the Moon and back—it is the only way.

He renames the concept Lunar Orbit Rendezvous (LOR) and presents the idea to the leaders of the space program. They say he's crazy and send him away. But Houbolt is determined. For two years he persists, even putting his job at risk, trying to present the idea of LOR.

And then it happens. In June 1962, in a meeting lasting six hours, Wernher von Braun relents. Lunar Orbit Rendezvous, championed by John Houbolt, will be the chosen method for getting a man to the Moon and back.

On July 20, 1969, when Neil Armstrong and Buzz Aldrin touched down on the surface of the Moon, Houbolt received what he considered to be the biggest reward of his career. Von Braun, seated in front of him in Houston's Mission Control, turned around and said, "Thank you, John."

Lunar Orbit Rendezvous

The beauty of LOR is the efficiency of its design. The rocket and spacecraft will shed the parts they no longer need, and the associated weight, at every step. The entire craft gets smaller and lighter along the way, requiring less and less fuel to complete the mission.

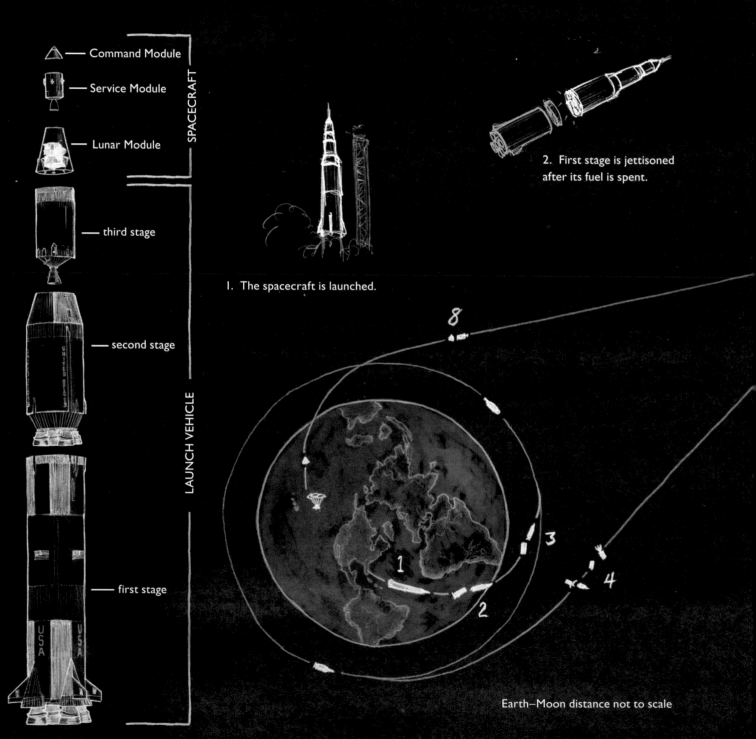

Command Module

Service Module

Lunar Module

SPACECRAFT

third stage

second stage

LAUNCH VEHICLE

first stage

USA

1. The spacecraft is launched.

2. First stage is jettisoned after its fuel is spent.

Earth–Moon distance not to scale

5

7

6. The Ascent Stage of the LM returns to the orbiting CSM, leaving the Descent Stage on the lunar surface.

7. Once the astronauts transfer back into the CSM, the Ascent Stage of the LM is jettisoned.

8. Before reentering our atmosphere the Service Module (SM) is jettisoned, leaving only the Command Module (CM) to return to Earth.

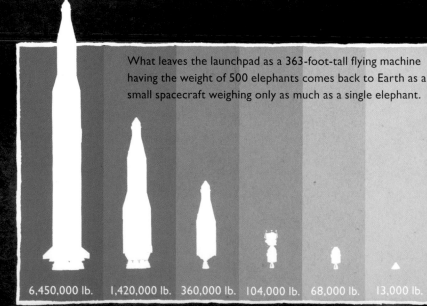

What leaves the launchpad as a 363-foot-tall flying machine having the weight of 500 elephants comes back to Earth as a small spacecraft weighing only as much as a single elephant.

| 6,450,000 lb. | 1,420,000 lb. | 360,000 lb. | 104,000 lb. | 68,000 lb. | 13,000 lb. |

The Payload Problem

Everything a rocket, also known as a launch vehicle, pushes up into space is called the payload. The larger a payload you have, the larger the rocket needs to be.

During the Mercury program, NASA is able to use a Redstone rocket to push Alan Shepard in his capsule up to a height of 116 miles. Later on in the program, the engineers use a larger Atlas rocket to push John Glenn into orbit around Earth. In the Gemini program, when two astronauts spend up to two weeks in Earth orbit, they use the Titan II rocket.

Now that von Braun and his team have committed to Lunar Orbit Rendezvous, it is clear that a three-person crew is needed to do all the things necessary for a Moon mission. The biggest concern is weight.

Everything hinges on this factor—starting with the weight of the astronauts themselves. They will have to bring all the supplies they need to survive in the unforgiving environment of space: oxygen, water, food, spacesuits, and tools. They will need extra fuel to break free of Earth's gravity and put them on a course for the Moon; add to that the fuel needed to go into lunar orbit, land on the Moon, take off from the Moon, and get home.

NASA's engineers know that the more weight they add to the top of the rocket, where the spacecraft is, the more fuel they'll need to launch it. Every pound added to the payload means adding up to 80 pounds of thrust to the engines in the launch vehicle. As the calculations are made, the rocket continues to grow.

Mercury-Redstone
Height   83 ft.
Diameter 6 ft.
Weight   66,000 lb.
Payload   4,000 lb.

Mission: Suborbital
Crew: 1
Duration: 15 minutes

Mercury-Atlas D
Height   94 ft.
Diameter 10 ft.
Weight   260,000 lb.
Payload   3,000 lb.

Mission: Earth orbit
Crew: 1
Duration: 34 hours

Gemini-Titan II
Height   109 ft.
Diameter 10 ft.
Weight   340,000 lb.
Payload   7,900 lb.

Mission: Earth orbit
Crew: 2
Duration: 2 weeks

Apollo-Saturn V
Height   363 ft.
Diameter 33 ft.
Weight   6,450,000 lb.
Payload   104,000 lb.

Mission: Moon landing
Crew: 3
Duration: up to 2 weeks

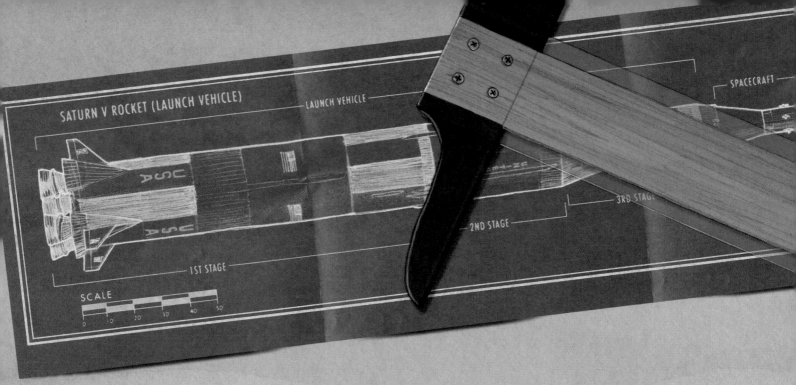

The Saturn V Rocket: The Launch Vehicle

After careful consideration of the mission, von Braun and his team calculate that it will take a gargantuan three-stage rocket to propel the spacecraft and its passengers on their journey to the Moon. It will be the largest flying machine ever built. The launch vehicle itself will be made up of three parts, or stages, which will work in sequence to get the spacecraft into orbit and on its way to the Moon.

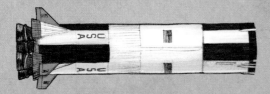

The first stage will be made up of two large fuel tanks and five of the most powerful rocket engines ever invented. Its job will be to create the over 7.5 million pounds of thrust needed to lift the entire vehicle off the launchpad and to a height of about 35 miles in the first 2.5 minutes, before running out of fuel and falling away into the ocean.

The second stage, also with two large fuel tanks and five engines, will propel the remainder of the vehicle up to a height of about 115 miles at a speed of four miles a second. It too will fall away into the ocean after its fuel is spent.

The third stage, with one engine, has two jobs. The first is to push what remains—the Apollo spacecraft—into orbit at a speed of 17,500 miles per hour. Then after one and a half orbits around Earth, it will fire again, bringing the velocity of the spacecraft up to a mind-boggling 25,000 miles per hour. This is the speed calculated to extend the spacecraft's orbit to a point where it will intercept the Moon.

The Apollo Spacecraft: The Payload

When it comes to designing the concepts for the Apollo spacecraft, NASA leans heavily on one of its most talented designers, Maxime A. "Max" Faget (see p. 99). Faget (pronounced fah-ZHAY), a quiet, eccentric man prone to wearing bow ties, was responsible for designing the Mercury capsule. He now has to help design a spacecraft to take three men to the Moon, land two of them, and return the trio safely to Earth.

To turn his ideas into drawings and models, Faget works with longtime collaborator Caldwell Johnson. As a boy, Johnson loved nothing more than building exquisite airplane models. His beautiful designs and attention to detail landed him a job at NACA when he was only 18 years old. By the time Apollo came into being, he had established himself as an indispensable designer of spacecraft.

Faget and Caldwell conceptualize the Apollo spacecraft as a modular system. This approach means that each part can be specific to a certain role during the mission. Once its task is complete, it can be discarded, making the overall craft smaller and lighter.

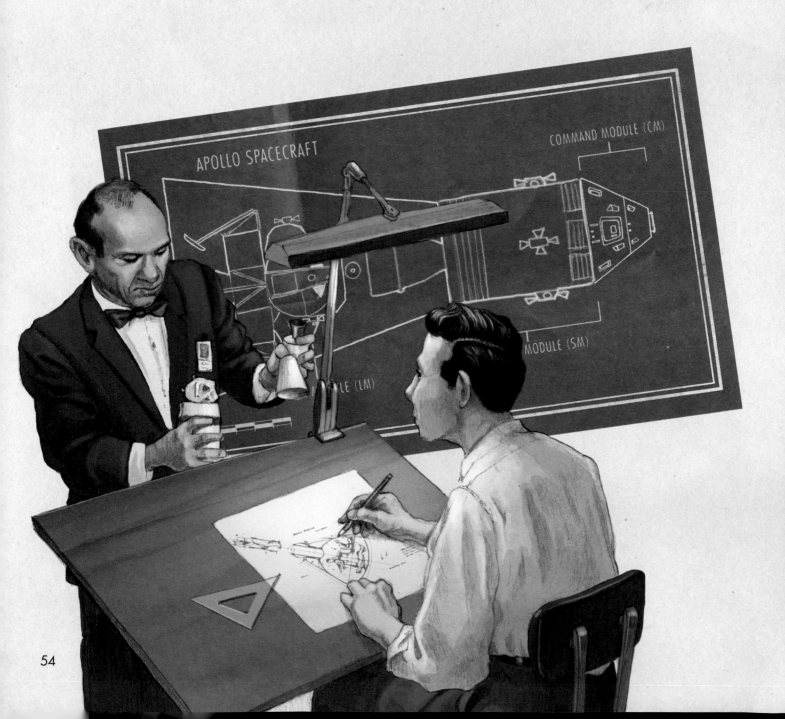

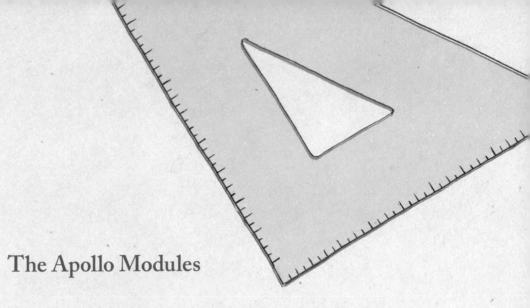

The Apollo Modules

The Command Module (CM) will be the crew compartment for the journey to and from the Moon. Its conical shape is designed with reentry in mind. The blunt end will be covered with a thick heat shield to protect the astronauts from the intense temperatures that build up during reentry into Earth's atmosphere. This will be the only part of the spacecraft to return to Earth.

The Service Module (SM), together with the CM, will make up the main part of the spacecraft. This is referred to as the Command and Service Module (CSM). Not everything the astronauts need for the two-week journey has to come back to Earth, so the SM will serve as a support trailer. It will house power, fuel, air, and many of the other necessary supplies. The SM can be discarded before reentry into Earth's atmosphere, making the spacecraft lighter, smaller, and, most important, safer.

The Lunar Module (LM) will be a lightweight craft that will ferry two of the astronauts from lunar orbit down to the surface of the Moon. It will consist of two parts: a Descent Stage, which will house the engine and fuel needed to land on the surface, and the Ascent Stage, which will detach from the Descent Stage to bring the astronauts back up to redock with the CSM in lunar orbit.

Hal Laning at the Massachusetts Institute of Technology (MIT) helps design the software for the Apollo Guidance Computer.

Over 6,000 construction workers help build Kennedy Space Center.

Dorothy Vaughan teaches "human computers" the new language of the digital computer.

Engineers at IBM assemble the Saturn Launch Vehicle Digital Computer.

The Apollo Workforce

A plan is in place. We now know how we are going to get to the Moon.

And a hugely ambitious plan it is. Thousands of blueprints have been drawn. Tens of thousands of documents, procedures, and design details have been written. In 1962, NASA begins to hire the help it needs to actually execute the plan.

A massive workforce will be required to build all the different parts of the launch vehicle and the spacecraft. We have to build places to test them. We have to construct a facility to put all the parts together. We need a launchpad and a control center. We need spacesuits and life support systems and training facilities for the astronauts. The list seems endless.

Frances "Poppy" Northcutt works on mission planning and analysis in Houston.

Engineers at Hamilton Standard design the life support system.

Thousands of engineers at North American Aviation work to build the Apollo spacecraft.

Dottie Lee helps design the heat shield on the Apollo CM.

Over the next several years, Apollo will employ thousands of different companies and over 400,000 workers to build and test everything it will take to launch a mission to the Moon.

Although the vast majority of workers are white men, it will be women who execute some of the most precise craftsmanship demanded by Apollo. NASA is also keenly aware that it has a responsibility to be a leader when it comes to racial equality, and so efforts are made to hire people of color for the program. This proves to be difficult, as many of NASA's facilities are located in southern states, where segregation and racism are prevalent.

The Apollo workforce comes from every corner of the United States. Engineers, mathematicians, scientists, construction workers, welders, seamstresses, programmers, mechanics, electricians, and more—all are dedicated to meeting President Kennedy's goal by the end of the decade.

Charles Smoot recruits African American engineering students to work at NASA.

Seamstresses work tirelessly to sew the parachutes for the CM.

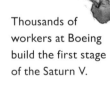

Thousands of workers at Boeing build the first stage of the Saturn V.

Seamstresses at ILC Dover assemble spacesuits.

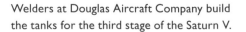

Welders at Douglas Aircraft Company build the tanks for the third stage of the Saturn V.

PART 3

Building a Launch Vehicle

"It takes sixty-five thousand errors before you are qualified to make a rocket."

—WERNHER VON BRAUN,
DIRECTOR OF NASA'S MARSHALL SPACE FLIGHT CENTER

The rocket required to send the Apollo spacecraft to the Moon will be taller than the Statue of Liberty and will hold enough propellant to fill over 100 tanker trucks. It will have to be strong enough to withstand the intense power of the largest rocket engines ever built, yet light enough to break free of Earth's gravity. It must be able to store the propellants in its tanks at hundreds of degrees below zero, then shoot them out at temperatures close to those at the surface of the Sun. The rocket will require a special system to keep it flying on course, and ways of keeping everyone safe if it doesn't work the way it should.

   Called the Saturn V, this rocket will be a perfect machine of raw power. It has only one chance to work right. And once it completes its task . . . it will be gone.

STAGE ONE (S-IC) and the Mighty F-1 Engine

In December 1961, the task of building the first stage of the Saturn V is awarded to Boeing, which has specialized in making airplanes since 1916. At its Michoud Assembly Facility in New Orleans, one of the largest manufacturing plants in the world, George H. Stoner supervises the development of the S-IC.

The S-IC consists primarily of two large tanks stacked one on top of the other, with a spacer in between called a skirt. At its base will be five F-1 engines made by Rocketdyne, which will burn through 559,000 gallons of propellants to lift the 6.5-million-pound rocket to a height of 35 miles and a speed of 5,300 miles per hour. It will take almost six years to develop and build the S-IC—and its purpose will be fulfilled in a mere 150 seconds.

Saturn V S-IC Facts

Height	**138** ft.
Diameter	**33** ft.
Weight (fully fueled)	**5,022,674** lb.
Weight (empty)	**288,750** lb.
Manufacturer	**Boeing**

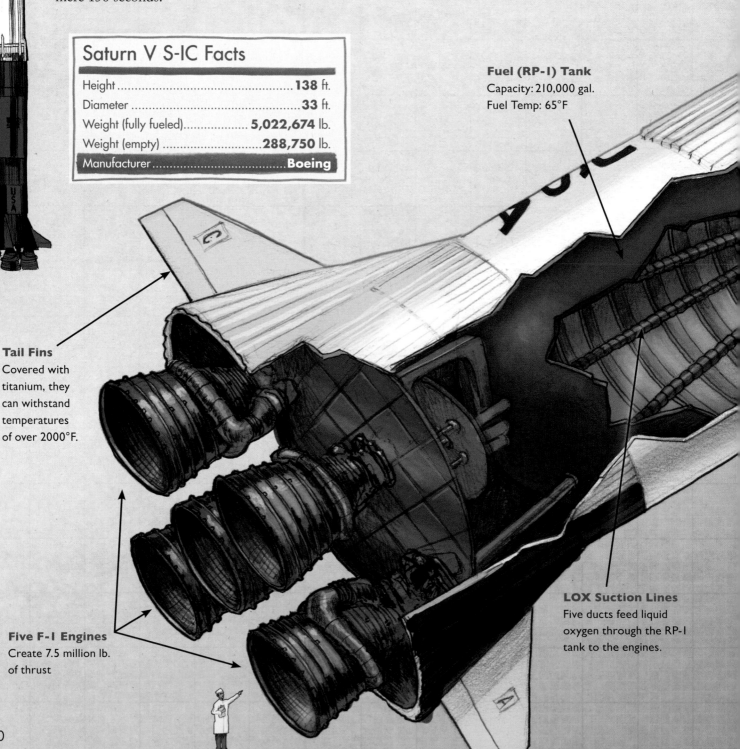

Fuel (RP-1) Tank
Capacity: 210,000 gal.
Fuel Temp: 65°F

Tail Fins
Covered with titanium, they can withstand temperatures of over 2000°F.

Five F-1 Engines
Create 7.5 million lb. of thrust

LOX Suction Lines
Five ducts feed liquid oxygen through the RP-1 tank to the engines.

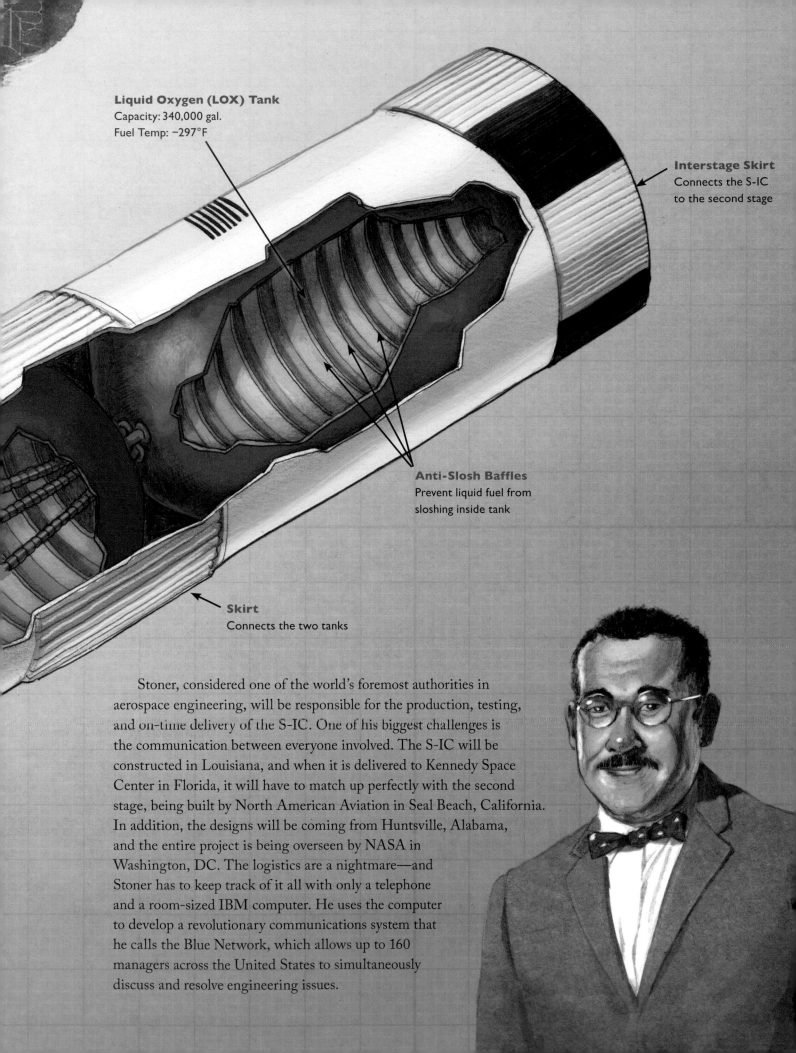

Liquid Oxygen (LOX) Tank
Capacity: 340,000 gal.
Fuel Temp: −297°F

Interstage Skirt
Connects the S-IC
to the second stage

Anti-Slosh Baffles
Prevent liquid fuel from
sloshing inside tank

Skirt
Connects the two tanks

Stoner, considered one of the world's foremost authorities in aerospace engineering, will be responsible for the production, testing, and on-time delivery of the S-IC. One of his biggest challenges is the communication between everyone involved. The S-IC will be constructed in Louisiana, and when it is delivered to Kennedy Space Center in Florida, it will have to match up perfectly with the second stage, being built by North American Aviation in Seal Beach, California. In addition, the designs will be coming from Huntsville, Alabama, and the entire project is being overseen by NASA in Washington, DC. The logistics are a nightmare—and Stoner has to keep track of it all with only a telephone and a room-sized IBM computer. He uses the computer to develop a revolutionary communications system that he calls the Blue Network, which allows up to 160 managers across the United States to simultaneously discuss and resolve engineering issues.

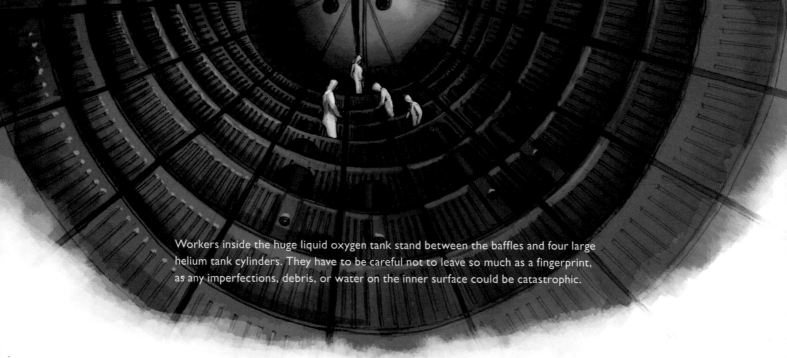

Workers inside the huge liquid oxygen tank stand between the baffles and four large helium tank cylinders. They have to be careful not to leave so much as a fingerprint, as any imperfections, debris, or water on the inner surface could be catastrophic.

The Tanks

Over 90 percent of the weight of the S-IC comes from the propellants it carries in its enormous tanks.

Problem! Sloshing

One of the issues that the Boeing team needs to resolve is the sloshing of propellants in the tanks. Sloshing is when the liquid in a container moves around in an irregular way due to motion. You may have experienced this when carrying a full glass of water across a room. Even the slightest shift can cause a spill.

The sloshing of over four million pounds of liquid fuel in a moving rocket would change the vehicle's center of gravity, causing instability or even complete destruction.

center of gravity

Solution! Baffles

Luckily, this problem has been dealt with for years in other large vehicles that carry liquids, such as ships, trains, tankers, and airplanes. Based on these earlier designs, the Boeing engineers install metal rings, called anti-slosh baffles, around the inside of the tank. These baffles work to reduce the sloshing by limiting the movement of the liquid, which allows the center of gravity to remain stable.

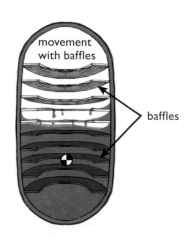

baffles

EXPERIMENT

Take an empty two-liter soda bottle, fill it one-third full of water, and put the cap back on. Briskly move it back and forth on a surface and let go. The water sloshing around will cause the bottle to continue to move as its center of gravity shifts, possibly even making it topple over.

Problem! Keeping the Tanks Pressurized

Because the tanks feeding the engines are a completely sealed system, the Boeing engineers need to find a way to fill the space left behind by the emptying propellants in order to maintain the proper pressure. Otherwise, a vacuum will be created, which will greatly reduce fuel flow and possibly cause the tanks—and therefore the rocket—to collapse inward.

You may have seen something like this when you drink from a plastic water bottle without allowing air in to replace the water you took out. The bottle begins to collapse on itself.

Solution! Pressurizing with Oxygen and Helium

For the liquid oxygen (LOX) tank, engineers pass a small amount of the supercold liquid oxygen through a heat exchanger in the engines; there, it expands into gaseous oxygen, which is fed back in through the top of the tank to fill the empty space there.

It is too dangerous to do this with the fuel, RP-1, because of the threat of combustion. Instead, helium stored in the supercold LOX tank is passed through the heat exchanger. The gaseous helium is then sent to fill the empty space in the fuel tank.

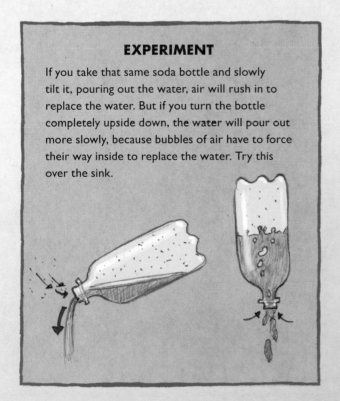

EXPERIMENT

If you take that same soda bottle and slowly tilt it, pouring out the water, air will rush in to replace the water. But if you turn the bottle completely upside down, the water will pour out more slowly, because bubbles of air have to force their way inside to replace the water. Try this over the sink.

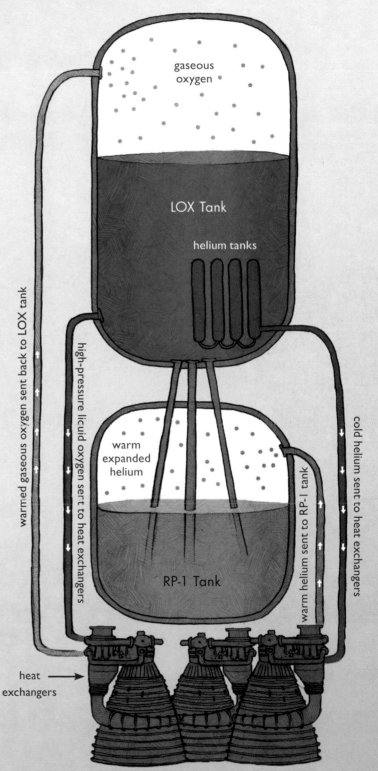

gaseous oxygen

LOX Tank

helium tanks

warm expanded helium

RP-1 Tank

warmed gaseous oxygen sent back to LOX tank

high-pressure liquid oxygen sent to heat exchangers

warm helium sent to RP-1 tank

cold helium sent to heat exchangers

heat → exchangers

The F-1 Engine

Wernher von Braun needs someone he can trust. He needs someone who can oversee the design and construction of the largest rocket engine ever imagined—someone who understands the challenge that managing this job will present.

A 28-year-old engineer named Sonny Morea is just that person.

Morea has been on von Braun's team for the past five years. He knows the pressures and temperatures the engine will have to withstand. The superhot gases it creates will explode out of its nozzle at almost 10 times the speed of sound. One of the biggest challenges of designing and building an engine this massive will be to keep it from self-destructing under the extreme forces it has to harness.

Simply scaling up earlier rocket engine designs won't be enough. New welding techniques will have to be developed, as well as new pumps that can handle the sheer volume of propellants. Ingenious methods for keeping the engine cool will also have to be invented. Morea knows that if they cannot get the engine to work, the whole Apollo program will be stuck on the ground.

F-1 Engine Facts

Length	**18** ft. **4** in.
Diameter	**11** ft. **11** in.
Weight	**18,000** lb.
Maximum Thrust	**1,522,000** lb.
Propellants	**LOX** and **RP-1**
Manufacturer	**Rocketdyne**

HOW THE F-1 ENGINE WORKS

The F-1 engine undergoes a complex series of operations that are designed not only to produce tremendous thrust but also to maintain stability during combustion.

1 Small amounts of the propellants are burned in a gas generator, and the combustion creates hot gases that spin a turbine. The exhaust then moves through a heat exchanger to warm the LOX and helium being used to pressurize the tanks.

2 A LOX pump and a fuel pump, powered by the turbine, now draw the propellants from the tanks to a mechanism called an injector plate.

3 The propellants are sprayed at high velocity through the injector plate and into a combustion chamber, where they mix and are ignited. The hot gases then explode out of a thrust chamber.

4 The cooled exhaust gases that have passed through the heat exchanger are now sent through a turbine exhaust manifold, creating a barrier around the inside of a nozzle extension (see p. 66).

5 The nozzle extension controls the direction of the flame and the exhaust created in the combustion chamber, increasing the efficiency of the engine.

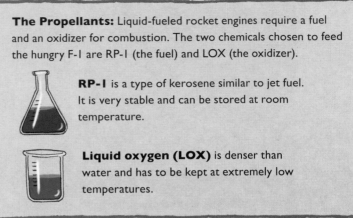

The Propellants: Liquid-fueled rocket engines require a fuel and an oxidizer for combustion. The two chemicals chosen to feed the hungry F-1 are RP-1 (the fuel) and LOX (the oxidizer).

RP-1 is a type of kerosene similar to jet fuel. It is very stable and can be stored at room temperature.

Liquid oxygen (LOX) is denser than water and has to be kept at extremely low temperatures.

turbopump
LOX pump
fuel pump
turbine

injector plate

The injector is a round steel plate lined with copper and filled with holes like a showerhead. RP-1 and LOX shoot through the holes and into the combustion chamber, where they ignite.

RP-1 being pumped from tank
LOX being pumped from tank

cold helium and LOX being sent to the heat exchanger

combustion chamber

3

thrust chamber

2

1

gas generator

heat exchanger

warm helium and gaseous oxygen being sent to pressurize the tanks

turbine exhaust manifold

4

nozzle extension

5

F-1 ENGINE

65

Keeping the F-1 Engine Cool

Problem! Temperature

To say that the F-1 engine runs hot is an understatement. In the combustion chamber, it is over 5000°F. All metal will melt at that temperature! The Rocketdyne engineers have to find a way to keep the structure of the engine cool during operation.

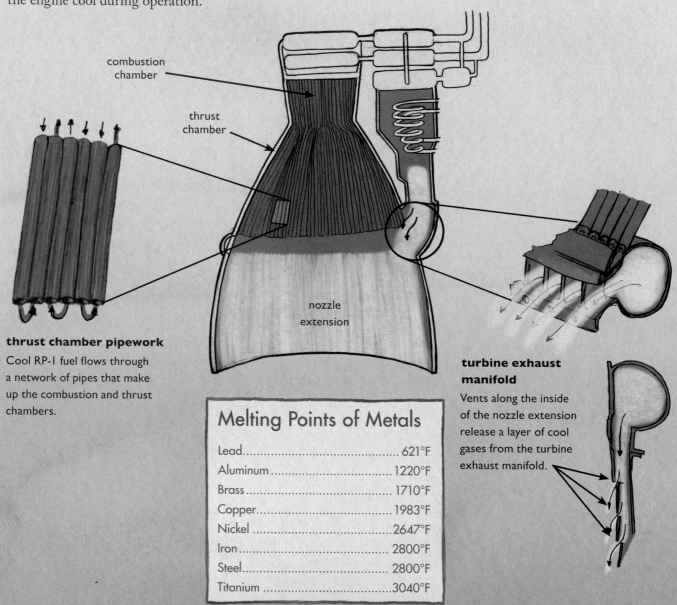

combustion chamber

thrust chamber

nozzle extension

thrust chamber pipework

Cool RP-1 fuel flows through a network of pipes that make up the combustion and thrust chambers.

turbine exhaust manifold

Vents along the inside of the nozzle extension release a layer of cool gases from the turbine exhaust manifold.

Melting Points of Metals

Lead	621°F
Aluminum	1220°F
Brass	1710°F
Copper	1983°F
Nickel	2647°F
Iron	2800°F
Steel	2800°F
Titanium	3040°F

Solution! Heat Transfer

The engineers create combustion and thrust chambers out of a series of nickel-alloy pipes. As the engine is firing, 70 percent of the high-pressure RP-1 fuel is sent through these pipes before it enters the fuel injector plate. This allows the fuel to carry the heat away from the metal, in a process called heat transfer (see p. 75).

To keep the nozzle extension cool, the exhaust gases that were previously cooled from the heat exchanger are released through a series of vents around the turbine exhaust manifold. This protects the nozzle extension by creating a layer of cooler gases—a barrier between the engine exhaust and the metal.

Saverio F. "Sonny" Morea (b. 1932)

Project Manager for the F-1 and J-2 Rocket Engines and the Lunar Rover

As a young boy in Queens, New York, Sonny Morea was fascinated by flight. He took his first airplane ride at 14 and knew he wanted to become a pilot. Since flying lessons were expensive, Morea spent every other Saturday working a construction job to pay for them. He earned his pilot's license by the time he was 17, when he was a junior at Brooklyn Technical High School.

After getting a degree in mechanical engineering from the City College of New York, he began his career working on airplanes before joining the army. At the age of 23, he was assigned to work with Wernher von Braun and his group of rocket scientists in Huntsville, Alabama. Morea became very skilled at managing projects, and five years later was put in charge of overseeing development of the F-1 rocket engine.

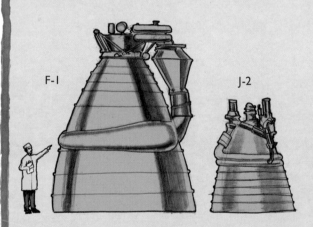

F-1 J-2

Morea went on to become the project manager for the J-2 engines used in the second and third stages of the Saturn V rocket. His final task for the Apollo program was to oversee the development of a car that the astronauts could drive on the Moon! This Lunar Roving Vehicle (LRV), or Lunar Rover, was used during the Apollo 15, 16, and 17 missions.

Later, after retiring from NASA, Sonny Morea went back to the thing he loved best: aviation. Working as a flight instructor, Morea shared his passion for flying with all his students.

THE LUNAR ROVING VEHICLE

Even before we land on the Moon, NASA is thinking of new ways to explore the lunar surface. An astronaut could venture only a short distance from the spacecraft on foot, so having a vehicle would allow them to explore much farther. This thinking leads to the development of the LRV—the Lunar Rover—for the last three Apollo missions. The crews can't bring the LRVs back with them because of their size and weight—so next time you look up at the Moon, know that there are three cars still sitting up there.

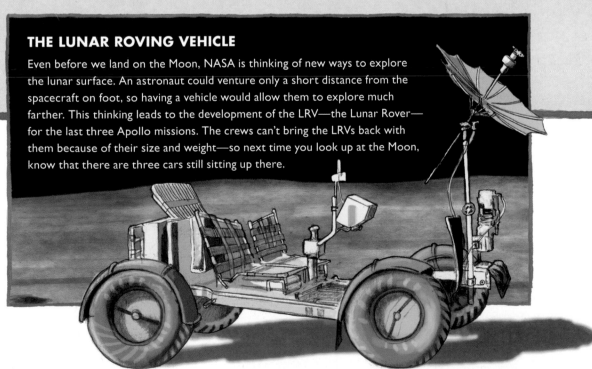

Saturn V Test Stand in Huntsville, AL

Saturn V Test Stand

The powerful F-1 engines need to be tested, just like every one of the millions of parts of the Saturn V rocket. In order to do so, engineers design test stands like this one in Huntsville, Alabama. Impressively massive in its own right, made from concrete and steel and nearly 300 feet tall, the stand is built to tolerate the 7.5 million pounds of thrust that the Saturn V's first stage will generate.

The exhaust will need to be directed away from the ground to prevent the test stand from being destroyed by the extreme forces coming from the five F-1 engines. To solve this, the engineers design what is called a flame bucket or flame deflector. It acts like a giant scoop, forcing the exhaust outward.

The first tests of the F-1 engines are so powerful that the shock waves shatter windows in downtown Huntsville, over five miles away!

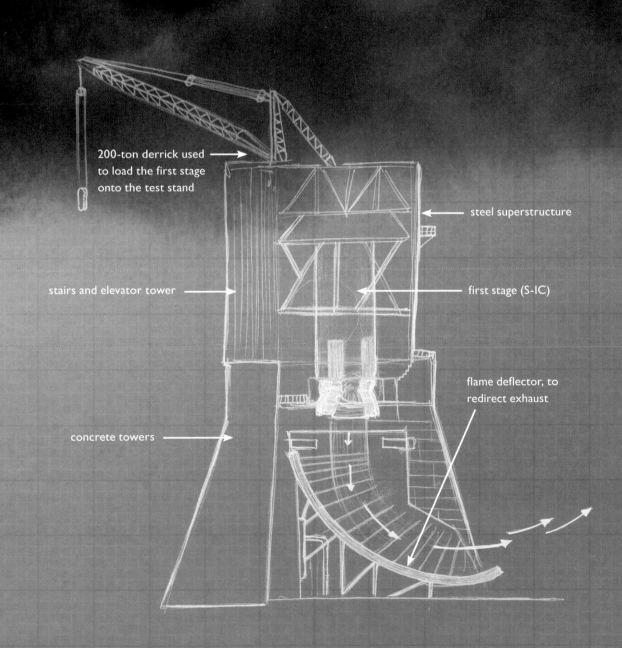

200-ton derrick used
to load the first stage
onto the test stand

steel superstructure

stairs and elevator tower

first stage (S-IC)

flame deflector, to
redirect exhaust

concrete towers

Problem! Combustion Instability

Once the test firings begin, Sonny Morea is horrified to learn that some of the F-1 engines are exploding. He and Paul Castenholz, an engineer at Rocketdyne, realize it's because of something they call combustion instability. This is when the flame becomes unstable and flickers back and forth like a candle. In the gigantic F-1, the instability is caused by pressure waves moving across the injector plate. These waves are causing the 12-foot-wide flame to rotate at a speed of 2,000 times a second, which eventually destroys the engine.

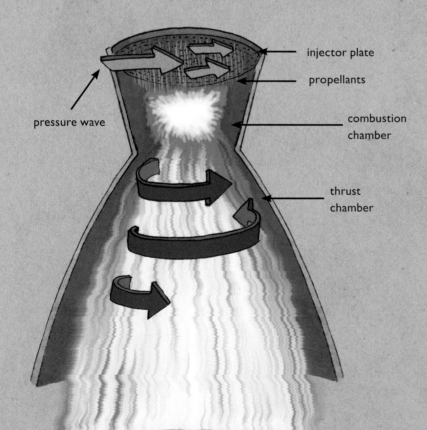

pressure wave

injector plate

propellants

combustion chamber

thrust chamber

The injector plate is a 40-inch circular piece of copper that looks like a giant showerhead. It has 29 rings with 2,816 holes drilled at angles so that the liquid oxygen and the fuel can meet a short distance away from the plate and ignite.

Original Injector Plate Design

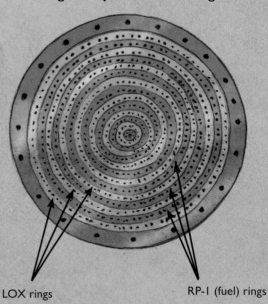

LOX rings

RP-1 (fuel) rings

Solution! Injector Plate Redesign

Morea and Castenholz quickly organize a team of expert engineers to work out this problem. They discover that they need to redesign how the propellants are injected into the combustion chamber. Dozens of different injector plate designs are produced to see which ones will be the most stable. In the future, engineers will simply build a computer model to test different designs to see which one works best, but the engineers at Rocketdyne have to rely on trial and error with actual engines.

Final Baffle Design

After months and months of testing, a solution is found by separating the injector plate into 13 parts using copper baffles. Instead of one giant showerhead of propellants, the injector plate becomes 13 smaller ones, which restrict the movement of pressure waves across the plate. To make sure their solution works, they set off a small bomb inside the thrust chamber during a test firing. It forces the flame to become unstable—and their new design works perfectly. The engine regains stability in less than half a second.

baffles

Redesigned Injector Plate with Baffles

Meanwhile, in Seal Beach, California, North American Aviation is overseeing the production of the second stage of the Saturn V. While the first stage has the job of lifting the entire rocket off the launchpad, its work is done two and a half minutes after launch.

The second stage (S-II) has to push what remains of the rocket to a height of 115 miles and attain a speed of 15,500 miles per hour. Like the first stage, the S-II is also made up of two tanks, but this time the fuel tank—filled with a much lighter and more dangerous fuel, liquid hydrogen (LH_2)—will be on the top, and the LOX tank will be on the bottom.

Loading the S-II with a quarter million gallons of one of the coldest substances known will require the creation of many intricate systems and valves—a job that will fall squarely on the shoulders of young mechanical engineers like 23-year-old Harvey LeBlanc.

Saturn V S-II Facts

Height	**82** ft.
Diameter	**33** ft.
Weight (fully fueled)	**1,059,171** lb.
Weight (empty)	**79,918** lb.
Manufacturer	**North American Aviation**

Interstage
Holds the S-II away from the S-1C stage, giving space for the engines

Thrust Structure
Holds the engines and propels the thrust to the S-II

Five J-2 Engines
Create a total of one million pounds of thrust

LOX Tank
Capacity: 87,440 gal.
Fuel Temp: −297°F

LH₂ Tank
Capacity: 264,172 gal.
Fuel Temp: −423°F

LIQUID HYDROGEN

Choosing LH₂ as the fuel for the second and third stages of the Saturn V has many benefits, including the fact that it is light—a cup of LH₂ weighs less than a cup of marshmallows. Unfortunately, the downside of LH₂ is that you have to keep it extremely cold. At any temperature higher than −423°F, it will boil off into gaseous hydrogen, which can ignite from as little as static electricity from your shoes. Hydrogen fires are invisible during daylight, so LeBlanc and his team have to carry straw brooms out in front of themselves as they walk alongside LH₂ pipes. If the broom catches on fire, they know to stop walking!

1 gallon
RP-1 (6.7 lb.)

12 gallons
LH₂ (6.7 lb.)

Forward Skirt
Connects to the bottom of the third stage

Harvey LeBlanc (b. 1939)
Design Engineer

Born and raised outside of Lafayette, Louisiana, Harvey LeBlanc never shied away from hard work—he started picking cotton when he was six years old. During college, he spent his summers working for an oil company, developing systems for handling gas and oil.

In 1962, right before graduating from the University of Southwestern Louisiana with a degree in mechanical engineering, LeBlanc and a few of his classmates were approached by a recruiter from North American Aviation, who asked if they wanted to go to Southern California to help build a rocket that would send men to the Moon. He even offered them money for first-class airfare and moving expenses. LeBlanc pocketed the cash, bought a cheap used car, threw a suitcase in the back, and drove the 1,800 miles to his new job at North American.

In part because of his experience with the oil company, he quickly rose to become the leader of the group that will design all the propellant loading systems for the S-II at the Mississippi Test Facility.

Problem! Weight

When North American Aviation is awarded the contract to build the S-II in the fall of 1961, the Apollo payload (the spacecraft) is already getting heavier in its design. This means that the launch vehicle has to get lighter. With both the first and third stages of the Saturn V too far along to be changed, the burden of shedding weight falls to the second stage—and every pound counts. For every pound added to the Apollo spacecraft, the second stage has to lose five pounds.

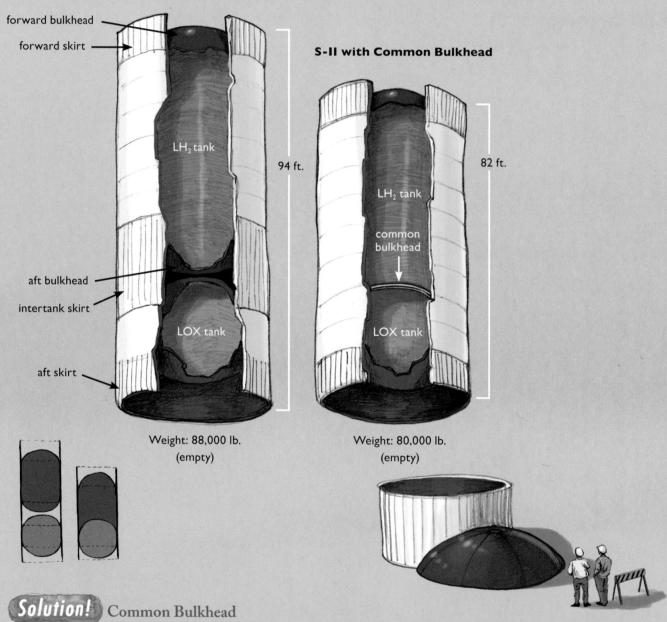

S-II with Separate Tanks

forward bulkhead

forward skirt

LH$_2$ tank

94 ft.

aft bulkhead

intertank skirt

LOX tank

aft skirt

Weight: 88,000 lb.
(empty)

S-II with Common Bulkhead

LH$_2$ tank

common bulkhead

LOX tank

82 ft.

Weight: 80,000 lb.
(empty)

Solution! Common Bulkhead

The fuel and liquid oxygen tanks are formed from cylinders and sealed with dome-shaped caps called bulkheads. The tanks are usually connected with skirts, which are also used as spacers between the stages. The engineers at North American realize that if they combine the two tanks and use a common bulkhead between them, they'll be able to lose the lower bulkhead of the LH$_2$ tank as well as the skirt between the two tanks—a brilliant idea that shortens the entire stage by 12 feet and makes it 8,000 pounds lighter.

74

HEAT TRANSFER

Heat will always move from a hot object (liquid, gas, or solid) to a cooler object. Understanding how that heat transfers from one object to another was important to the engineers as they designed and built the tanks for the S-II.

Heat energy is also called thermal energy, and temperature is the measurement of that energy. There are three ways that thermal energy can transfer from one object to another:

Thermal Radiation: The transfer of heat via light waves. An example of this is the heat from the Sun warming your face.

Thermal Conduction: The transfer of heat from one object to another when they touch. An example of this would be your hand touching a warm mug of hot chocolate.

Thermal Convection: The transfer of heat through a liquid or gas. An example of this is the warm air rising from a campfire.

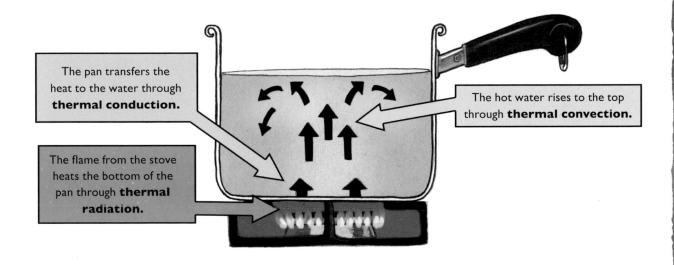

The pan transfers the heat to the water through **thermal conduction.**

The hot water rises to the top through **thermal convection.**

The flame from the stove heats the bottom of the pan through **thermal radiation.**

BOILING POINT

The boiling point is the temperature at which a liquid converts to a gas. A liquid's boiling point will vary depending on the surrounding atmospheric pressure. For example, water at sea level will boil at 212°F. If that same water were in the lower atmospheric pressure at the top of Mount Everest, it would boil at 160°F.

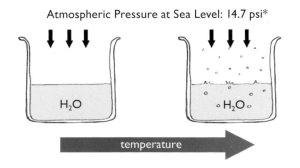

Atmospheric Pressure at Sea Level: 14.7 psi*

H_2O

H_2O

temperature

*psi = pounds per square inch

Problem! Fuel Loss

With the S-II propellant tanks now combined, there are two liquids of greatly different temperatures sharing a common bulkhead less than an inch thick. Even though the liquid oxygen is incredibly cold, it is still 126°F warmer than the liquid hydrogen. This means that heat from the LOX will move into the LH_2 tank through thermal conduction. This is a problem because if any LH_2 gets warmer than −423°F it will boil and turn into a gas, which will vent out of the tank, resulting in a loss of fuel.

If that weren't bad enough, the engineers also have to consider where the rocket will be launched. The Florida air outside the walls of the tanks will be considerably warmer than the liquids inside. And that means heat will transfer from the outside air to both tanks, causing the propellants to boil off even faster.

The engineers have to take steps to prevent both types of heat transfer. Otherwise, by the time of the launch, there will be no fuel left in the tanks.

air
75°F

The heat from the air outside transfers through the tank walls toward the cold liquids inside.

LH_2
−423°F

The warmer LOX transfers heat to the LH_2 above through the tank wall.

LOX
−297°F

It is not safe to vent hydrogen into the air, so when the LH_2 boils off, the gaseous hydrogen is sent through pipes to a nearby pond and burned at its surface.

When liquid oxygen boils off, the steam (gaseous oxygen) is released into the atmosphere.

Solution! Insulation

To slow down the heat transfer that causes the propellants to boil off, the engineers at North American rely on a new type of insulation: fiberglass honeycomb, filled with a heat-resistant foam. They also decide to build the tanks from a special aluminum alloy that has the unique property of getting stronger as it gets colder. Now, having the supercold propellants in direct contact with the metal will allow for thinner, lighter walls.

Because of this, the tank insulation is applied to the *outside* of the tank. The bulkhead insulation is sandwiched between two layers of the aluminum alloy.

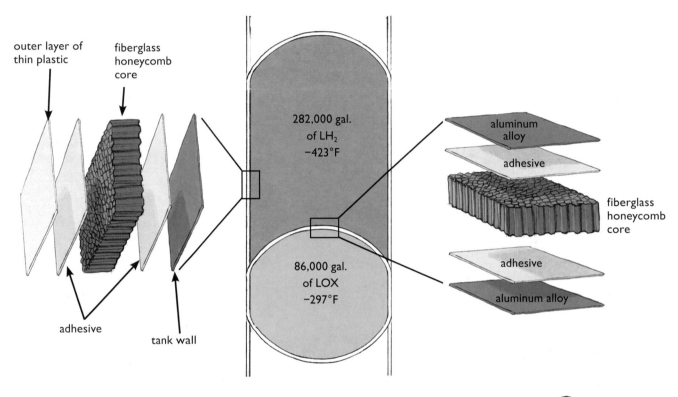

outer layer of thin plastic

fiberglass honeycomb core

adhesive

tank wall

282,000 gal. of LH$_2$ −423°F

86,000 gal. of LOX −297°F

aluminum alloy

adhesive

fiberglass honeycomb core

adhesive

aluminum alloy

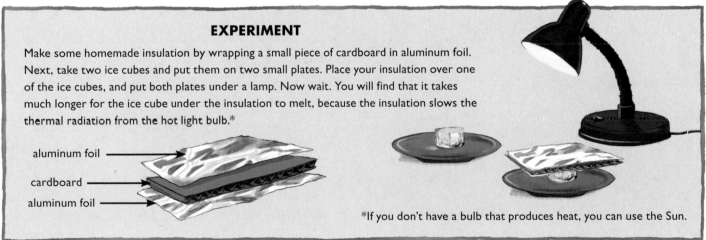

EXPERIMENT

Make some homemade insulation by wrapping a small piece of cardboard in aluminum foil. Next, take two ice cubes and put them on two small plates. Place your insulation over one of the ice cubes, and put both plates under a lamp. Now wait. You will find that it takes much longer for the ice cube under the insulation to melt, because the insulation slows the thermal radiation from the hot light bulb.*

aluminum foil

cardboard

aluminum foil

*If you don't have a bulb that produces heat, you can use the Sun.

Spray Foam

If the insulation tiles are not shaped and placed perfectly, pockets of air between the tiles and the tank wall will liquefy from the intense cold. This makes the tiles pop off, causing drastic delays and expensive repairs. By Apollo 13, the engineers will come up with a solution: spray foam. It turns out that spray-on foam will adhere directly to the tanks, eliminating air pockets. The foam is also lighter and has better insulating qualities than the fiberglass honeycomb.

In Huntington Beach, California, engineers at the Douglas Aircraft Company are putting together the third stage of the Saturn V, the S-IVB. It was originally meant to be the fourth stage of an earlier rocket design, which is why it has the roman numeral four in its name.

The third stage has two important jobs. The first is to fire its single J-2 engine to push the Apollo spacecraft into orbit around Earth. Once it does this, the engine will shut down, with over half of its propellants still remaining, and coast in orbit until it is called upon to fire again. That's the S-IVB's other important job. The second firing will bring the spacecraft up to a speed of over 25,000 miles per hour, allow it to break free of its Earth orbit, and send it hurtling toward the Moon. This is called Translunar Injection (TLI).

The challenge of building a machine that will restart in space presents several complex problems, but the solutions the engineers come up with are elegantly simple in design.

Saturn V S-IVB Facts

Height	**58** ft. **5** in.
Diameter	**21** ft. **8** in.
Weight (fully fueled)	**260,523** lb.
Weight (empty)	**25,000** lb.
Manufacturer	**Douglas Aircraft Company**

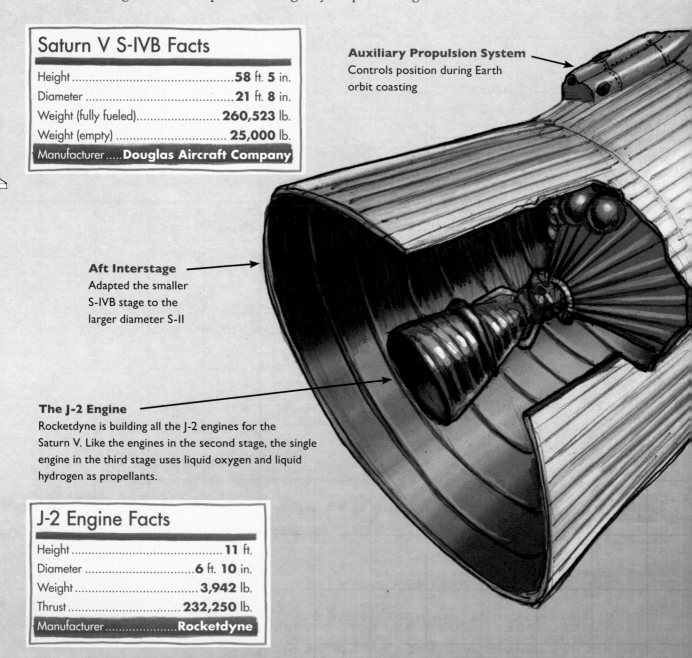

Auxiliary Propulsion System
Controls position during Earth orbit coasting

Aft Interstage
Adapted the smaller S-IVB stage to the larger diameter S-II

The J-2 Engine
Rocketdyne is building all the J-2 engines for the Saturn V. Like the engines in the second stage, the single engine in the third stage uses liquid oxygen and liquid hydrogen as propellants.

J-2 Engine Facts

Height	**11** ft.
Diameter	**6** ft. **10** in.
Weight	**3,942** lb.
Thrust	**232,250** lb.
Manufacturer	**Rocketdyne**

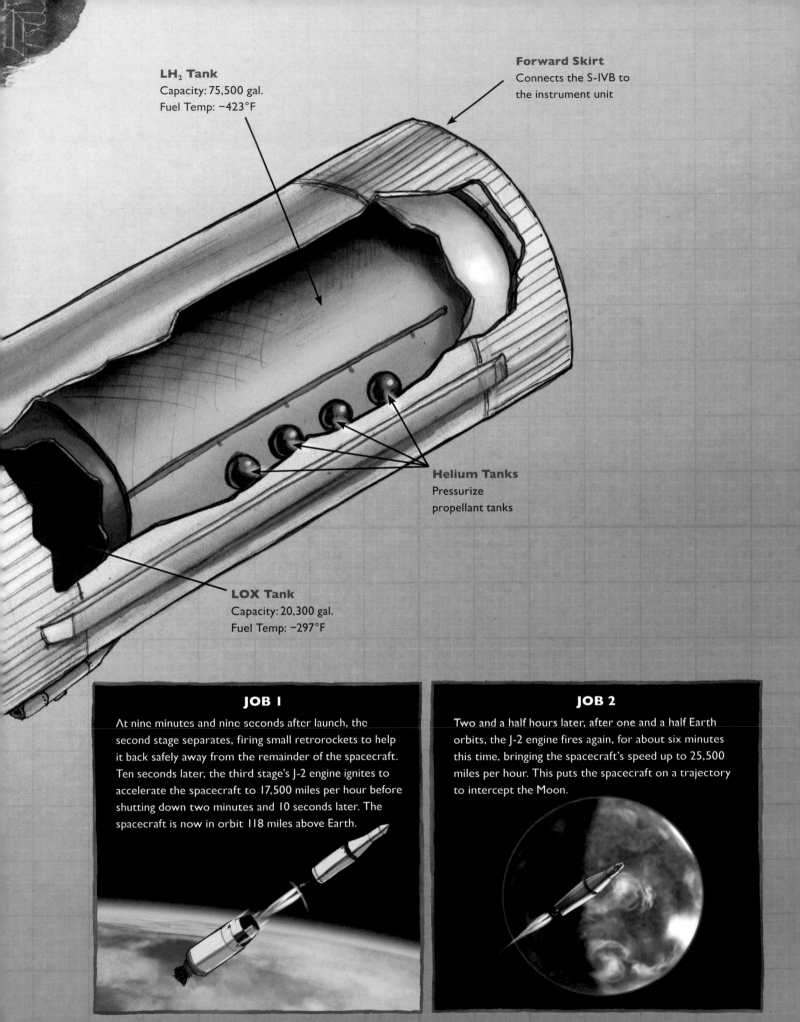

LH₂ Tank
Capacity: 75,500 gal.
Fuel Temp: −423°F

Forward Skirt
Connects the S-IVB to
the instrument unit

Helium Tanks
Pressurize
propellant tanks

LOX Tank
Capacity: 20,300 gal.
Fuel Temp: −297°F

JOB 1

At nine minutes and nine seconds after launch, the second stage separates, firing small retrorockets to help it back safely away from the remainder of the spacecraft. Ten seconds later, the third stage's J-2 engine ignites to accelerate the spacecraft to 17,500 miles per hour before shutting down two minutes and 10 seconds later. The spacecraft is now in orbit 118 miles above Earth.

JOB 2

Two and a half hours later, after one and a half Earth orbits, the J-2 engine fires again, for about six minutes this time, bringing the spacecraft's speed up to 25,500 miles per hour. This puts the spacecraft on a trajectory to intercept the Moon.

Going into Orbit

At first, the engineers at Douglas think that once the S-IVB engine ignites, it will send the spacecraft directly on a course to intercept the Moon. But at a meeting with NASA in 1964, rocket scientist Ernst Geissler reminds them why going into Earth orbit first, before the translunar injection burn, is critical.

He states that there are a number of factors that determine when it is best to launch. Knowing where you are launching from and where on the lunar surface you want to land are only the beginning. The timing of the landing is also important. The crew needs to land when the Sun is low on the lunar horizon, he explains, allowing the shadows to clearly define the craters and rocks. He says it's also best to launch from Earth during the day if possible.

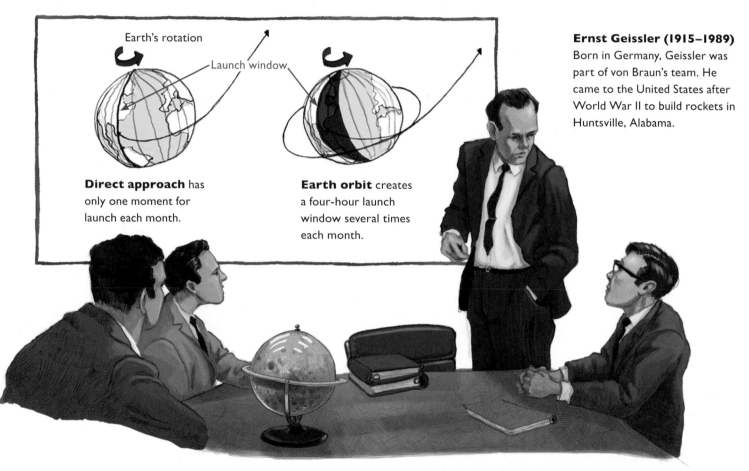

Earth's rotation

Launch window

Direct approach has only one moment for launch each month.

Earth orbit creates a four-hour launch window several times each month.

Ernst Geissler (1915–1989)
Born in Germany, Geissler was part of von Braun's team. He came to the United States after World War II to build rockets in Huntsville, Alabama.

Once the engineers consider all of this, it becomes clear: flying *directly* to the Moon from launch can be accomplished only during one precise moment each month, when the locations of Earth and the Moon create the perfect trajectory.

However, if we first go into an orbit around Earth, it allows us to choose the moment we start our trajectory toward the Moon. This method will give us several potential launch days each month, as well as a wider window of time (up to four hours) to launch within. This is important because there can be many delays during a countdown due to inclement weather or technical problems.

It will also give the astronauts time to make sure everything is in proper working condition before they hurl themselves 240,000 miles across space.

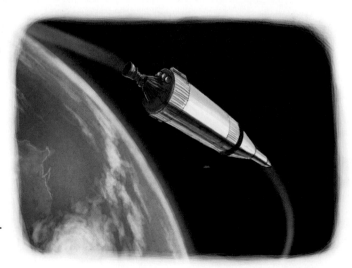

Free-Return Trajectory

The fastest way to get to the Moon is to carry enough propellants to keep the spacecraft's engines running all the way there. Unfortunately, the weight of that much propellant would make it impossible to get off the ground. Instead, the plan is to fire the S-IVB's engine for about six minutes, enabling it to gather enough speed to propel itself on a path to intercept the Moon.

The spacecraft and crew will then coast along for three days, gradually slowing from the pull of Earth's gravity. When they get within 40,000 miles of their target, the Moon's gravity will take over and begin to pull them in. As the spacecraft gets pulled around the far side of the Moon, the crew will fire its engine again, slowing down the spacecraft enough to allow Lunar Orbit Insertion (LOI).

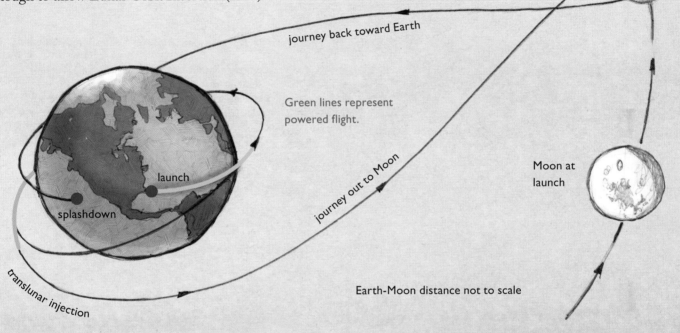

Moon at landing

journey back toward Earth

Green lines represent powered flight.

launch

splashdown

journey out to Moon

Moon at launch

translunar injection

Earth-Moon distance not to scale

If for some reason the engine does not fire, the spacecraft will simply whip around the Moon and begin a long fall back to Earth, gradually picking up speed as it gets closer. This is called a free-return trajectory—"free" because it will not cost any fuel to get back to Earth.

The free-return trajectory is an elegant solution for crew safety. The Russians proved that it worked in October 1959, when they launched an unpiloted spacecraft called Luna 3 to photograph the Moon's far side. Using a gravity assist from the Moon, Luna 3 came flying back toward Earth two weeks later without the use of fuel. In 1963, NASA adopts free-return trajectory as part of the Apollo mission plan.

Free-Return Trajectory to the Rescue

"Okay, Houston, we've had a problem here."—Jack Swigert, astronaut

An oxygen tank exploded on the Apollo 13 spacecraft as it was headed toward the Moon on April 11, 1970. Because of possible damage to the main engine, Mission Control did not want to risk using it, and had to rely upon the LM's engine to put them back on a free-return trajectory to get the crew home. On April 17th, after six days of coasting over a half million miles through space, commander Jim Lovell, Lunar Module pilot Fred Haise, and Command Module pilot Jack Swigert returned safely to Earth.

HAVING THE RIGHT ATTITUDE

The orientation, or position, of an aircraft or a spacecraft is called its attitude. In order to control the attitude, a spacecraft has to be able to move around on three different axes, called roll, pitch, and yaw. An aircraft has the benefit of moving through air, so a pilot can use controllable flaps or fins to redirect that air and change the airplane's attitude. In space, there is nothing for flaps or fins to push against, so spacecraft have to use other means to control attitude.

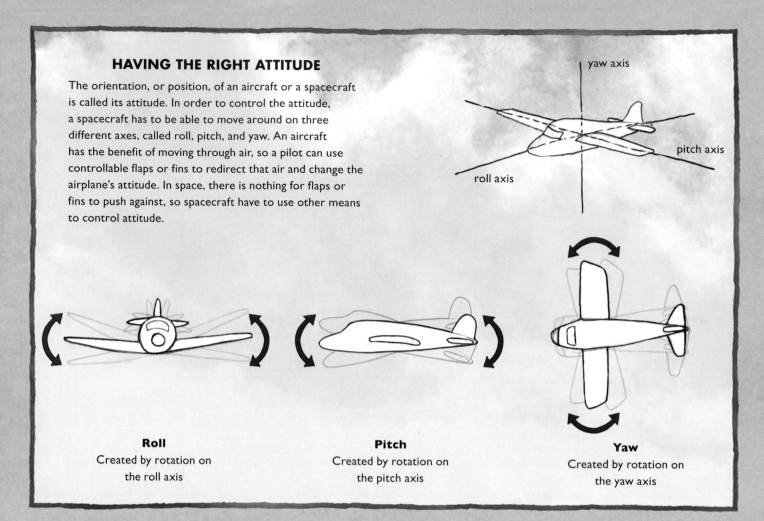

Roll
Created by rotation on the roll axis

Pitch
Created by rotation on the pitch axis

Yaw
Created by rotation on the yaw axis

Problem! Controlling the Attitude of the S-IVB

Controlling the attitude of a rocket while it is in flight is possible because the engine nozzles on all three stages of the rocket can swivel, or gimbal, to steer the rocket in the direction you want it to fly in. The first and second stages, having more than one engine, can also gimbal their engines in a way to create roll. The S-IVB, with its single engine, cannot. It also has no way of controlling its attitude while the engine is off and it is coasting in orbit.

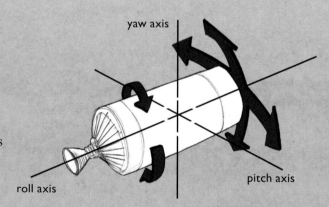

Full Three-Axes Attitude Control: Rotating around one of these three axes allows the S-IVB to orient itself.

Like the engines on the S-IC and S-II stages, the single engine on the S-IVB can be aimed to change the pitch or yaw of the spacecraft.

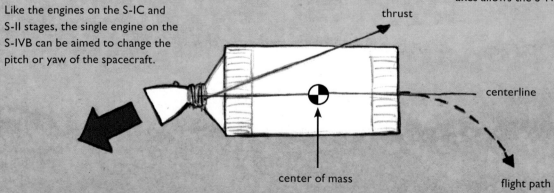

Solution! Auxiliary Propulsion System (APS)

In Redondo Beach, California, engineers at Thompson Ramo Wooldridge (TRW) design two self-contained systems, called Auxiliary Propulsion Systems, to mount on opposite sides of the S-IVB. Together these allow for complete control of the spacecraft while in orbit. Each APS has four engines, which control roll, pitch, yaw, and ullage.

Ullage is the unfilled space in a container. (The word was first used by brewmasters to describe the unfilled section of a beer barrel.) Once in orbit, the S-IVB will have a large amount of ullage in its tanks since a considerable amount of the propellants have already been depleted during the first engine burn. It's important to make sure all the liquid propellants are at the bottoms of the tanks before firing the engine again.

A short burst from the two ullage engines will give the spacecraft a forward push, settling the propellants to the bottoms of the tanks. Then the main engine can be fired to send the spacecraft on a path to intercept the Moon.

pitch

roll

yaw

APS on either side of the aft skirt

High-Pressure Helium Tank
Provides constant pressure to the propellant tanks. The propellants are contained inside Teflon bladders, and the helium will pressurize the space between the tank wall and the bladder.

Fuel Tank
Contains monomethylhydrazine (CH_3NHNH_2)

Oxidizer Tank
Contains nitrogen tetroxide (N_2O_4)

Pitch Engine
Can orient the spacecraft along its pitch axis with its 150 pounds of thrust

Yaw and Roll Engines
Can be sequenced to orient the spacecraft along its yaw or roll axis. On opposite sides of the APS, each engine has 150 pounds of thrust.

Ullage Engine
Settles the propellants in the S-IVB's tanks to their bottoms

ullage

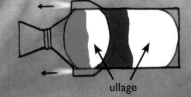

ullage

The Instrument Unit (IU): The Critical Stage

Piloting a 6.5-million-pound rocket into orbit and then on a course for the Moon is an impossible task for three crew members riding in a tiny capsule at the top of a spacecraft. There are too many variables, too many steps, and too many perfectly timed events that need to occur in order to make it work.

The Saturn V needs an autopilot, a machine that knows where the rocket is, where it wants to go, what it needs to do to get there, and how to carry out those commands. Luckily, in a small laboratory at the Massachusetts Institute of Technology (MIT), there is a man who knows how to design such a device. His name is Charles Stark Draper, and on August 9, 1961, NASA awards his instrumentation laboratory the very first Apollo contract to design and build an automated guidance system.

Saturn V IU Facts

Height	**3** ft.
Diameter	**21** ft. **8** in.
Weight (at launch)	**4,400** lb.
Manufacturer	**IBM**

POWER SYSTEM

Uses four silver-zinc batteries to power all the electronics on the IU

ENVIRONMENTAL CONTROL SYSTEM (ECS)

Carries the heat away from the electronics using a process called sublimation (see pp. 90–91)

84

This system will become the brains of the launch vehicle. It will be mounted in a three-foot-tall ring called the Instrument Unit (IU), which contains all the electronic systems for the Saturn V. The IU, designed by NASA and manufactured and assembled by IBM, will provide all the information and commands to the three stages below, controlling everything the Saturn V does from launch through the final engine burn. Similar guidance systems, also made by Draper's lab, will be placed in the Command Module and the Lunar Module.

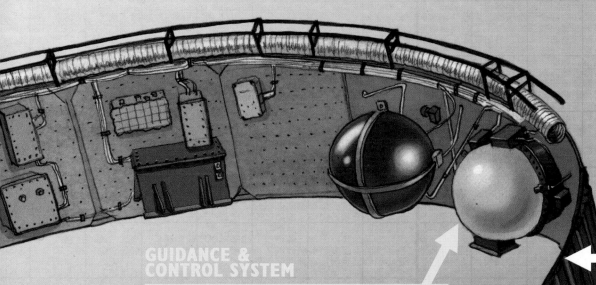

STRUCTURE

Unlike the rest of the Saturn V, the outer layer of the IU is built more like the Apollo spacecraft that sits above it. The walls are formed from a lightweight aluminum honeycomb sandwiched between two sheets of aluminum alloy.

GUIDANCE & CONTROL SYSTEM

Inertial Platform
Measures the acceleration and attitude of the Saturn V

Launch Vehicle Digital Computer (LVDC)
Receives the measurements from the inertial platform and calculates guidance equations

Analog Flight Control Computer
Issues the commands to steer the vehicle

EMERGENCY DETECTION SYSTEM (EDS)

Commands an automatic abort sequence to save the crew if something goes wrong with the rocket

TELEMETRY SYSTEM

Gathers important information about the vehicle's status and transmits it back to Mission Control for monitoring

Charles Stark "Doc" Draper (1901–1987)

The Father of Inertial Navigation

Doc Draper was a quirky genius. He was a champion ballroom dancer, an amateur boxer, a pilot, a teacher, a psychologist, *and* a scientist. While studying electrochemical engineering at MIT, Draper started flying small planes. He immediately noticed the limitations of their instrumentation and felt that it could be improved. This led him to teach courses in aircraft instrumentation at MIT in the late 1920s. By the 1930s, Draper had founded the MIT Instrumentation Laboratory, where he and his team researched and developed guidance systems for flight navigation.

Using gyroscopes and accelerometers (see p. 89), Draper developed the Inertial Guidance System. It could measure both the direction and acceleration of a moving object, and would later be adopted for use in aircraft, submarines, and space vehicles—but first, Draper had to prove it could work.

In 1953 in Bedford, Massachusetts, Draper boarded a B-29 bomber equipped with his Inertial Guidance System. Once it got into the air, the pilot left his seat and the controls. If all went well, the Inertial Guidance System would tell the autopilot how to steer the plane 3,000 miles across the country, to an airfield in Los Angeles.

Hours passed. All was going smoothly until suddenly the plane banked to the right. Draper was alarmed. Why would the plane bank? Was his machine not doing its job? When they came down through the clouds, there was Los Angeles, right below them, exactly where the system was supposed to bring them. It turned out that side winds had pushed the plane off course, and Draper's Inertial Guidance System had merely been doing its job of self-correcting the plane's flight.

It worked perfectly.

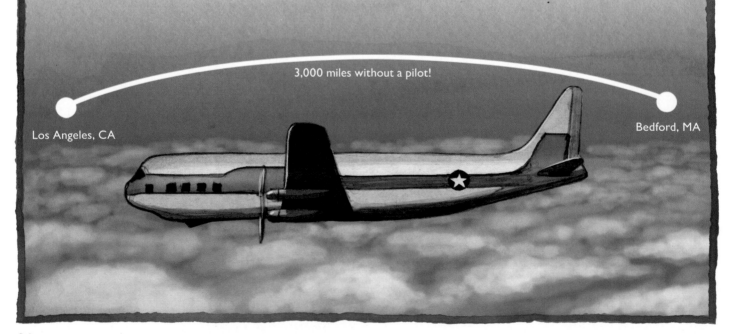

3,000 miles without a pilot!

Los Angeles, CA

Bedford, MA

The Guidance and Control System

Where am I? Where do I want to go? What do I need to do to get there?

These are the questions that drove Draper and his team to develop an Inertial Guidance System. The idea is simple: if you know exactly where you start from and you keep track of how fast and in which direction you are traveling, you will know your exact location at all times. And if you know that, you can calculate the course needed to get to where you want to go.

In order to make these calculations, Draper needs three pieces of critical information:

STARTING POINT

Draper knows that for a mission to the Moon, the crew will need to know where the spacecraft is relative to a fixed position in space, using stars. You cannot use a fixed point on Earth, because Earth itself is not fixed—it is spinning, and rotating around the Sun.

CHANGES IN ATTITUDE

If you can measure how much the spacecraft is rotating around the pitch, yaw, and roll axes, then you can know which direction you are going in.

CHANGES IN ACCELERATION

If you can measure acceleration on all three axes, then you will know how far you are going over time.

Doc Draper demonstrates that a gyroscope (essentially a spinning wheel) nested inside a framework of gimbals doesn't change its attitude no matter how much he moves the outer frame. This device will prove critical in building a guidance system that can measure changes in attitude.

Inertial Platform

To measure changes in attitude and acceleration, Draper and his team build an instrument called an inertial platform. *Inert* means "motionless," and the inertial platform's job will be to stay perfectly still, no matter how much the vehicle it's in changes its attitude. In order to do this, three gyroscopes are mounted on the platform: one to stabilize the pitch of the platform, one for the roll, and one for the yaw.

A framework of gimbals allows the platform to remain stationary while the vehicle it is mounted in moves freely on all three axes. As the vehicle changes position, the gimbals will rotate, and this rotation can be measured. These measurements tell the computer system how the vehicle's attitude has changed from where it began.

An engineer works on the inertial platform

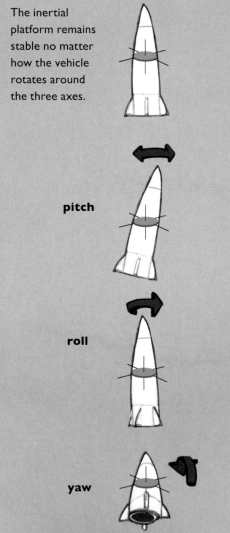

The inertial platform remains stable no matter how the vehicle rotates around the three axes.

pitch

roll

yaw

Schematic of Inertial Platform

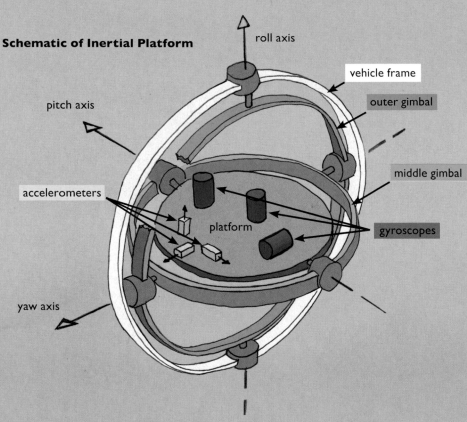

roll axis

pitch axis

vehicle frame

outer gimbal

middle gimbal

accelerometers

gyroscopes

platform

yaw axis

Three accelerometers measure the speed in all directions and send that information to the computer system as well. Using this data, the computer knows whether any changes need to be made to keep the vehicle on the predefined course.

How a Gyroscope Works to Keep a Platform Stable

The gyroscope, invented by French physicist Léon Foucault in 1852, is a spinning wheel mounted on an axis and held within a frame. The spinning wheel resists change in orientation and has a stabilizing effect similar to the wheels of a bicycle in motion.

Balancing on a bicycle that is stationary is difficult.

Balancing on a bicycle that is moving is much easier, because the spinning wheels held within the framework of the bike help to stabilize it.

EXPERIMENT

A. Hold a bicycle wheel by its axle, and rotate it by pushing one side outward. You will find this to be fairly easy.

B. Now try the same movement with the wheel spinning briskly. You will find that this takes much more effort. That is because a wheel in motion resists change.

How an Accelerometer Works to Measure Acceleration

An accelerometer measures changes in acceleration. Invented by English physicist George Atwood in the late 18th century and called the Atwood machine, it was designed to verify Newton's three laws of motion.

To understand how an accelerometer works, think of yourself sitting in the back seat of a moving car. If the car suddenly slows down or speeds up, you will feel yourself slide either forward or backward. How much force you feel will be relative to how quickly the car decelerates or accelerates. Accelerometers measure this force.

constant speed   acceleration   deceleration

Accelerometers and gyroscopes are used today in many devices, like smartphones and handheld game consoles, to detect movement and tilting motions. For example, a smartphone will orient the display depending on whether you are holding it vertically or horizontally, and a racing game will allow you to steer your car by tilting your game console from side to side.

Problem! Keeping the Electronics Cool

Over time, electronic devices get hot. For example, you may have felt the heat of a laptop computer on your legs. That is because all the metals and wiring used in electronics have an attribute called resistance. When electricity passes through these metals, the resistance causes energy to build up, which turns into heat. The wires in a toaster use this resistance to build up enough heat to toast bread. The engineers at IBM need to figure out a way to remove the heat from all the different electronic and computer systems in the Saturn V Instrument Unit (IU).

A toaster uses the resistance in the wires to create heat when electricity passes through them.

CHANGING STATES OF MATTER

Most matter exists in one of three states: solid, liquid, or gas. Temperature affects these states by changing how the molecules bond together. You're familiar with the process of an ice cube melting. That's when the water molecules change from a solid to a liquid form. When that water is then boiled on a stove, those molecules move more rapidly, evaporating into a gaseous state called steam. It is also possible for a solid to sublimate, turning directly into a gas. You may have seen this happen with solid carbon dioxide, also known as dry ice.

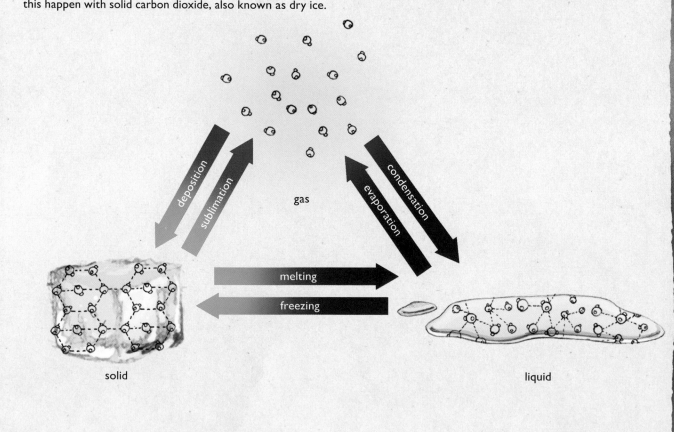

Solution! Sublimators and Cold Plates

In 1963, at a company called Hamilton Standard in Windsor Locks, Connecticut, engineers John S. Lovell and George C. Rannenberg are working on the problem of how to keep the Apollo spacesuit cool. They know that if you expose ice to the vacuum of space it will turn into a gas and carry the heat away with it. Together, Lovell and Rannenberg develop an arrangement of metal plates pierced with microscopic holes that make them porous. In space, if they fill these plates with water, it freezes and sublimates out of the holes. They call their invention a sublimator, and it is so effective that it is not only used to keep the spacesuit cool but also adopted for the Saturn V Instrument Unit (IU) and the Apollo spacecraft.

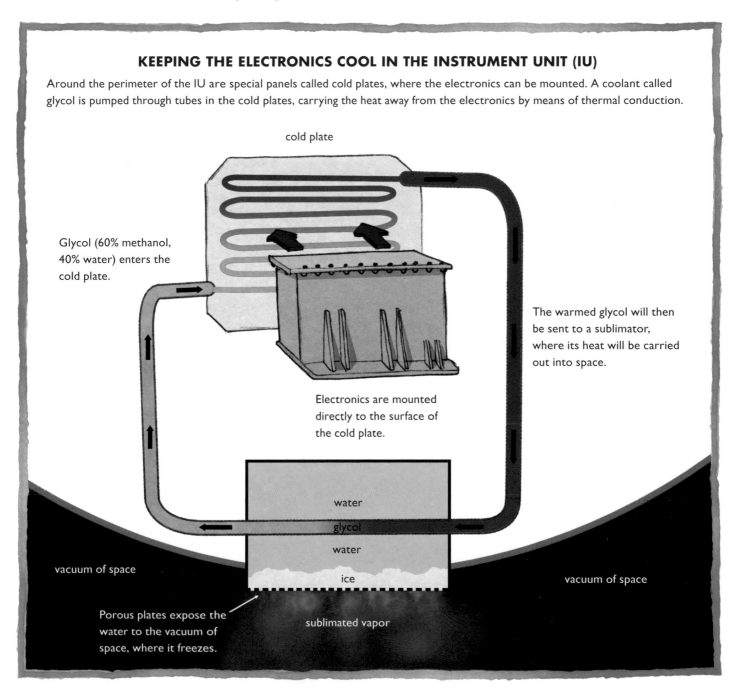

KEEPING THE ELECTRONICS COOL IN THE INSTRUMENT UNIT (IU)

Around the perimeter of the IU are special panels called cold plates, where the electronics can be mounted. A coolant called glycol is pumped through tubes in the cold plates, carrying the heat away from the electronics by means of thermal conduction.

cold plate

Glycol (60% methanol, 40% water) enters the cold plate.

The warmed glycol will then be sent to a sublimator, where its heat will be carried out into space.

Electronics are mounted directly to the surface of the cold plate.

water

glycol

water

vacuum of space

ice

vacuum of space

Porous plates expose the water to the vacuum of space, where it freezes.

sublimated vapor

Now that the IU has a way to stay cool, the Saturn V has a fully functioning "brain" that can pilot the rocket into space and on to the Moon. Its digital computer will send signals 25 times a second to keep the rocket on course, giving NASA the ability to test the entire rocket without a crew aboard.

Command and Service Module (CSM)

Command
Module (CM)

Service Module (SM)

Descent Stage

Ascent Stage

Lunar Module (LM)

PART 4

Building a Spacecraft

*"The whole idea of going into space was new and daring.
There were no textbooks, so we had to write them."*

—KATHERINE JOHNSON, MATHEMATICIAN

With the construction of the Saturn V launch vehicle in progress, NASA now has a way to send a spacecraft on a trajectory to the Moon. The next task is to build one that can carry the astronauts close to a million miles through space, allow them to land on another world, and bring them safely back to Earth. Apollo's inventive design will end up being not one spacecraft but four—each made from millions of parts and designed to perform a specific set of tasks.

The Apollo spacecraft will be one of the most sophisticated machines ever built, designed to accomplish something that has never been done: take human beings to the Moon and bring them back to Earth.

The Command Module (CM): A Home in Space

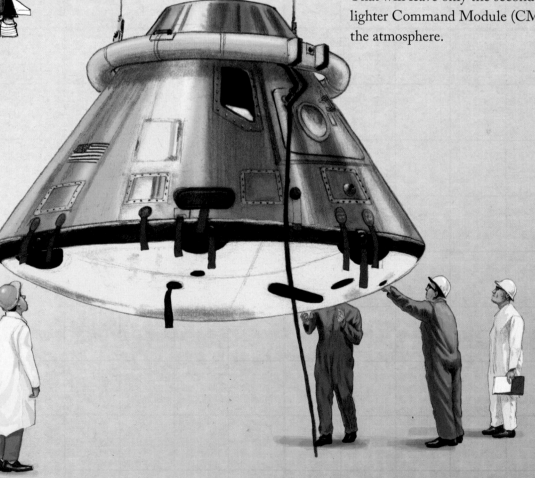

On November 28, 1961, the contract to build the Apollo spacecraft is awarded to North American Aviation. It is a well-respected company—only two years ago, they built the X-15 plane, which test pilots like Neil Armstrong flew to the edge of space.

North American has to create a home for three crew members to live in for up to 14 days. The spacecraft needs to hold everything the crew requires to survive the journey—oxygen, food, water, batteries, an environmental control system, waste management, fuel, a propulsion system, and other controls. It will also need parachutes for a safe landing, and survival equipment in case the astronauts land in a remote area on Earth, far from rescue. All of these things could make the spacecraft large and heavy, causing it to generate too much heat as it slams back into Earth's atmosphere—and potentially burn up like a meteorite during reentry.

How can North American cut down on weight?

The engineers realize that not everything needed during the mission has to return to Earth, so they decide to build a two-part Command and Service Module (CSM). The first part, the Service Module (SM), which houses many of the necessary life support systems and fuel, can be jettisoned right before reentry. That will leave only the second part, the smaller, lighter Command Module (CM), to come through the atmosphere.

Apollo CM Facts

Height	**10** ft. **7** in.
Diameter	**12** ft. **10** in.
Weight (including crew)	**13,000** lb.
Weight (splashdown)	**11,700** lb.
Manufacturer	**North American Aviation**

The CM has only 210 cubic feet of room inside it, but it is very spacious compared to the cramped Mercury and Gemini capsules. During launch and reentry, the crew will lie on their backs, on what the engineers call "couches." For the bulk of the mission, the center couch will be folded up, allowing the astronauts to float freely through the space.

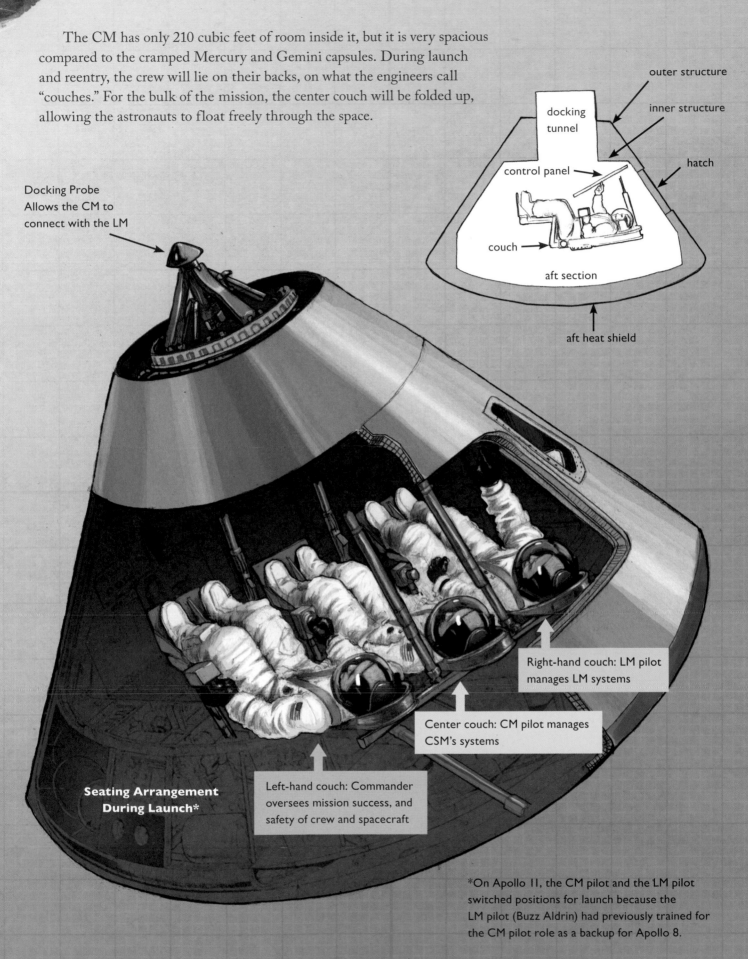

outer structure

docking tunnel

inner structure

control panel

hatch

couch

aft section

aft heat shield

Docking Probe
Allows the CM to
connect with the LM

Right-hand couch: LM pilot
manages LM systems

Center couch: CM pilot manages
CSM's systems

Left-hand couch: Commander
oversees mission success, and
safety of crew and spacecraft

**Seating Arrangement
During Launch***

*On Apollo 11, the CM pilot and the LM pilot
switched positions for launch because the
LM pilot (Buzz Aldrin) had previously trained for
the CM pilot role as a backup for Apollo 8.

95

COMMAND MODULE MAIN CONTROL PANEL

The CM Main Control Panel includes hundreds of switches, indicators, and instruments. From their couches, the three crew members can control almost every aspect of their spacecraft.

1 A) **Entry displays**

1 B) **Displays and manual controls for boost, entry, and abort**

1 C) **Flight attitude indicator No. 1**

1 D) **Switches and indicators for flight control of the spacecraft**

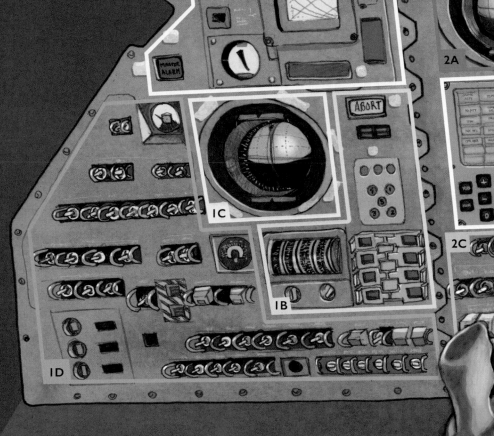

2 A) Flight attitude indicator No. 2

2 B) **Display and keyboard for Apollo Guidance Computer (AGC)**

2 C) **Switches for abort, boost, and entry**

left-hand couch

center couch

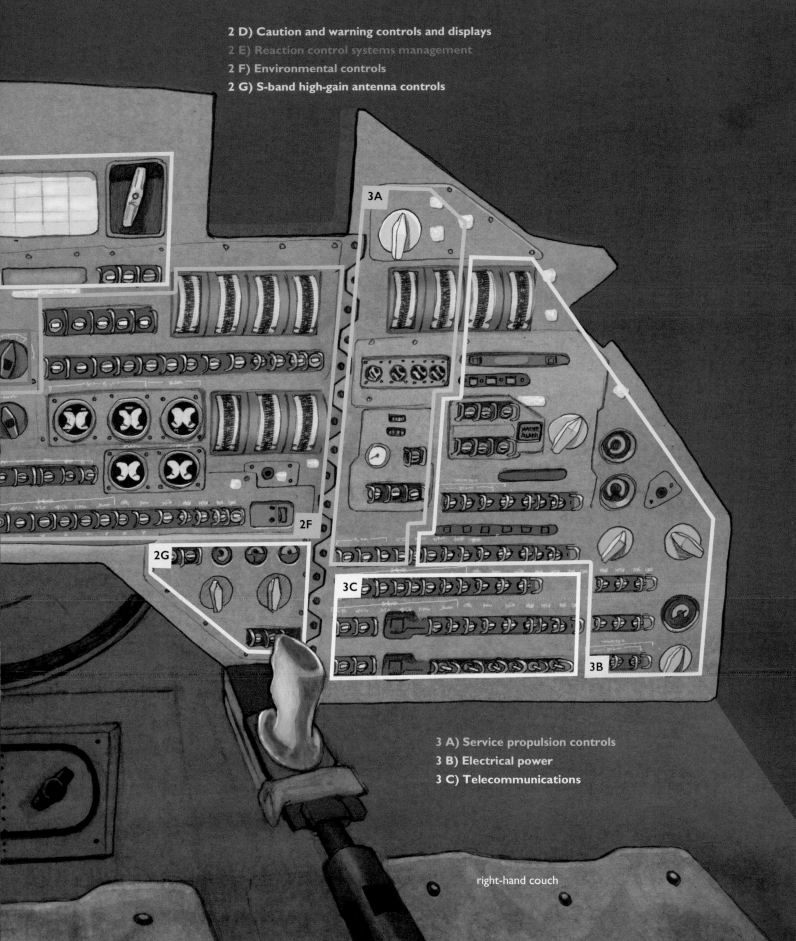

2 D) Caution and warning controls and displays
2 E) Reaction control systems management
2 F) Environmental controls
2 G) S-band high-gain antenna controls

3A

2F

2G

3C

3B

3 A) Service propulsion controls
3 B) Electrical power
3 C) Telecommunications

right-hand couch

97

The Launch Escape Tower (LET)

Problem! An Exploding Rocket

Rockets sometimes blow up. Everyone involved with Apollo knows this. Many unpiloted rocket tests before and during Project Mercury ended with a spectacular explosion. During the Gemini program, each astronaut had an ejection seat, similar to what you might find on a military jet. If something went wrong, the seats would explode out of the capsule, allowing the Gemini crew to parachute to safety. But it was far from being a safe option, and it was lucky that the astronauts never had to use it.

The danger has grown with the size of the rockets. If a Saturn V rocket were to blow up, the fireball would be enormous and having the crew eject out of the CM would be deadly.

Solution! Ejection Seat for the Entire Command Module

Developed by Max Faget in 1958 and first used during Project Mercury, the Launch Escape Tower (LET) is an elegant, innovative solution. In the case of an explosion, a solid rocket motor attached to a tower would fire for 3.5 seconds, which would pull the entire CM— with the crew inside—away from the exploding rocket, to a sufficient height to deploy its parachutes.

Electrical sensors down the sides of the rocket would trigger the LET if something were to go wrong, either on the launchpad or during the first three and a half minutes of the flight. The crew also has a manually activated abort trigger in the CM. When the Saturn V reaches the height of 295,000 feet, the crew can utilize their Service Module for aborts, so the LET would be jettisoned. It would take with it the protective forward heat shield, finally giving the crew some larger windows to look out of.

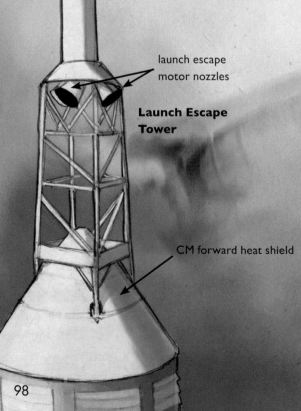

tower jettison motor nozzle

launch escape motor nozzles

Launch Escape Tower

CM forward heat shield

The LET was first introduced during Project Mercury, but the new Apollo launch escape tower has more thrust than the entire rocket that sent Alan Shepard into space.

During an unpiloted test of the Apollo LET, the rocket starts to explode and the LET works perfectly to pull the CM away. Even though none of the Apollo piloted missions will ever make use of the LET, it sure makes everyone more comfortable knowing that it's there.

Maxime A. "Max" Faget (1921–2004)
Chief Engineer, Manned Spacecraft Center

"It's hard to tell people how you invent something. You see a problem—you solve a problem. I enjoy solving problems."

The Mercury capsule, the Launch Escape Tower, and the Space Shuttle all have one thing in common: they were born from the imagination of Max Faget.

Faget, the son of an American doctor who studied tropical diseases, was born in British Honduras (now Belize). As a child, he was fascinated with building model airplanes, and he went on to get a degree in mechanical engineering from Louisiana State University in Baton Rouge. During World War II, Faget saw combat duty as a naval officer inside cramped submarines in the Pacific. In 1946, on a whim, he applied for a job at the National Advisory Committee for Aeronautics (NACA) and was hired as a research engineer.

Faget was small in stature, but he had an unforgettable presence—sometimes leaping over chairs as he jogged into a meeting, or doing headstands to improve blood circulation to his brain. Unlike most engineers, who worked out problems sitting at a drafting table and doing complex mathematics, Faget would figure things out in his head and then start building models.

When the space race got under way in 1957, Faget's idea for a one-person space capsule was adopted for the Mercury program. It was a simple design, and it allowed NASA to move quickly in its effort to put a man in space. Faget's brilliant ideas were a key factor in the success of the US space program.

Max Faget holding a model of a reusable spacecraft. His design was the initial inspiration for what would eventually become the Space Shuttle, which first flew in 1981.

How the Command Module Can Fly Without Wings

After traveling over 240,000 miles back from the Moon, the Apollo spacecraft will have to enter the atmosphere at a very precise angle called the entry corridor, which is only about 15 miles wide. That's like sinking a basketball through a hoop mounted on a moving car almost five miles away!

With a too-shallow approach, the CM and the crew inside will skip off the atmosphere like a flat stone off a pond. After that, without fuel or an engine to slow them down, they will continue to orbit Earth until they run out of supplies. With a too-steep approach, the CM will burn up upon reentry. Either way will mean certain death for the crew. Having the ability to fly the CM is critical to allow the crew to have control over their reentry.

Faget knows that at 400,000 feet, the air molecules in the atmosphere will begin to hit the surface of the CM, creating drag, which will act to slow down the spacecraft. He realizes that a blunt-ended craft is a perfect solution. The air molecules bombarding the blunt end will create lift, turning the entire CM into a wing. This will allow the crew to control the spacecraft.

Max Faget was once seen flinging pairs of paper plates, taped together, from a second-story balcony to study the aerodynamics of a so-called blunt body shape. Later studies, and tests performed in a special wind tunnel, proved that a blunt-shaped Command Module was capable of controlled flight.

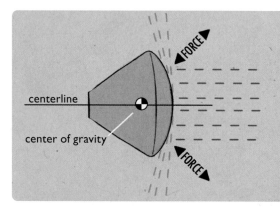

The center of gravity of an object is the averaged location of all its weight and is also considered its balance point. If the center of gravity is in the exact middle along the CM's centerline, it will meet air molecules head-on, and the force created will be the same on all sides. This approach would not allow control of the CM.

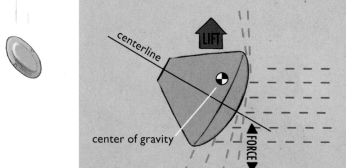

If you place the heavier equipment in the CM toward one side, it moves the center of gravity off the centerline. This will force the CM to meet air molecules on an angle, creating an upward lift as more air molecules are directed downward. This approach would allow control of the CM.

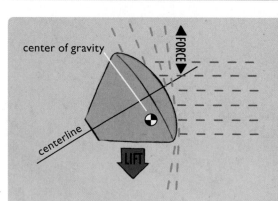

Using the CM's roll thrusters, crew members can rotate the CM around its centerline to change the direction of lift. This gives them the ability to steer the craft in pitch and yaw—and thus adjust their flight path during reentry.

Since the CM will be landing in the ocean, ships will be stationed in specifically targeted areas to retrieve the crew and the CM after splashdown. If there is a problem in the initial landing area, such as inclement weather, having the ability to fly the CM enables the crew to extend its flight by as much as 400 miles.

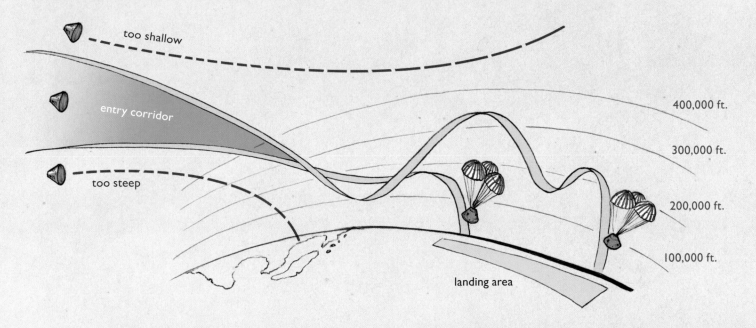

too shallow

entry corridor

too steep

400,000 ft.

300,000 ft.

200,000 ft.

100,000 ft.

landing area

Ann D. Montgomery (b. 1946)

Flight Crew Equipment Engineer

There was only one woman who had clearance to go out to the Apollo launchpad, and even she was often stopped by security guards until they saw her credentials. Her name was Ann Montgomery, and her job was to manage where everything was stowed on the CM.

Food, TV cameras, experiments, lunar rock boxes, tools, and a myriad of other equipment had to be loaded inside 24 hours before liftoff. Where it was stowed was crucial, because the CM's center of gravity had to be in a specific spot in order for it to fly during reentry.

Montgomery made sure that everything was stowed in the correct place prior to launch. Throughout the mission any weight changes would be tracked by Mission Control, as some things were going to be left behind on the Moon (equipment and trash), and other things, like lunar rocks, were going to be brought back, so every fraction of an ounce had to be accounted for.

Montgomery started at NASA in June 1968, shortly after graduating from the University of Florida with a mathematics degree. She continued working for NASA while she earned a master's degree in engineering. Montgomery was only 21 years old when she worked on her first mission—Apollo 7. She worked on every Apollo mission to the Moon and on many Space Shuttle missions before retiring from NASA in 2002.

Ann Montgomery inside the White Room, preparing to load equipment into the CM

The Heat of Reentry

The burning and charring ablative material melts and carries the heat away from the spacecraft.

Problem! Extreme Temperatures

Have you ever felt a bicycle pump after you've inflated a tire? It is warm to the touch. That's because the compression of air molecules creates heat. When the Command Module slams into the atmosphere at 24,500 miles per hour, it will compress the air in front of it, creating temperatures of over 5000°F. How can you protect the astronauts and their spacecraft from these extreme temperatures so that they won't burn up like a meteorite?

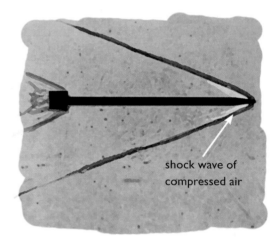

shock wave of compressed air

Initial Dartlike Shape (Early 1950s)

Solution! A Blunt Body with a Heat Shield

From his work on the Mercury and Gemini capsules, Max Faget understands that a blunt body design will work best. The blunt shape will not only allow the crew to steer, it will also compress the air into a shock wave in front of the spacecraft, keeping most of the heat away from it.

To combat the rest, the engineers design a heat shield. It is made from a material that will char, melt, and then fall off the CM, carrying the heat away with it. This process is called ablation. As it burns away, it will also emit a vapor that will help insulate the CM from the fiery inferno.

The heat shield is formed from a fiberglass honeycomb whose cells are filled with a type of plastic called phenolic epoxy resin. In addition to the heat shield, this resin-filled honeycomb also covers the rest of the CM, although not as thickly.

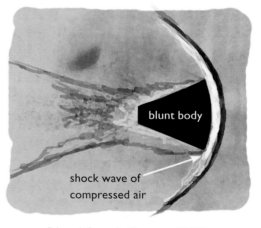

blunt body

shock wave of compressed air

Piloted Capsule Concept (1957)

Early testing in high-speed wind tunnels during the Mercury program showed that a blunt body shape was best for reentry.

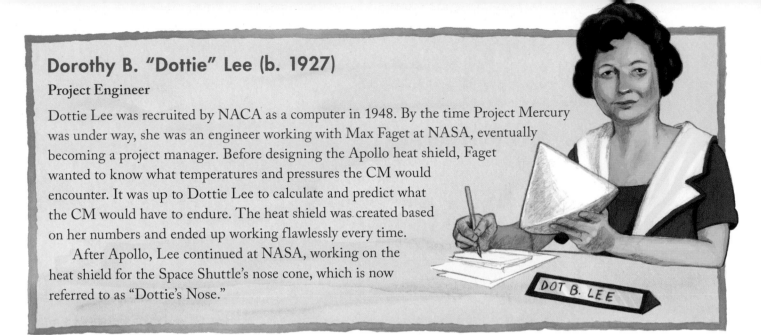

Dorothy B. "Dottie" Lee (b. 1927)
Project Engineer

Dottie Lee was recruited by NACA as a computer in 1948. By the time Project Mercury was under way, she was an engineer working with Max Faget at NASA, eventually becoming a project manager. Before designing the Apollo heat shield, Faget wanted to know what temperatures and pressures the CM would encounter. It was up to Dottie Lee to calculate and predict what the CM would have to endure. The heat shield was created based on her numbers and ended up working flawlessly every time.

After Apollo, Lee continued at NASA, working on the heat shield for the Space Shuttle's nose cone, which is now referred to as "Dottie's Nose."

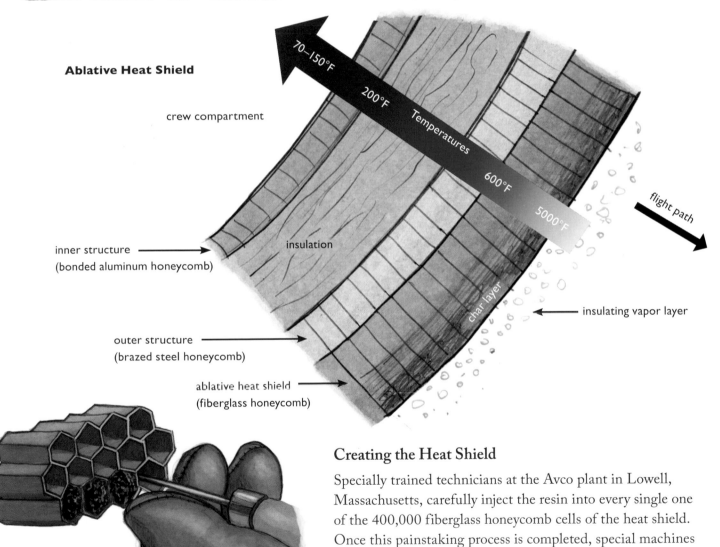

Ablative Heat Shield

crew compartment

70–150°F

200°F

Temperatures

600°F

5000°F

flight path

inner structure
(bonded aluminum honeycomb)

insulation

char layer

insulating vapor layer

outer structure
(brazed steel honeycomb)

ablative heat shield
(fiberglass honeycomb)

Creating the Heat Shield

Specially trained technicians at the Avco plant in Lowell, Massachusetts, carefully inject the resin into every single one of the 400,000 fiberglass honeycomb cells of the heat shield. Once this painstaking process is completed, special machines carve off all the excess to the desired thickness—the blunt aft section is two inches thick, whereas the top sections are closer to one-half-inch thick. Each finished section is x-rayed to make sure it is filled perfectly. The smallest imperfection can cost the lives of the crew, so an inspector will mark any flaws to be drilled out and redone.

103

Attached to the Command Module, the Service Module is basically a supply depot with a rocket engine. Its job is to house all the oxygen, power, and fuel that the crew needs on its long journey. Its engine, called the Service Propulsion System (SPS), has the critical job of slowing the spacecraft down once it goes behind the Moon, so that it can fall into lunar orbit. When the astronauts return from the lunar surface, the SPS has to fire again to send the spacecraft on a trajectory toward Earth. This engine has no backup, so if it fails to restart, the crew will have no way to get home.

Apollo SM Facts

Height (including engine nozzle)	**24** ft. **7** in.
Diameter	**12** ft. **10** in.
Weight (fully fueled)	**55,000** lb.
Weight (empty)	**11,500** lb.
Manufacturer	**North American Aviation**

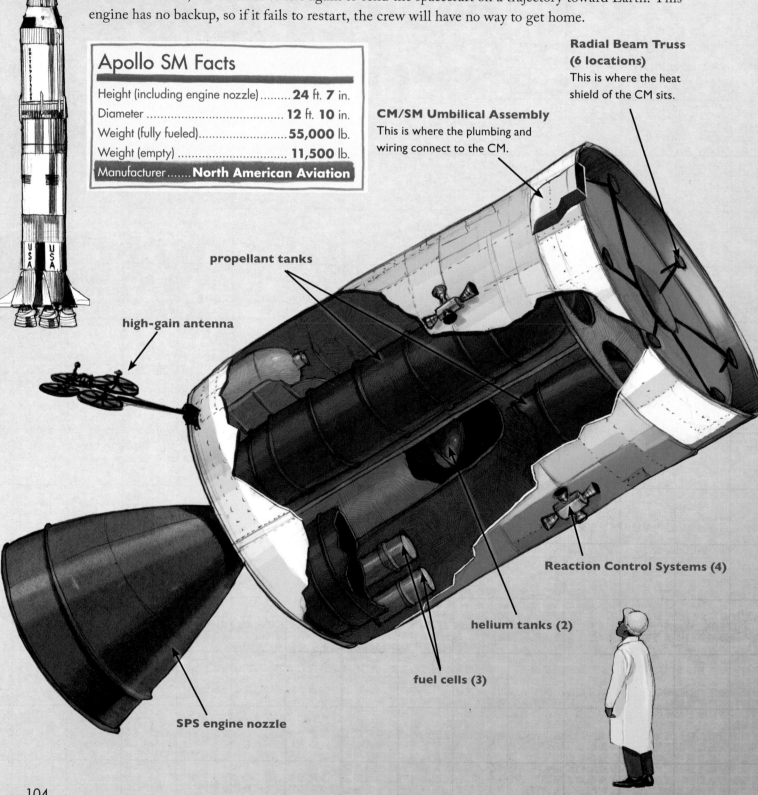

Radial Beam Truss (6 locations)
This is where the heat shield of the CM sits.

CM/SM Umbilical Assembly
This is where the plumbing and wiring connect to the CM.

propellant tanks

high-gain antenna

Reaction Control Systems (4)

helium tanks (2)

fuel cells (3)

SPS engine nozzle

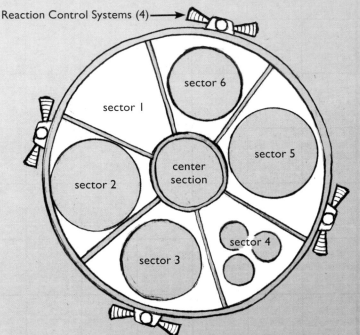

Reaction Control Systems (4) →

The SM is a 12-foot-wide cylinder made from one-inch thick aluminum-alloy honeycomb panels. The outside is covered in silver Mylar, the same substance used for party balloons, which helps protect its components from the extreme temperatures in space. The inside is divided into six pie-slice-shaped sections with a circular section down the center. To command the spacecraft's attitude, it has four Reaction Control Systems (RCS), each having four nozzles, or motors, that produce 100 pounds of thrust apiece.

Sector 1: Ballast (weight) to maintain the proper center of mass. On Apollo 15–17, it will hold scientific instruments.
Sectors 2 and 3: SPS oxidizer tanks
Sector 4: Oxygen tanks, hydrogen tanks, and fuel cell batteries
Sectors 5 and 6: SPS fuel tanks
Center Section: SPS engine and helium tanks

THE SERVICE PROPULSION SYSTEM: THE MOST RELIABLE ENGINE EVER BUILT

What do you do when you have to design an engine able to start in space   240,000 miles from Earth—and must not fail? You think simple. The fewer the parts and mechanisms, the fewer the things there are that could go wrong. This approach inspires the engineers' use of hypergolic propellants. Hypergolics are two different chemicals that ignite upon contact with each other, even in the vacuum of space. Helium is used to force the propellants (the oxidizer and the fuel) into the combustion chamber, where they will mix and ignite.

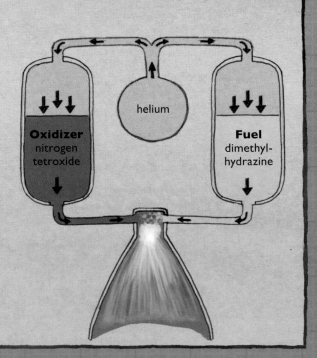

Creating Electricity

Problem! Not Enough Power

The crew will need a lot of electricity to run the computers, lights, environmental controls, and life support systems for a Moon mission that could last eight days or more. The obvious solution is batteries. The CM contains five batteries that will be used after the SM is jettisoned shortly before reentry. But powering the spacecraft for the entire journey would require a much larger supply of batteries, and that would mean a lot of added weight.

Solution! Fuel Cells

The engineers turn to the idea of using fuel cells. A fuel cell uses hydrogen (or another chemical) and oxygen to produce a reaction that creates electricity. The advantage of using fuel cells for Apollo is that as long as they have a supply of hydrogen and oxygen, they will continue to produce power for the entire trip—with a weight a lot less than with batteries. The other benefit is that the reaction between hydrogen and oxygen also creates drinkable water. In fact, the three fuel cells on Apollo will produce more than 50 gallons of water during its mission to the Moon—enough for the needs of all three crew members for the entire trip. This will result in a tremendous weight savings, because they won't have to bring water with them.

Engineers at Pratt & Whitney testing an Apollo fuel cell

HOW A BATTERY WORKS

Electricity is the flow of electrons through a conductive path (for example, a wire) called a circuit. Batteries have three parts: an anode (−), a cathode (+), and an electrolyte. When an electrical circuit connects the cathode and the anode, a chemical reaction takes place, causing a buildup of electrons at the anode. The electrons will want to move toward the cathode to balance things out, but the electrolyte prevents this, so the electrons must move through the circuit to get there, creating electricity. Most batteries don't last very long because the chemical process causes fewer and fewer electrons to be produced over time.

A fuel cell can keep producing electricity for as long as its supply of chemicals lasts. The Apollo fuel cells, built by Pratt & Whitney, use hydrogen and oxygen to create electricity, water, and heat.

Typical Flashlight Battery

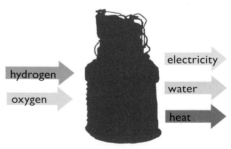

Fuel Cell

Temperature Control

Problem! Heat Shield Damage

On a voyage to the Moon and back, the Apollo spacecraft will be exposed to extreme temperatures. The side of the spacecraft facing the Sun can heat up to 280°F, and the side in its shadow will cool down to –240°F. The engineers at North American test the spacecraft at these temperatures and discover that long exposure to the extreme cold causes the heat shield to become brittle and crack. They discuss their options, which range from creating special radioactive heaters to redesigning the heat shield altogether. All the possible solutions are both expensive and time-consuming to develop.

–240°F

280°F

Solution! Barbecue Roll

NASA manager Joe Shea comes up with a simple yet brilliant solution. If having one side of the spaceship in the cold shadow is the problem, he reasons, then why not keep slowly rotating it all the way out to the Moon and back? That way, the heat shield will always stay warm. The engineers call the technique Passive Thermal Control (PTC), but the astronauts call it "barbecue roll" or "rotisserie mode."

This rotation will have little or no effect on the crew, as there is no up or down in space. And it won't use much fuel, because once you start the spacecraft rotating, it won't stop unless acted upon by another force. (See Newton's first law of motion, p. 29.)

To start PTC, the crew will fire the reaction control engines in a short burst, which initiates the rotation of the spacecraft at a rate of about three revolutions per hour.

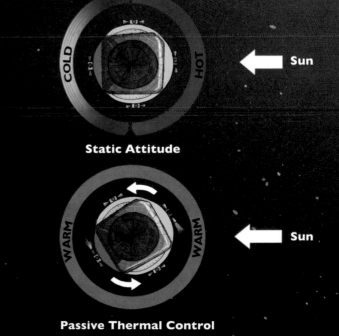

COLD HOT Sun

Static Attitude

WARM WARM Sun

Passive Thermal Control

Computers will carry out most of the critical steps during the mission to the Moon. The spacecraft will need computers that can store multiple programs to calculate and control the firing of the engines, also known as an engine burn, stabilize its attitude, and a myriad of other tasks. The entire mission—all nine days of it—will have to be preprogrammed or scripted out, and the astronauts will need a way to communicate with the computer to input and receive information. The programs will also need the flexibility to allow the crew to cope with unanticipated problems that could arise during the mission.

The only computers available fill entire floors of office buildings. Now MIT must build a computer that will handle all the tasks of a Moon mission—and be no larger than a couple of shoeboxes. This computer is called the Apollo Guidance Computer, or the AGC.

AGC Facts

Dimensions	**24** by **12.5** by **6.5** in.
Weight	**70** lb.
Design	**MIT Instrumentation Laboratory**
Manufacturer	**Raytheon**

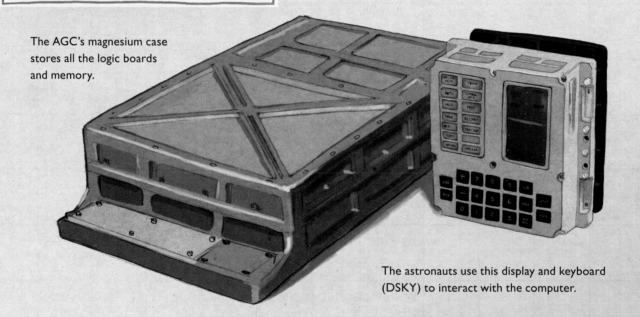

The AGC's magnesium case stores all the logic boards and memory.

The astronauts use this display and keyboard (DSKY) to interact with the computer.

THE AGC VS. THE MODERN SMARTPHONE

By today's standards, the AGC was incredibly simple and not that powerful, but its design laid the foundation for all computers to come. It is considered the great-grandfather of the modern computers and smartphones we use today.

Today's modern smartphone has hundreds of thousands of times the power and capability of the AGC. In fact, the phone in your pocket has more computing power than all the computers at NASA during the time of the Apollo missions! However, what is important to understand is that the AGC was built to handle very specific tasks and was highly economical in its design. It couldn't show you a video of a cute cat, but it could get astronauts to the Moon.

For the sake of understanding how far we have come with computing power, here is a side-by-side comparison.

	AGC	Smartphone
Transistors	16,800	1.6 billion (95,000 times more)
Random-Access Memory (RAM)	4 KB	1 GB (250,000 times more)
Read-Only Memory (ROM)	72 KB	128 GB (1.7 million times more)*
Processing Speed	1.024 MHz	1.4 GHz (1,400 times faster)

1 bit = a 1 or a 0   8 bits = 1 byte   1,024 bytes = 1 kilobyte (KB)   1,024 kilobytes = 1 megabyte (MB)   1,024 megabytes = 1 gigabyte (GB)

*The AGC could store only 18 pages of text, whereas the smartphone can store over a hundred million pages!

DSKY Interface

The astronauts need a way to interact with the AGC in order to give and receive information, so engineers at MIT design a guidance computer display and keyboard, or DSKY (pronounced DIS-key). Punching certain numerical buttons on the keypad will run different programs and call up specific data. By the time the mission is completed, the astronauts will have altogether logged over 10,500 button pushes.

Warning Lights
These warning lights alert the crew to a problem or give them information about the state of the vehicle or the computer itself.

Verb/Noun Communication
MIT engineers develop a numerical system of verbs and nouns for the astronauts to use. The verbs represent the action to take, and the nouns represent the thing to be acted upon. There are hundreds of sets of verb/noun pairs that the crew can request. For example:
If the astronaut wants to know the time of the next engine burn, he can enter VERB 06 (meaning "display") and NOUN 33 (meaning "time of ignition"). The computer will then run the appropriate program and display the hours, minutes, and seconds until the time of ignition.

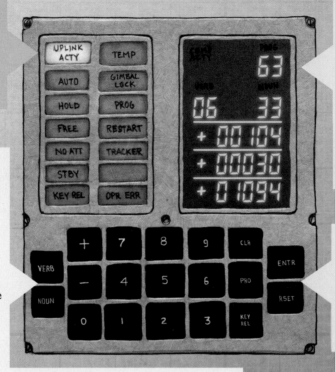

Display
Using numbers, the digital display shows the astronauts the information they've requested from whichever program they are running. The computer calculates all numbers using metric values, but because the astronauts are American, it converts them to imperial values for the display. (For example, distances are displayed in feet or nautical miles, not meters and kilometers.)

Keypad
Used in combination with the verb/noun buttons, this keypad is where the crew will input data. The buttons are much larger than on a normal keyboard, to allow for the large gloved fingers of the astronauts.

Ramon L. Alonso (b. 1930)
Apollo Guidance Computer Designer

Born in Argentina, Ramon Alonso received his PhD in applied mathematics from Harvard University. In 1958, he joined MIT's Instrumentation Lab, where he designed computers for spaceflight. One of the biggest challenges was figuring out how astronauts could easily communicate with the AGC. Alonso remembered when, as a child, he was learning to speak English as a second language. His first attempts had involved fitting together verbs and nouns, and he realized that a verb/noun approach would be an easy way for astronauts to learn to "speak" with the AGC. He assigned numbers to each verb and noun, allowing the crew to communicate commands—such as "Fire rocket" (verb, noun) or "Display time" (verb, noun)—by simply punching numbers into the DSKY.

The IBM 7090

The computer being used at NASA for the Apollo program takes up the entire floor of a building. This computer, the IBM 7090, is used to calculate all sorts of information vital to the program, including launch trajectories, burn rates, and hundreds of simulations. IBM computers are so new to the program that many of the calculations are double-checked by the human computers to make sure the numbers are accurate.

IBM 7090 Facts

Storage Capacity .... **128** MB
Processing Speed .... **229,000** instructions per second*
Price (in 1960).........**$2.9** million ($20 million in today's dollars)
*A modern laptop computer can execute 1.8 billion instructions per second.

Binary Language

All the information a computer uses is represented by electrical signals. Electricity passing through a wire can be either on or off. A computer calls this electrical signal a 1 or a 0. Any number can be represented by a series of 1s and 0s (or a bunch of wires that are either on or off), and the more wires you have, the more numbers you can store. This language is called binary.

To handle all of these 1s and 0s, a computer has circuits, which will add, subtract, multiply, or divide the 1s and 0s to get new results. These circuits represent the logic of a computer. The more circuits a computer has, the more calculations it can perform.

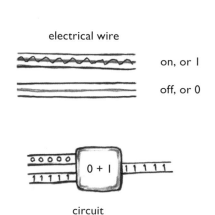

electrical wire

on, or 1

off, or 0

circuit

Problem! Shrinking a Computer to Go to the Moon

In 1961, when MIT gets its Apollo contract, computers use large vacuum tubes and transistors to handle the electrical signals. The computers are slow and cumbersome, and bigger than a school bus. Now, MIT is charged with creating a computer for the Moon mission that can fit into a one-cubic-foot space.

vacuum tube

for scale

Solution! Integrated Circuits

Eldon C. Hall, the lead designer of the AGC, proposes the idea of using integrated circuits, which are a relatively new invention. These integrated circuits pack many tiny circuits into a much smaller space—a microchip—making them much faster at processing information than transistors or vacuum tubes. Their reliability is still being tested, but Hall feels that the reward outweighs the risk. In the fall of 1962, he convinces a reluctant NASA to embrace this new technology and proceeds to build the world's first digital portable computer.

transistor

a single integrated circuit

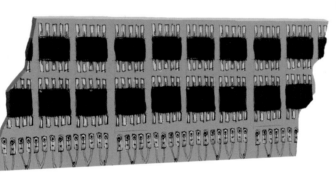

a logic board containing many integrated circuits

This logic module contains 120 integrated circuits.

Twenty-four modules will fit into the AGC container.

Eldon Hall started working at the MIT Instrumentation Laboratory in 1952.

Today, integrated circuits have become smaller and more complex, with billions of circuits in each one. You can find them in everything from toasters to smartphones.

Core Rope Memory

Every computer must contain a place where important instructions, or programs, are stored. The programs in the AGC tell it how to process all the information that the astronauts input. A time-tested, reliable solution is used to store all the AGC programs: core rope memory. The instructions are literally woven together, using wires and doughnut-shaped magnets called cores. A wire containing an electrical current will either pass through the center of the magnet, creating a 1, or it will pass around it, creating a 0. Thousands of these magnetic cores and miles and miles of wire are packed into the AGC.

core rope memory

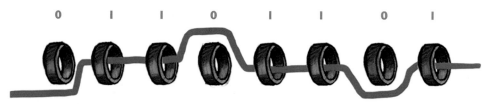

Wires woven through or around the magnetic cores indicate the 1s and 0s.

Core Rope Memory Weavers

Now that MIT has a solution for the memory that the AGC will use, someone has to actually weave the programs through all of those tiny magnets. When just one misplaced 1 or 0 could get the astronauts killed, accuracy is critical. Raytheon, the company responsible for core rope memory production, hires experienced weavers to handle the task. Nicknamed the Little Old Ladies (because most of them are grandmothers), they painstakingly work the tiny wires through and around the doughnuts according to the layout of a particular program. Each program takes at least six weeks to weave, and then it is put through months of rigorous testing. This means that all the weaving for a particular mission must be completed 10 months prior to a launch.

Weavers at Raytheon work on the core rope memory.

Margaret Hamilton (b. 1936)

Lead Apollo Flight Software Engineer

Before the weavers could start their work, someone had to write the programs. One of the many people to do this was mathematician Margaret Hamilton.

Hamilton was the very first programmer that MIT hired for Apollo, and her job was to help design the software programs for the AGC to run. One of the first things she did was change her job title from programmer to software engineer, as she believed that she was just as much of an engineer as the men who were building the spacecraft.

She would continually test the software inside a mock-up of the Command Module (CM), basically doing what the astronauts would be doing on a mission. Hamilton was a working mother, and she sometimes brought her daughter, Lauren, to MIT with her. One day, Lauren, who enjoyed playing astronaut, crashed the computer by pushing the wrong set of buttons on the DSKY. This innocent mistake led Hamilton to ask NASA if she could design a fail-safe system, which would warn the astronauts if they entered the wrong set of commands. NASA responded that the astronauts were too highly trained to make such a mistake and refused her request.

Hamilton and her daughter, Lauren

Margaret Hamilton inside the CM simulator

On the way back from the Moon during the Apollo 8 mission in 1968, while inputting star sightings into the DSKY, astronaut Jim Lovell accidentally did what Margaret Hamilton's daughter had done—and it made the computer think that the spacecraft was back on the launchpad. It took Mission Control over two frantic hours to fix the problem. The crew was very lucky this mistake hadn't taken place during a vital maneuver, or it might have been disastrous.

After that, NASA immediately gave Hamilton the go-ahead to design her fail-safe warning system. This proved crucially important on future missions when astronauts got tired and did occasionally end up pushing the wrong buttons.

In all, Hamilton not only pioneered the building blocks of software engineering; she gave it its name.

The CM will be traveling over 24,000 miles per hour when it reenters Earth's atmosphere. Over the next several minutes, the atmosphere will slow the spacecraft down to a speed of 320 miles per hour, pressing the crew members deep into their couches with the force of over six times that of Earth's gravity. Then, after having traveled almost a million miles through space, the CM's safe landing will completely depend upon the parachutes.

The parachutes are the most important part of the Earth Landing System (ELS). They are not a backup system for safety, like the Launch Escape Tower. For the crew inside the spacecraft, the parachutes will be the primary thing keeping them safe.

Of the 36,000 people working at North American Aviation in Downey, California, the only one with enough expertise to design Apollo's parachutes is Charles "Chuck" Lowry.

In January 1962, Lowry is contracted with Northrop's Ventura Division to work on the parachutes for the CM. Starting with small models in a vertical wind tunnel, Lowry tests different prototypes as the specifications of the CM keep changing. As it gets heavier and heavier, the test parachutes to slow it down get bigger and bigger.

Lowry and his team decide that instead of one large parachute, like the Mercury and Gemini capsules had, two 85-foot-diameter parachutes will provide a soft landing for the Apollo capsule. However, design policy at NASA dictates that even if one part fails, the mission cannot fail, so Lowry and his team add a third parachute, in case one of the two doesn't open.

One of the issues concerning the team is that if the three main parachutes open when the spacecraft is going 320 miles per hour, they will shred into bits. So they design smaller drogue parachutes to slow the CM down before deployment of the main parachutes. Altogether, there will be a system of nine parachutes that work to safely land the CM.

It takes six years of work and 139 drop tests to develop the final parachutes, and it will now be up to a team of meticulous seamstresses to turn acres of thin nylon into the finest parachutes ever made.

Main Parachute Facts

Diameter	**85** ft.
Weight (each chute)	**130** lb.
Manufacturer	**Northrop Ventura**

Chuck Lowry inspects the parachute compartment of a recently flown Command Module.

Making and Packing the Parachutes

Dozens of highly skilled seamstresses machine-sew miles of tape and webbing into each parachute, tasked with executing over two million stitches without a single flaw. Every spool of thread they use is dated and numbered so that any failure can be traced back to the source. A complete set of parachutes will contain over 10 miles of thread and enough nylon fabric to cover an entire football field. The seamstresses know that their sewing is a crucial step in getting the astronauts safely back to Earth.

Problem! Fitting the Parachutes into the Command Module

The most efficient way to pack a parachute is in a tube or cylinder. Unfortunately, the only free space left in the CM is between the access tunnel and the sides of the forward heat shield. The three main parachutes, along with over four and a half miles of nylon cords, have to somehow fit into this small, awkwardly shaped space.

The engineers at Northrop Ventura devise a high-strength nylon mold whose interior is the exact size and shape as the allotted space. The packing process involves folding the parachutes extremely carefully and feeding them into the mold. Then, using a hydraulic press, they slowly squeeze the fabric and the many miles of cord, bit by bit. The whole process takes an entire week. Once completed, each parachute, perfectly compressed into the molded shape, is as solid and dense as a block of hardwood.

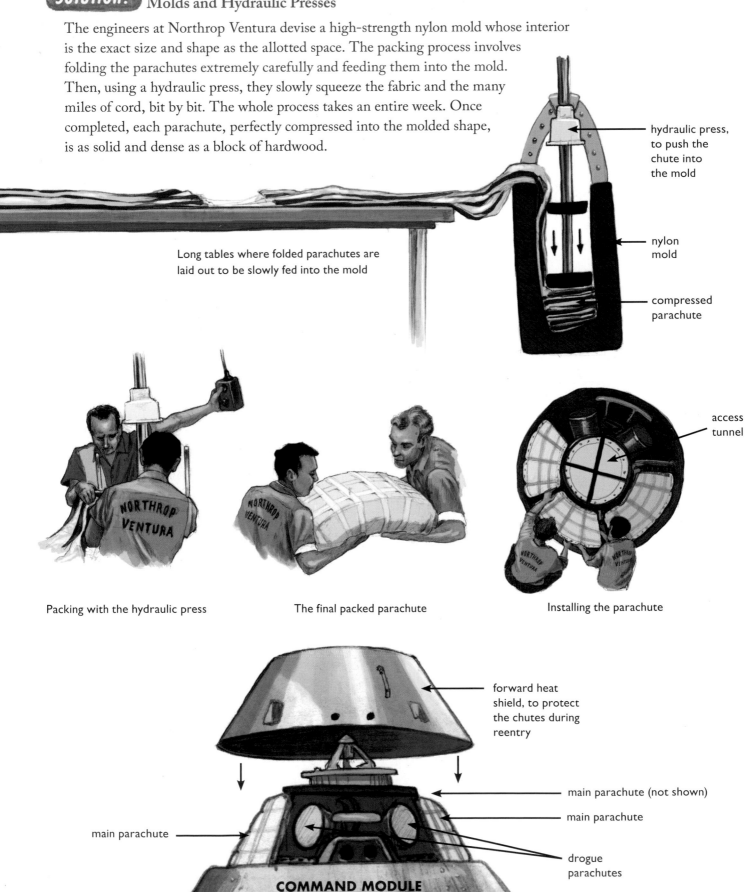

hydraulic press, to push the chute into the mold

nylon mold

compressed parachute

Long tables where folded parachutes are laid out to be slowly fed into the mold

access tunnel

Packing with the hydraulic press

The final packed parachute

Installing the parachute

forward heat shield, to protect the chutes during reentry

main parachute (not shown)

main parachute

main parachute

drogue parachutes

COMMAND MODULE

How the Parachute System Slows Down the Spacecraft

1

At 24,000 feet, the forward heat shield, which protects the parachutes from the extreme temperature of reentry, disconnects and is pulled clear by a small parachute.

2

Two drogue parachutes are shot out by explosive mortars 1.6 seconds later. These chutes, which are a little over seven feet in diameter, slow the spacecraft from 320 miles per hour to 160 miles per hour. This will both stabilize the spacecraft and prevent the main chutes from shredding when they open.

3

At 11,000 feet, three pilot chutes deploy as the drogue chutes are cut away by pyrotechnics. The pilot chutes' job is to pull the main chutes out of the CM.

4 The main chutes begin to fill with air.

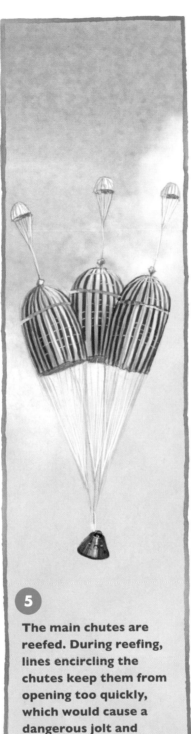

5 The main chutes are reefed. During reefing, lines encircling the chutes keep them from opening too quickly, which would cause a dangerous jolt and possibly damage them.

6 After 10 seconds, the reefing lines are cut by pyrotechnic charges and the main chutes fully open, slowing the spacecraft down to 21 miles per hour for splashdown.

7 When the spacecraft hits the water, the Lunar Module pilot will push a button that will disconnect the main parachutes from the CM.

Impact Attenuation System

Problem! Impact

During months of CM drop tests, the engineers at North American Aviation discover that hitting the water at 21 miles per hour damages the spacecraft and could easily injure the three crew members inside. And if the reentry is off target, there is a possibility that the spacecraft will come down on land, which would be even worse.

Solution! Crushable Bumpers and Shocks

The engineers design an internal solution and an external solution. The external solution involves adding four crushable ribs at the base of the pressurized inner structure of the spacecraft. Made from corrugated aluminum, these ribs will collapse upon impact, almost like a bumper on a car. Internally, the couches the astronauts are strapped into will be suspended and supported by eight struts, or shock absorbers. Together, the two solutions will absorb most of the impact of splashdown, protecting the crew and the spacecraft.

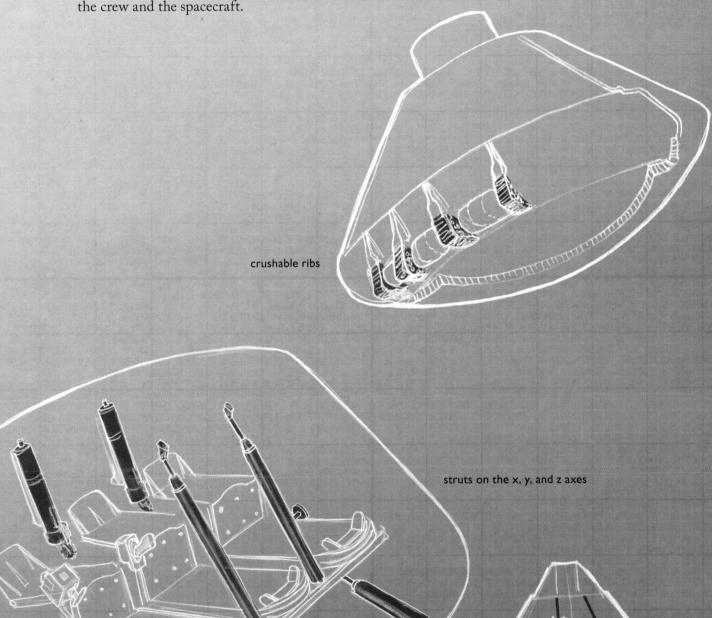

crushable ribs

struts on the x, y, and z axes

The Lunar Module (LM): World's First Spaceship

In July 1962, when NASA announces that Lunar Orbit Rendezvous (LOR) is the mode that it is going to use to land on the Moon, nine different companies compete for the chance to build the Lunar Module, or LM (pronounced lem). It will be the only part of Apollo that will land on the Moon.

Tom Kelly, an engineer at a small aircraft company called Grumman, has been thinking about the problem for a while. Kelly knows that unlike airplanes and rockets, which are designed to be aerodynamic and streamlined, the LM will be built to operate only in the vacuum of space and can be any shape at all. His idea is that form follows function. Simply put, the LM's appearance should be a direct result of what it has to accomplish: bring two men safely down to the surface of the Moon and then bring them back up to reconnect with the orbiting CSM.

Apollo LM Facts

Height	**22** ft. **11** in.
Diameter	**31** ft.
Weight (fully fueled, with crew)	**36,000** lb.
Weight (empty)	**10,800** lb.
Manufacturer	**Grumman Corporation**

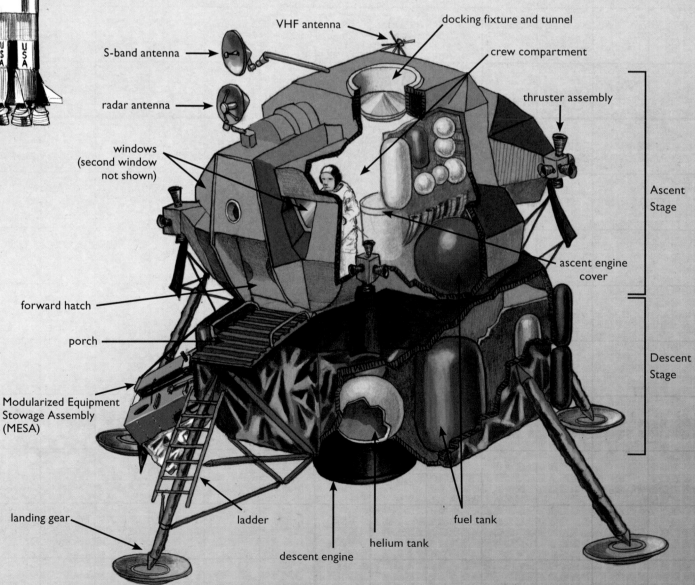

- VHF antenna
- docking fixture and tunnel
- S-band antenna
- crew compartment
- radar antenna
- thruster assembly
- windows (second window not shown)
- Ascent Stage
- ascent engine cover
- forward hatch
- porch
- Descent Stage
- Modularized Equipment Stowage Assembly (MESA)
- landing gear
- ladder
- fuel tank
- helium tank
- descent engine

Kelly also has the unique idea to make the LM a two-stage spacecraft. The top half, called the Ascent Stage, is where the two-man crew will live and work during their time on the Moon. The heavier bottom half, called the Descent Stage, with all the landing gear and the descent engine, will carry the LM down to the surface. When the astronauts are done exploring, they can use the Descent Stage as a launch platform to return to the CSM in the Ascent Stage.

On November 7, 1962, Grumman wins the contract to build the LM for Apollo, and its engineers are now tasked with creating the world's first true spaceship.

A TWO-STAGE SPACECRAFT

A. Once the spacecraft is in lunar orbit, the commander and the Lunar Module pilot climb through the docking tunnel into the LM. They undock from the orbiting CSM and use thrusters to move safely away. The Command Module pilot will stay inside the CM, which will continue to orbit the Moon.

B. They fire the LM's descent engine in the direction of their orbit, which slows them down, allowing the Moon's gravity to pull them out of orbit and toward the surface.

C. As they approach the lunar surface, the LM orients itself so that the astronauts can look through the windows to see where they are landing.

D. The descent engine then throttles down, allowing the LM to make a soft landing.

E. The astronauts explore the Moon, set out scientific experiments, and collect samples to bring back to Earth.

F. They return to the LM and, using the Descent Stage as a launchpad, fire the ascent engine to fly back to the CSM.

Problem! Weight

One of the biggest challenges the engineers face when designing the LM is the issue of weight. Initial calculations state that for every pound the LM weighs, it will need over three pounds of propellant to complete its mission. Any added weight will have a snowball effect all the way down the rocket, so every pound added to the LM will mean adding 400 pounds of fuel to the Saturn V launch vehicle.

Grumman's initial LM design is a solid structure with large windows in the front of the Ascent Stage for the crew to look out of during landing, similar to a helicopter. It also has five landing legs, for a more stable landing platform, as well as chairs that can swivel, giving the crew access to all the controls. Although a good design, it would be extremely heavy.

1963 Initial Grumman Design

Solution! Take Out the Seats

In 1963, NASA engineers ask Grumman to look at the possibility of having the LM crew stand rather than sit. There is only one-sixth gravity on the Moon, so their knees could easily absorb the shock of the landing. Removing the bulky seats would also give the crew much more cabin space, and lighten the LM. Even better, a standing crew could be closer to the windows. This means that much smaller windows could provide them with the same field of view. These smaller windows would save a tremendous amount of weight.

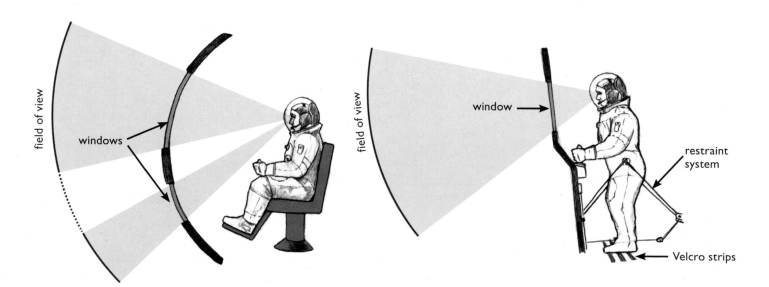

A seated crew would be farther from the windows. To have the field of view needed for landing, the windows would need to be large.

A standing crew would have the same field of view with much smaller windows. The two astronauts would be kept stable during flight using a restraint system of cables and pulleys, and Velcro strips to hold the astronaut's boots to the floor.

1967 Final Grumman Design

Over the course of the next four years, Tom Kelly and his Grumman team refine the LM's design, removing the seats and looking for additional ways to shed weight. Through a series of tests, they discover that if they use four landing legs instead of five, the weight savings is worth the added risk. They also discover that using several layers of Mylar (the superthin material covering the Service Module) creates a perfect insulation against the extreme temperatures of space. This allows them to replace the heavy outer walls of the Descent Stage. After over 40,000 drawings done by over 3,000 engineers and countless prototypes and tests, the final design is complete. It may appear to be an ugly spacecraft, but it's the perfect machine for the job.

EXPERIMENT

Take a piece of paper or cardboard and cut out a square window four inches by four inches in the center. Now, holding the piece of paper at arm's length, pay attention to how much you can see through the window. This is your field of view. Next, move the window closer to you (the way the astronauts moved closer to the windows by standing). Your field of view expands, allowing you to see much more through the same size window.

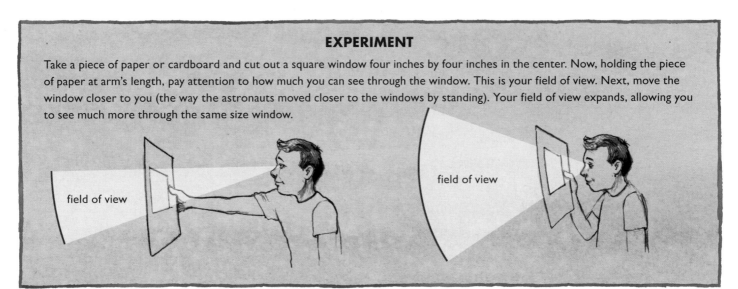

field of view

field of view

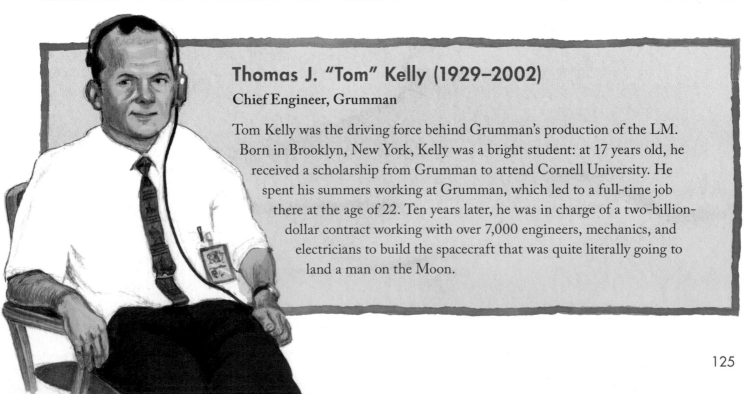

Thomas J. "Tom" Kelly (1929–2002)

Chief Engineer, Grumman

Tom Kelly was the driving force behind Grumman's production of the LM. Born in Brooklyn, New York, Kelly was a bright student: at 17 years old, he received a scholarship from Grumman to attend Cornell University. He spent his summers working at Grumman, which led to a full-time job there at the age of 22. Ten years later, he was in charge of a two-billion-dollar contract working with over 7,000 engineers, mechanics, and electricians to build the spacecraft that was quite literally going to land a man on the Moon.

Inside the LM Ascent Stage

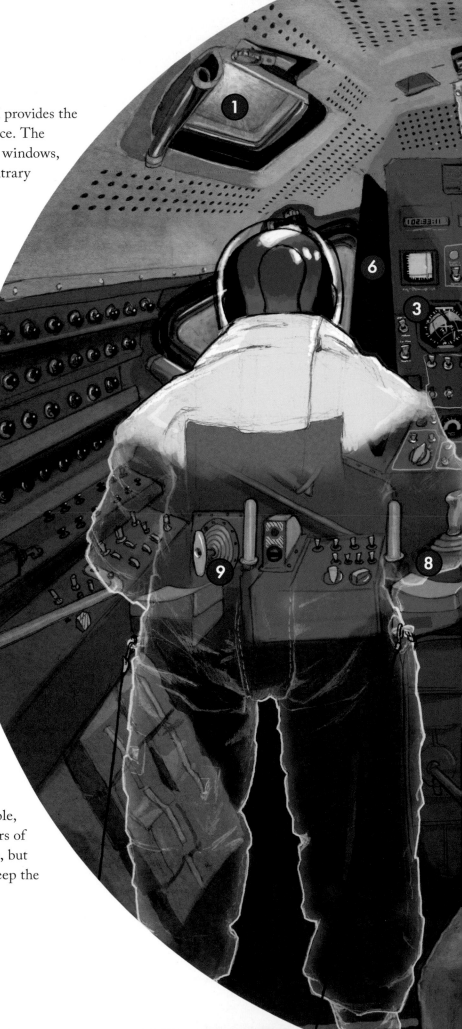

The cramped crew compartment of the LM provides the two astronauts with only 160 cubic feet of space. The commander stands on the left side, facing the windows, and the Lunar Module pilot to the right. Contrary to his title, the Lunar Module pilot does not fly the LM. His job is to watch the DSKY and the control panel while calling out the altitude, velocity, and propellant levels as the commander watches out a window during the descent to the lunar surface. If need be, the commander will take partial control of the automated computer using his attitude and thrust controllers.

The front of the crew compartment (shown here) has all the controls the astronauts will need to land on and take off from the Moon. Behind them are all the environmental controls, the life support systems, and the storage areas for the helmet visors and life support backpacks they will use during their moonwalk. Above and slightly behind them is the overhead hatch, where they will access the CM after redocking.

The crew compartment on the LM is pressurized, so after the astronauts land, they will put on their life support backpacks and depressurize the compartment before opening the forward hatch to exit onto the Moon. Once back inside, they will repressurize the LM before removing their backpacks and helmets.

In order to keep the LM as light as possible, the walls of the cabin are as thin as three layers of aluminum foil. This might seem unbelievable, but it is enough to maintain cabin pressure and keep the astronauts safe from the vacuum of space.

1. **Docking Window and Shade:** allows the commander to see the CSM during docking maneuvers

2. **Alignment Optical Telescope:** allows for star sightings, to align the gyroscopes in their Inertial Guidance System. The surrounding handle helps stabilize the astronauts while they are working.

3. **Artificial Horizon Indicators (8-Balls):** display the LM's orientation relative to the horizon of the Moon

4. **Main Cabin Floodlights** (both sides)

5. **Sequence Camera:** films the landing sequence and surface activity of the astronauts

6. **Glare Shield** (both windows)

7. **Apollo Guidance Computer Display and Keyboard**

8. **Attitude Controllers (right hand):** allow the crew to fire the thrusters, which control the attitude of the LM

9. **Thrust/Translation Controllers (left hand):** control the thrust of the descent and ascent engines

10. **Ingress/Egress Hatch:** the "door" the astronauts use for moonwalks

11. **Portable Life Support System (PLSS):** the backpacks the crew use for moonwalks. One is stowed on the floor, and one behind them on the wall.

Throughout the Apollo program, the astronauts are highly involved in spacecraft development. The development of the Lunar Module is no exception. When astronauts Pete Conrad and Ed White visit the Grumman factory to see the progress in the LM design, several issues come up:

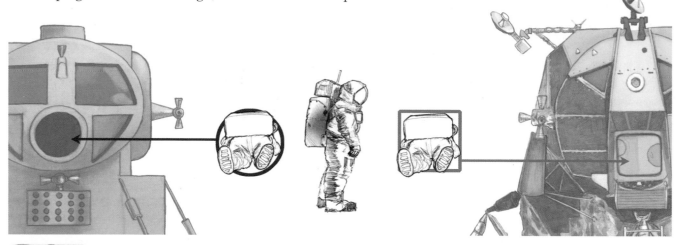

Problem! **Square Peg in a Round Hole**

In October 1963, astronaut Pete Conrad dons his full Apollo spacesuit and backpack and practices getting in and out of the LM. The Grumman design has a circular forward entrance hatch similar to the docking hatch that connects the CM to the LM. But when Conrad attempts to get through the LM hatch wearing his large square life support backpack, he can't fit through the door.

Solution! Square Hole

When the engineers see what the astronauts will be wearing during spacewalks, they design a new hatch that fits the profile of an astronaut.

Problem! Rope Ladders

Ed White visits the Grumman factory to practice the process of getting from the lunar surface to the LM hatch, which is almost 10 feet off the ground. He dons his Apollo spacesuit and connects himself to the Peter Pan rig, a set of wires and pulleys designed to simulate the one-sixth gravity of the Moon. Grumman engineers, in an effort to conserve weight, have White try using both a knotted rope and a roped block-and-tackle system to lift himself up. He struggles without any success, even injuring the ligaments in one of his feet in the process.

Solution! Metal Ladder

Tom Kelly realizes they might have gone too far with the lightweight rope solutions. He quickly works with his engineers to design a metal ladder that will be attached to the front leg of the Descent Stage.

The World's First Rocket Engine You Can Throttle

Up till this point, all rocket engines are either on or off—full blast or nothing. But to land on the Moon, the astronauts will need the ability to slowly adjust the thrust of the LM's descent engine to make a nice, soft landing, just like a helicopter. TRW aerospace engineer Peter Staudhammer accomplishes this by creating a mechanical throttle that controls the amount of propellants that go into the combustion chamber—similar to a gas pedal on a car. It has to work perfectly, though, because they have only enough fuel for one landing attempt.

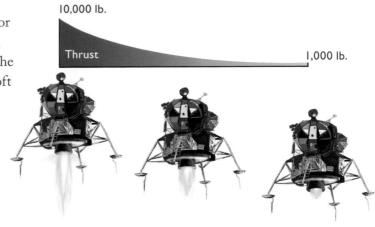

10,000 lb.

Thrust

1,000 lb.

A Thoroughly Tested Machine

No one has ever built a spacecraft like this before, and Grumman will have to construct every part from scratch. This also means that every part will have to be checked out extensively. Thousands of tests and millions of work hours will go into the development and construction of the final design, and Grumman will be responsible for building a total of 13 flight-ready Lunar Modules in all. Many of these will be used for various tests, and six of them will eventually land astronauts on the Moon. A seventh LM will serve as the Apollo 13 astronauts' "lifeboat" after an explosion severely damages their Command Service Module.

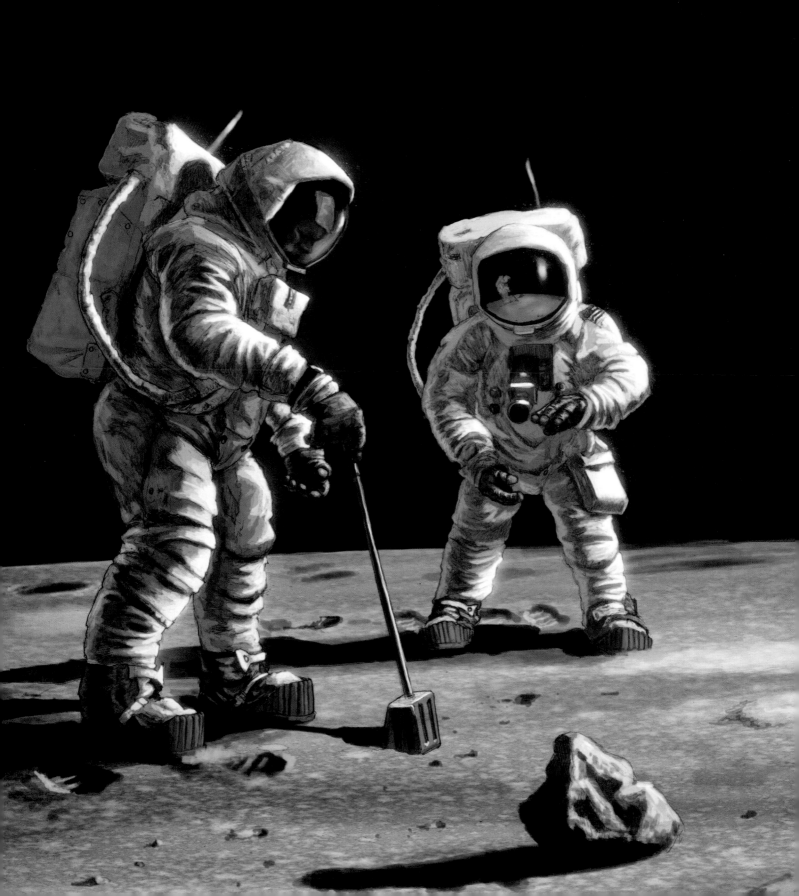

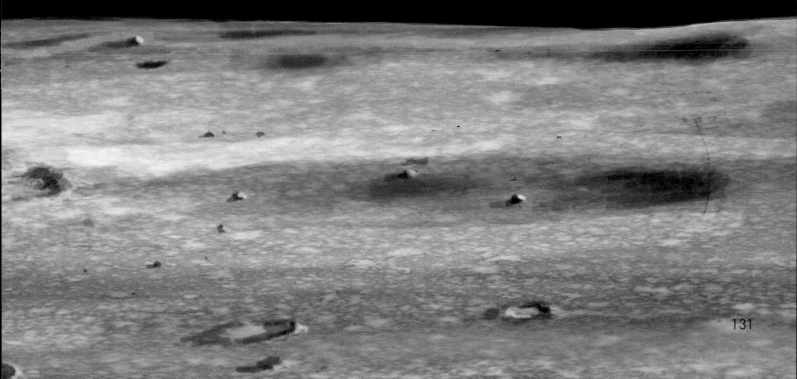

Living here on Earth, there are certain things we take for granted: oxygen to breathe, air pressure to keep the gases in our bloodstream from expanding and boiling away, and an atmosphere that protects us from being cooked by solar radiation and pelted by micrometeoroids traveling thousands of miles an hour.

Space has none of these things. It is an airless vacuum that can kill you in 90 seconds or less.

Engineers will have to design and construct life support systems that can protect the astronauts in the harsh environment of space. These systems need to provide the three-man crew with everything required to survive for up to two weeks. And the two moonwalkers, who will venture outside the cabin to explore the lunar surface, will need spacesuits that can produce air pressure and oxygen, and allow them to communicate.

The engineers designing and building these systems will work tirelessly for years, because they know that everything must function perfectly—or the crew will die.

131

The Life Support Systems

Designing life support systems for the three astronauts who are going to be living inside the tiny, sealed Command Module presents some serious challenges. It isn't just about making sure the crew members survive. They also need to be comfortable, nourished, and able to do the work necessary to carry out their mission. In order to accomplish this, the engineers need a clear understanding of what goes in and what comes out of a human body.

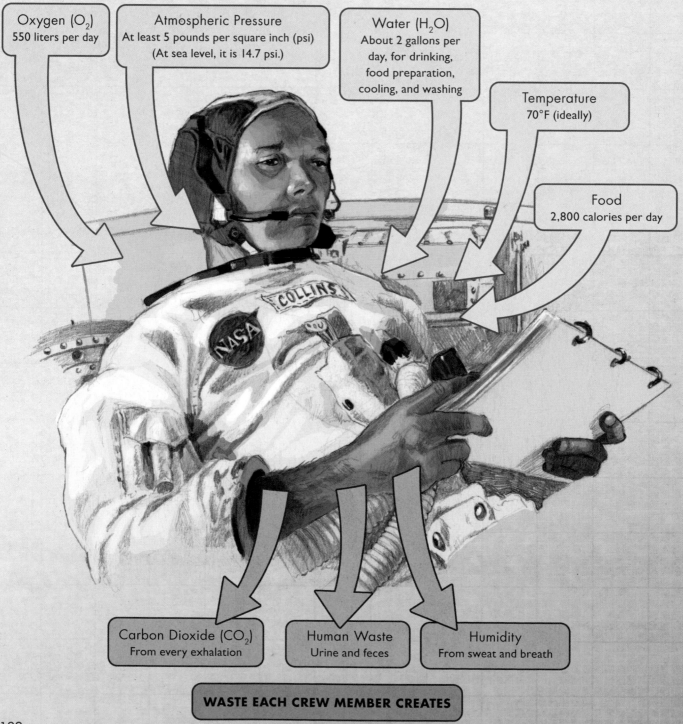

THINGS EACH CREW MEMBER NEEDS

Oxygen (O_2)
550 liters per day

Atmospheric Pressure
At least 5 pounds per square inch (psi)
(At sea level, it is 14.7 psi.)

Water (H_2O)
About 2 gallons per day, for drinking, food preparation, cooling, and washing

Temperature
70°F (ideally)

Food
2,800 calories per day

Carbon Dioxide (CO_2)
From every exhalation

Human Waste
Urine and feces

Humidity
From sweat and breath

WASTE EACH CREW MEMBER CREATES

Environmental Control System (ECS)

For each Apollo module, an Environmental Control System (ECS) is being built. The one for the Command Module is being developed by North American Aviation, and the other, for the Lunar Module, by Hamilton Standard. Although each ECS will serve a similar function, the system for the CM will be spread throughout the cabin, while the one for the LM (shown below) will be a singular unit.

The LM ECS is a dense network of pipes, filters, pumps, and fans that work together to provide the astronauts with everything they need, while removing everything they don't.

MAJOR FUNCTIONS OF THE ECS:

Spacecraft Atmosphere Control
- Regulates pressure and temperature of cabin and spacesuit gases
- Maintains desired humidity by removing water from cabin and spacesuit gases
- Removes CO_2 from cabin
- Removes odors and particles from air

Water Management
- Collects and stores sterilized drinkable water from fuel cells
- Delivers chilled and heated water for crew to consume
- Disposes of excess water by transferring it to wastewater system and dumping it overboard

Thermal Control
- Removes excess heat generated by crew and equipment

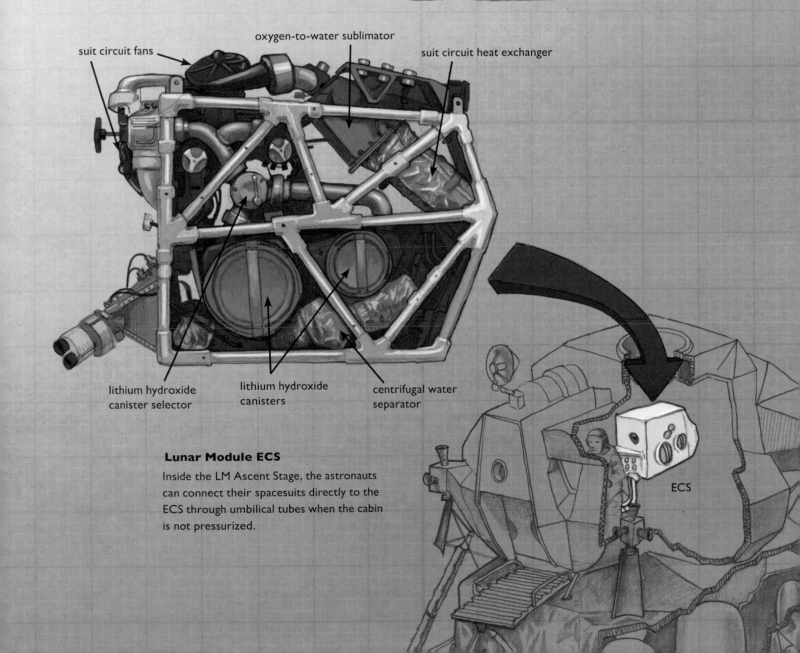

suit circuit fans

oxygen-to-water sublimator

suit circuit heat exchanger

lithium hydroxide canister selector

lithium hydroxide canisters

centrifugal water separator

ECS

Lunar Module ECS

Inside the LM Ascent Stage, the astronauts can connect their spacesuits directly to the ECS through umbilical tubes when the cabin is not pressurized.

Atmospheric Pressure

The weight the atmosphere exerts on our bodies is called atmospheric pressure. At sea level on Earth, there is a constant 14.7 pounds per square inch of this pressure. Fortunately, our bodies exert that same amount of pressure back, so we don't even feel it. Higher altitudes have much less atmospheric pressure. This is why your ears "pop" when you go up in a plane; your body is equalizing with the change in pressure. (Commercial aircraft are pressurized to 11 pounds per square inch.) In space and on the Moon, there is no atmosphere, and thus no atmospheric pressure. But our bodies need at least two pounds per square inch of atmospheric pressure to prevent the liquids in our tissues from boiling away.

The air we breathe at sea level is only about 21 percent oxygen. (That means of the 14.7 pounds per square inch of atmosphere pressing down on us, only three pounds of it is pure oxygen.) In a spacecraft, there is no need to supply the other gases that make up our atmosphere, because we need only the oxygen to function.

In space, the CM and LM crew compartments will be pressurized with only five pounds per square inch of pure 100 percent oxygen, but that's enough to supply the crew with the same concentration of oxygen as we breathe here on Earth.

If there were to be a leak, perhaps from a meteorite puncturing the spacecraft, a cabin pressure regulator would keep the pressure at a steady 3.5 pounds per square inch, giving the crew up to 15 minutes to breathe normally while they put on their spacesuits.

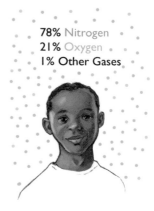

78% Nitrogen
21% Oxygen
1% Other Gases

14.7 psi on Earth at sea level

100% Oxygen

5 psi in pressurized spacecraft

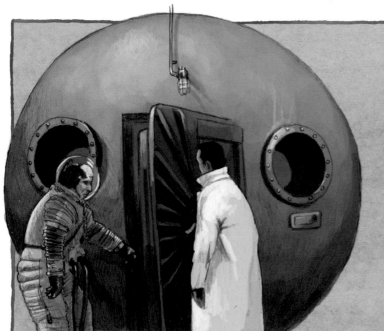

Vacuum Chamber Accident

On December 14, 1966, spacesuit technician Jim LeBlanc put on one of the latest Apollo spacesuit designs and entered a vacuum chamber at a NASA test facility. The chamber was completely depressurized to simulate the environment of the Moon. Suddenly, an umbilical hose disconnected, and the pressure inside his suit dropped to 0.1 pound per square inch. Within seconds, LeBlanc lost consciousness.

Technicians knew he would be dead in 90 seconds from lack of air pressure if they didn't act fast. Normally, it is safer to repressurize the chamber slowly, but this time they did it in less than a minute and a half.

After LeBlanc regained consciousness, he said the last thing he remembered was the saliva on his tongue starting to boil. Luckily, besides an earache from the sudden repressurization, he suffered no other effects.

Problem! Carbon Dioxide Poisoning

Every time you exhale, you release carbon dioxide (CO_2) into the atmosphere, but carbon dioxide is a toxic gas. On Earth, our plants and trees help clean the air of CO_2 through a process called photosynthesis. But in an enclosed spacecraft where three crew members are living, the buildup of CO_2 could reach deadly levels very quickly. Just 1 percent of CO_2 could cause dizziness, and 8 percent could cause unconsciousness or death.

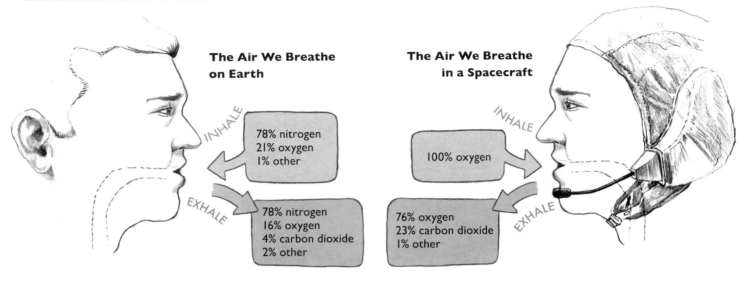

The Air We Breathe on Earth

INHALE
78% nitrogen
21% oxygen
1% other

EXHALE
78% nitrogen
16% oxygen
4% carbon dioxide
2% other

The Air We Breathe in a Spacecraft

INHALE
100% oxygen

EXHALE
76% oxygen
23% carbon dioxide
1% other

Solution! Lithium Hydroxide

The engineers create filter cartridges called CO_2 scrubbers that clean the CO_2 out of the air. As the cabin air gets pumped through the filters, a compound inside called lithium hydroxide (LiOH) interacts with the CO_2 molecules in a chemical reaction that traps them. The now-filtered air, still having plenty of oxygen, will then be pumped back into the spacecraft to be rebreathed. The astronauts will have to change the filter cartridges every 24 hours during the mission.

Command Module CO_2 filter

Lunar Module CO_2 filter

Filter Problems on Apollo 13

Because the Environmental Control Systems on the LM and the CM were built by different companies, they had differently shaped filter cartridges. This became a critical issue on Apollo 13 when, after an explosion in the SM, the crew had to move into the LM and use it as a lifeboat for the journey home. The LM was designed for only two astronauts. With three men on board, there was more CO_2 in the air, so they needed to change the filters more often. Unfortunately, the extra filters from the CM did not fit. Soon, the CO_2 would build up to deadly levels.

The engineers back in Houston quickly designed a workaround, and using only voice commands, they helped the crew build an adapter out of plastic bags, duct tape, and hoses on board the LM. The adapter allowed them to use the CM's square filter, which saved their lives.

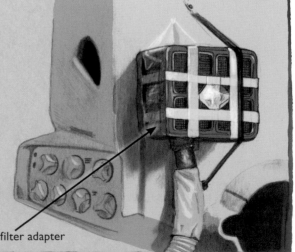

modified filter adapter

135

AS-204 (Apollo 1)

January 27, 1967

A plugs-out test. That's what they call the completely routine procedure when the astronauts sit inside a Command Module at the top of a Saturn V while it is on the launchpad. All the umbilical cables that provide electricity, environmental control, and communications are disconnected for the purpose of seeing how the spacecraft can manage under its own power.

At 1 p.m., astronauts Roger Chaffee, Ed White, and Gus Grissom enter the CM of the spacecraft known as AS-204 for the test. During an actual mission, the CM would have more pressure inside than the vacuum of space, so in order to simulate this on the ground, the cabin is filled with almost 17 pounds per square inch of pure oxygen.

This is a fatal mistake. Everyone involved overlooks the fact that in an environment of pure oxygen at that pressure, a single spark can start a fire so hot and furious that even certain metals will burn.

Roger Chaffee　　　　**Ed White**　　　　**Gus Grissom**

Five and a half hours into the test, a fire erupts inside the cabin. It consumes everything remotely flammable within seconds. Temperatures spike to over 1000°F. The pressure builds to over 1,500 pounds per square inch. The astronauts struggle to get out, but they cannot pull the hatch open.

The crew perishes in less than 18 seconds. It takes technicians outside over five minutes to get the hatch open.

The astronauts' families, the other astronauts, and all the other people working for NASA are devastated. The nation is stunned. The fire nearly brings the Apollo program to an end. Everyone involved knew the dangers of spaceflight, but they never for an instant thought they would lose astronauts on the ground.

Less than a week later, on February 3, NASA administrator Jim Webb puts together an accident review board, which includes Gemini 7 astronaut Frank Borman. The burned-out spacecraft is meticulously dismantled bolt by bolt, screw by screw, in hopes of determining the cause of the fire.

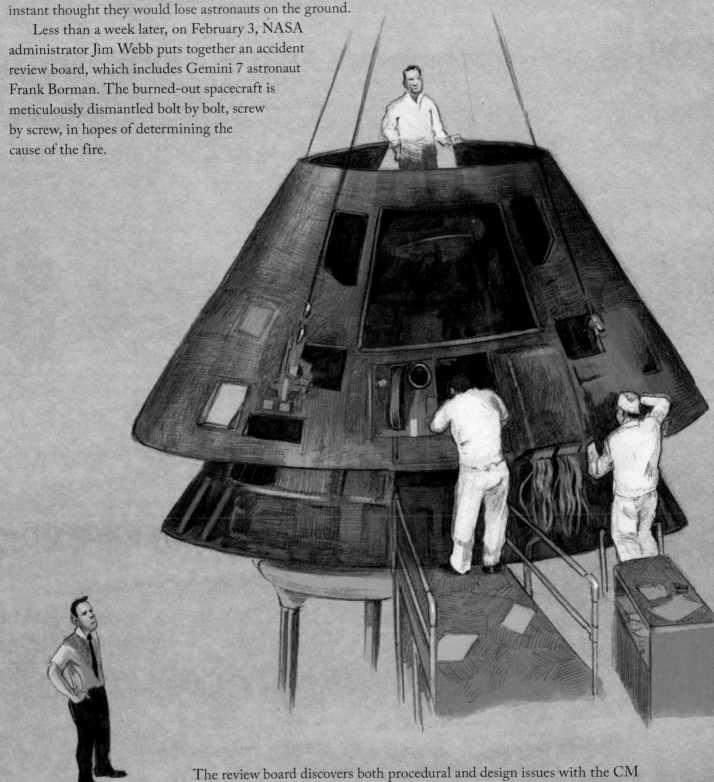

The review board discovers both procedural and design issues with the CM that led to the disaster. Before NASA can move forward with piloted spaceflight, the engineers need to solve all of those problems.

Problem! They Couldn't Open the Hatch

The hatch on the CM was designed to open inward. It was a three-part system where internal pressure helped seal the hatch. In ideal conditions, the crew could exit in 60 seconds. But escaping the fire would have been impossible because the immense build-up of pressure sealed the hatch shut.

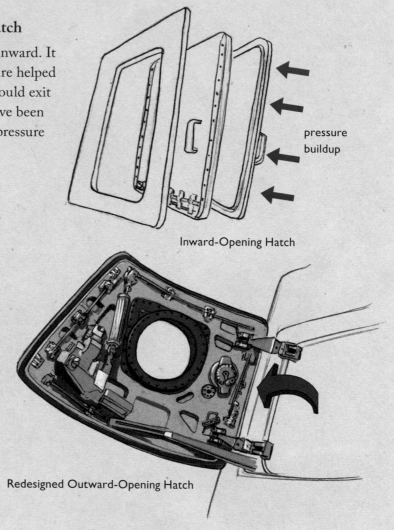

pressure buildup

Inward-Opening Hatch

Solution! Outward-Opening Hatch

A new single-piece hatch is designed to open outward in seven seconds, allowing the astronauts to get out quickly in an emergency.

Redesigned Outward-Opening Hatch

Problem! Too Many Combustible Materials

A fire requires fuel and oxygen. The astronauts had placed Velcro throughout the CM in order to keep loose items from floating around the cabin in zero gravity. In the pure-oxygen environment of 16.7 psi, almost everything becomes a fuel—including Velcro, the netting for holding cargo, and even the insulation on the wires.

Solution! Fire-Resistant Materials

Engineers utilize a new fireproof form of Velcro and change many of the other materials to fireproof or fire-resistant ones. All wiring is now protected from damage by covers, and wires carrying electrical power are wrapped with nonflammable Teflon tape.

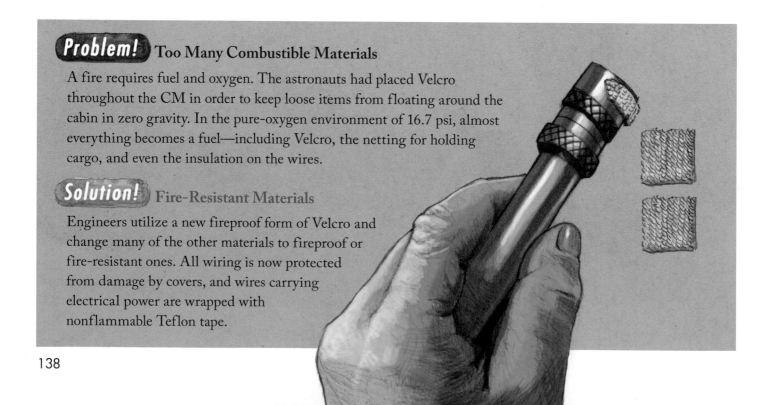

Problem! A Pure-Oxygen Environment

The most lethal issue was the pure-oxygen environment. No one working on Apollo had given it a second thought, because they used this same method throughout the Mercury and Gemini programs. After the fire, however, the danger posed by a high-pressure pure-oxygen environment on the launchpad seems like a painfully obvious oversight.

100% oxygen environment

Solution! A Mixture of Gases

Instead of filling the CM with 100 percent oxygen at 16.7 pounds per square inch on the launchpad, it will be filled with a safer mixture of 60 percent oxygen and 40 percent nitrogen, which is similar to the air we breathe on Earth. As the spacecraft leaves our atmosphere, the nitrogen will be bled out and the CM will be left with the five pounds per square inch of pure oxygen that the astronauts require.

60% oxygen/40% nitrogen environment

The fire stops all NASA spaceflight activity for 20 months. Three men lost their lives on the launchpad, and NASA and its contractors move forward with new resolve to never let anything like this happen again.

At the request of the wives of the fallen astronauts, the spacecraft's name is changed from AS-204 to Apollo 1.

Tough and Competent

On the Monday morning after the fire, 33-year-old flight director Gene Kranz calls a meeting of his team and gives a speech that will never be forgotten by anyone in Mission Control:

"From this day forward, Flight Control will be known by two words: 'tough' and 'competent.' 'Tough' means we are forever accountable for what we do or what we fail to do. 'Competent' means we will never take anything for granted. We will never be found short in our knowledge and in our skills. When you leave this meeting today, you will go to your office and the first thing you will do there is to write 'tough and competent' on your blackboards. It will never be erased. Each day when you enter the room, these words will remind you of the price paid by Grissom, White, and Chaffee. These words are the price of admission to the ranks of Mission Control."

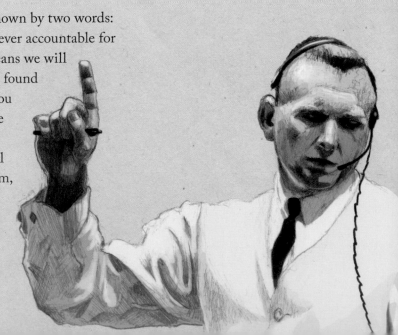

Space Food

The astronauts will have to bring all the food they will need for their long journey. The food must be lightweight, compact, and edible in zero gravity. Crumbs and spills are of major concern, because bits can float around the crew cabin and possibly get into the electronics of the spacecraft, causing damage. Food also has to be "low residue" so the crew creates as little waste as possible.

Rita M. Rapp (1928–1989)
Leader of the Apollo Food Systems Team

"I like to feed them what they like, because I want them healthy and happy."

Early space food was unappetizing, to say the least. Mercury astronauts squeezed pureed meats and vegetables into their mouths from toothpaste-like tubes. Gemini astronauts ate small freeze-dried sandwiches they had to moisten with the saliva in their mouths.

In 1966, physiologist Rita Rapp joined the Apollo Food Systems team and helped change that. Working with the Whirlpool Corporation, Rapp and her team developed special "spoon bowls"— pouches of food that astronauts could rehydrate, cut open, and then eat with a spoon. The team also used a new method of thermostabilizing food (processing food with heat to destroy bacteria), allowing it to be stored "ready to eat" in a can.

Rapp coordinated with the astronauts to create menus that met their nutritional needs but that they also enjoyed. They all loved her sugar cookies and used them as currency to barter with during missions. Rapp even figured out how to give the crew of Apollo 8 a special Christmas dinner in space—with real turkey, gravy, and cranberry sauce.

Dehydrated food is light and easy to pack. An astronaut injects a food pouch with hot or cold water from a water gun, then massages the pouch and waits until the food is rehydrated, cuts the bag open, and eats the meal with a metal spoon. The moist food now has a consistency that makes it stick to the spoon so it won't float away. After eating, a germicidal tablet is dropped inside the bag and mixed with anything left over to prevent bacterial growth and the formation of odors.

dehydrated beef with vegetables

"Wet-pack" food is ready to eat. A can of spreadable beef can be eaten with a spoon or spread on a piece of bread that has been coated in gelatin to prevent crumbs.

spreadable beef

brownies

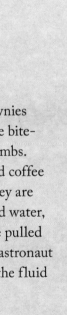
water gun

Other foods, like brownies or fruitcake, come in dense bite-sized pieces to prevent crumbs. Dehydrated juices, tea, and coffee come in pouches. Once they are rehydrated with hot or cold water, a wide plastic straw can be pulled out of the pouch, and the astronaut uses the straw to squeeze the fluid directly into his mouth.

rehydrated beef with vegetables
ready to be consumed

Each astronaut has his own menu, which includes some of his favorite items.

*Day 1 consists of Meal B and C only
**Spoon-Bowl Package
***Wet-Pack Food

APOLLO XI (ARMSTRONG)

MEAL	DAY 1*, 5	DAY 2	DAY 3	DAY 4
A	Peaches Bacon Squares (8) Strawberry Cubes (4) Grape Drink Orange Drink	Fruit Cocktail Sausage Patties** Cinn. Tstd. Bread Cubes (4) Cocoa Grapefruit Drink	Peaches Bacon Squares (8) Apricot Cereal Cubes (4) Grape Drink Orange Drink	Canadian Bacon and Applesau Sugar Coated Corn Flakes Peanut Cubes (4) Cocoa Orange-Grapefruit Drink
B	Beef and Potatoes*** Butterscotch Pudding Brownies (4) Grape Punch	Frankfurters*** Applesauce Chocolate Pudding Orange-Grapefruit Drink	Cream of Chicken Soup Turkey and Gravy*** Cheese Cracker Cubes (6) Chocolate Cubes (6) Pineapple-Grapefruit Drink	Shrimp Cocktail Ham and Potatoes*** Fruit Cocktail Date Fruitcake (4) Grapefruit Drink
		Meat Sauce** ...tatoes**	Tuna Salad Chicken Stew** Butterscotch Pudding	Beef Stew** Coconut Cubes (4) Banana Pudding Grape Punch

Waste Management: Going to the Bathroom in Space

Of all the daily activities the astronauts will have to deal with in space, going to the bathroom is probably the worst. First off, there's absolutely no privacy in the confined space of the CM or the LM. Secondly, in zero gravity, body waste does not naturally fall away from you. The final challenge: you have to put it somewhere once you are done.

Three astronauts spending two weeks in a tiny spacecraft can produce quite a lot of waste—not to mention smell—and the engineers have to figure out how to deal with this.

rubber roll-on cuff

**Urine
Transfer
System**

tube
attachment

collection bag

The system for urination is somewhat straightforward. Each astronaut is provided with a device called a Urine Transfer System (UTS). After rolling on a special cuff, he will urinate into the collection bag. The rubber roll-on cuff is replaced each day, and each astronaut has 10 color-coded cuffs to use on the journey. The urine is transferred by tube to a tank. Then, during what is called a "urine dump," it is vented from the tank out into space, where it will instantly freeze into thousands of tiny crystals that float around the spacecraft exterior and shimmer like stars. Astronaut Wally Schirra jokingly referred to it as "the Constellation Urion."

**Urine Collection and Transfer
Assembly (for EVAs)**

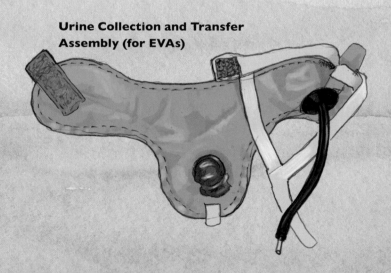

While the astronauts are doing extravehicular activities (EVAs), they will each wear a Urine Collection and Transfer Assembly (UCTA), or "pee pouch," under their suit. The collection bladder can either be drained through a valve while the astronaut is wearing the suit, or into the tank back in the spacecraft after the suit is removed.

The fecal collection system is a little more complicated. It consists of two plastic bags (a fecal bag and a fecal/vomit bag), tissue wipes, and a germicidal packet. The fecal bag "poo pouch" has a wide circular opening along with a circle of tape used to adhere it to the buttocks. Because there is zero gravity in space, a finger-shaped indent in the bag, called a finger cot, provides the astronaut with a way to push the fecal matter to the bottom of the bag. The bag is then removed and the wipes used for cleanup are added to it. To prevent gas buildup in the bag, a germicidal packet is dropped inside, broken open, and massaged through the waste. The bag is then sealed, put inside the fecal/vomit bag, rolled up tight, and stored inside the waste stowage compartment. Unlike liquids, which can be easily vented into space, the solids have to be saved. Once the astronauts return to Earth, the bags of waste will be given to scientists for analysis.

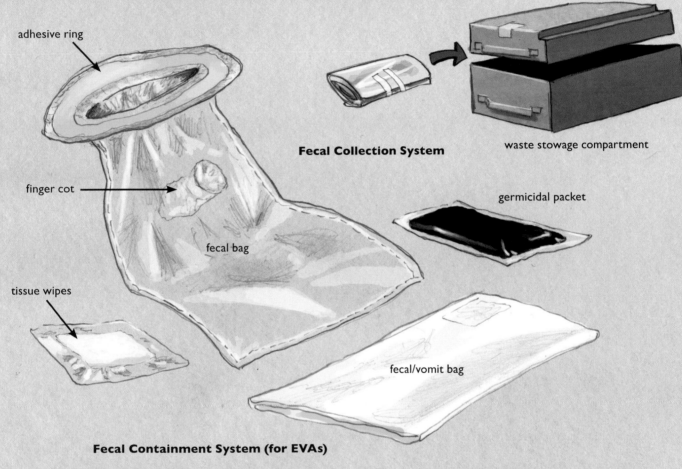

adhesive ring

finger cot

fecal bag

tissue wipes

Fecal Collection System

waste stowage compartment

germicidal packet

fecal/vomit bag

Fecal Containment System (for EVAs)

ARMSTRONG

Obviously, such a time-consuming and difficult task would be impossible while wearing a spacesuit, so each astronaut on a spacewalk could wear a Fecal Containment System (FCS). That is NASA's fancy term for a diaper. Don't you appreciate Earth toilets now? Gravity isn't so bad, either.

Landing on the Moon isn't enough. The astronauts are going to get out and walk around—explore the surface, collect rocks, and leave footprints on the lunar soil. To allow them to do this, engineers at the International Latex Corporation (ILC) and Hamilton Standard need to work together to design a spacesuit that will give the astronauts the same kind of protections they have inside the crew cabin. They need to create nothing less than a wearable spacecraft.

The spacesuit will need to be fully pressurized to protect the astronauts from the vacuum of space. It has to defend them from the tiny particles called micrometeoroids that zip through space at thousands of miles per hour and could damage or even puncture the spacesuit. Temperatures on the Moon will fluctuate between 260°F in the sunlight and –280°F in the shadow, so the suit will require insulation. Finally, the astronauts will need a way to control the environment inside the suit so they don't overheat.

What Happens to the Human Body When Exposed to the Vacuum of Space?

- Lack of oxygen will lead to hypoxia (lack of oxygen to the brain), and you will become unconscious in about 12 seconds.
- Your body will swell to twice its normal size as all the liquids inside you start to vaporize.
- All the gases inside you, including the air in your lungs, will rush out of your body as they try to equalize with the outside air pressure (which is zero!).
- Death will occur after 90 seconds.

WHY THE LIQUIDS IN YOUR BODY WILL BOIL IN A VACUUM

When you open a can of soda, it fizzes and the liquid bubbles. This is because it is aerated: carbon dioxide was injected into the liquid under high pressure. The CO_2 molecules stay embedded in the liquid while it remains unopened—and under pressure. Once the can is opened, the CO_2 molecules bubble up and escape because the pressure outside the can is so much less than the pressure inside. In other words, the pressure equalizes. So in a vacuum, where there is virtually no pressure, the liquids in your body boil immediately.

14.7 psi*

50 psi

*psi = pounds per square inch

The Three-Layered Apollo Spacesuit (A-7L)

Two different companies work together to create one of the most remarkable garments ever imagined. Designed to be as tough as armor yet supple enough to allow astronauts the necessary mobility to accomplish all the tasks they will need to perform on the Moon, the spacesuit is a work of art. Each astronaut will receive three custom-built suits: one for training, one for the mission, and one as a backup. Each suit will take hundreds of engineers, seamstresses, and technicians around 5,000 work hours to produce.

Oxygen Purge System (OPS)
Sitting on top of the PLSS is a backup supply of oxygen to be used only in emergencies if the PLSS fails.

1. Integrated Thermal Micrometeoroid Garment (ITMG)
The outer layer of the spacesuit is made up of a number of different materials that will protect the astronaut from the extreme temperatures of space as well as from the micrometeoroids constantly bombarding the lunar surface from deep space.

Portable Life Support System (PLSS)
This backpack provides oxygen, communications, and thermal control.

2. Pressure Garment Assembly (PGA)
This airtight inner layer, also called a flexible pressurized suit, is pressurized with oxygen to protect the astronaut from the pure vacuum of space. The elbows, shoulders, wrists, and knees are made to be easily flexible for better mobility.

3. Liquid Cooling Garment (LCG)
This long-john-like garment is made of thin netting interwoven with hundreds of feet of spaghetti-like tubing that can carry cold water pumped from the backpack to cool down the astronaut who is wearing all these heavy layers while working on the Moon.

At 180 pounds, the Apollo spacesuit and portable life support system together weigh more than the average astronaut, but in the Moon's gravity, they will weigh only 30 pounds.

145

The Development of the Apollo Spacesuit

Spacesuits of Science Fiction

Science-fiction writers have been putting their characters in all varieties of spacesuits since the 19th century. The designs were far from practical, but they often became a jumping-off point for actual spacesuit designs.

First Pressure Suit (1934)

With the help of the B. F. Goodrich Company, American aviator Wiley Post developed the first true pressure suit. The suit had an inner rubber bladder that could be pressurized, along with an outer layer made of rubberized parachute fabric. The outer layer was glued to a jointed frame that allowed Post the limited movement he needed to operate his plane's flight controls. The helmet, made from aluminum and plastic, was similar to a diver's helmet.

On September 5, 1934, Post flew to an altitude of 40,000 feet—where the air is so thin that the atmospheric pressure is less than three pounds per square inch—and his pressure suit worked perfectly.

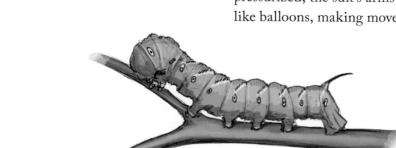

Wiley Post in his pressure suit

XH-5 "Tomato Worm" Suit (1943)

B. F. Goodrich continued to do pioneering work in the field of pressure suits. Inspired by the movements of the segmented tomato worm, engineer Russell Colley came up with the XH-5 design. One of the downfalls was that once pressurized, the suit's arms and legs expanded like balloons, making movement cumbersome.

XH-5 suit

tomato worm

Playtex advertisement from the 1940s

From Girdles and Bras to Spacesuits

Playtex, a division of ILC, specializes in making rubber garments that move with the body. It has been making rubberized girdles since the 1940s. So in March 1962, when NASA starts searching for a company to make spacesuits, the leaders of ILC see an opportunity to take their expertise to the Moon. Although there are many other companies in the aerospace industry fighting for the same opportunity, ILC has been developing something that no one else has: the convolute.

Convoluted Joint

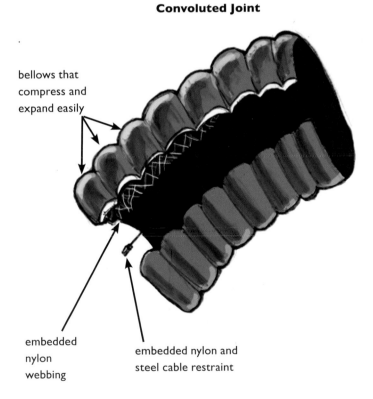

bellows that compress and expand easily

embedded nylon webbing

embedded nylon and steel cable restraint

The convolute is a segmented natural latex bladder similar to the XH-5. The big difference: the convolute has embedded nylon and steel restraints and nylon webbing that prevent the bladder from expanding and blowing up like a balloon once pressurized. This restraint system allows for a freedom of movement that no other company can compete with.

147

Pressure Garment Assembly (PGA)

The design for the flexible pressurized suit takes ILC over 10 years to develop. It uses convoluted joints for the shoulders, elbows, hips, knees, wrists, and ankles, allowing the astronauts all the mobility they will need during a moonwalk. It has a polycarbonate helmet, known as a bubble helmet, that is so strong you can't break it with a hammer. Inside the helmet is a rubber piece called a Valsalva device that the astronaut can press his nose against in order to "pop" his ears during launch and reentry as cabin pressure changes. Inside the suit, along the neck ring, is a water nozzle, allowing the astronaut to drink from a water bag worn inside the suit, called an In-Suit Drinking Device. The feed port on the helmet is designed so that the fully suited astronaut can always insert a water gun or food probe in an emergency. The suit is equipped with a special pressurized zipper that runs from the back of the neck down to the crotch, allowing the astronaut to easily get inside. The gloves and the helmet are attached to the suit using locking aluminum rings.

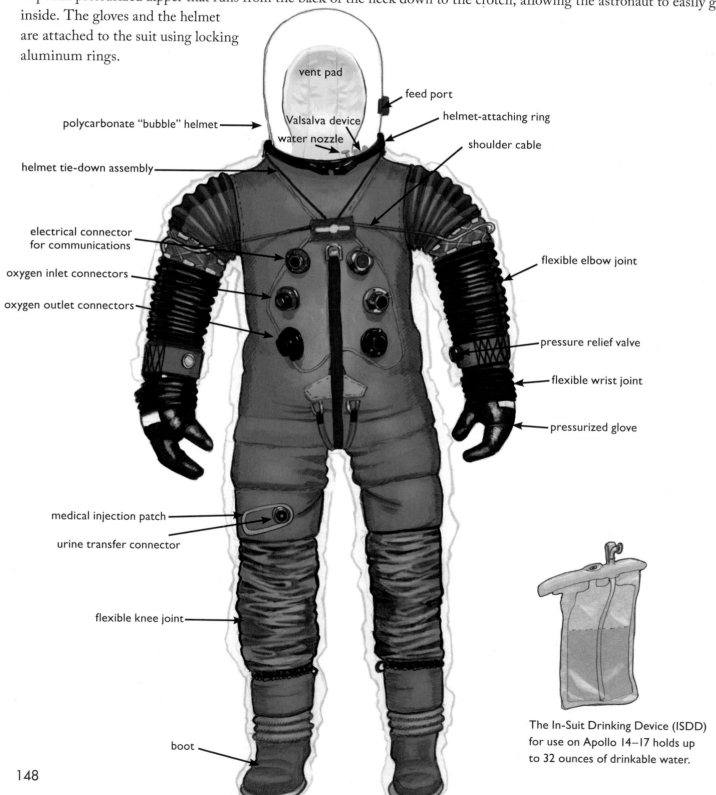

vent pad

feed port

Valsalva device

helmet-attaching ring

polycarbonate "bubble" helmet

water nozzle

shoulder cable

helmet tie-down assembly

electrical connector for communications

oxygen inlet connectors

oxygen outlet connectors

flexible elbow joint

pressure relief valve

flexible wrist joint

pressurized glove

medical injection patch

urine transfer connector

flexible knee joint

boot

The In-Suit Drinking Device (ISDD) for use on Apollo 14–17 holds up to 32 ounces of drinkable water.

Integrated Thermal Micrometeoroid Garment (ITMG)

Worn over the pressurized suit, the Integrated Thermal Micrometeoroid Garment is made of materials the seamstresses doing the stitching and gluing have never worked with before. All 14 layers of the ITMG are designed to protect the astronauts from extreme temperatures and micrometeoroid punctures. The outermost layers, known as beta cloth, are made from flameproof fiberglass silicon and Teflon.

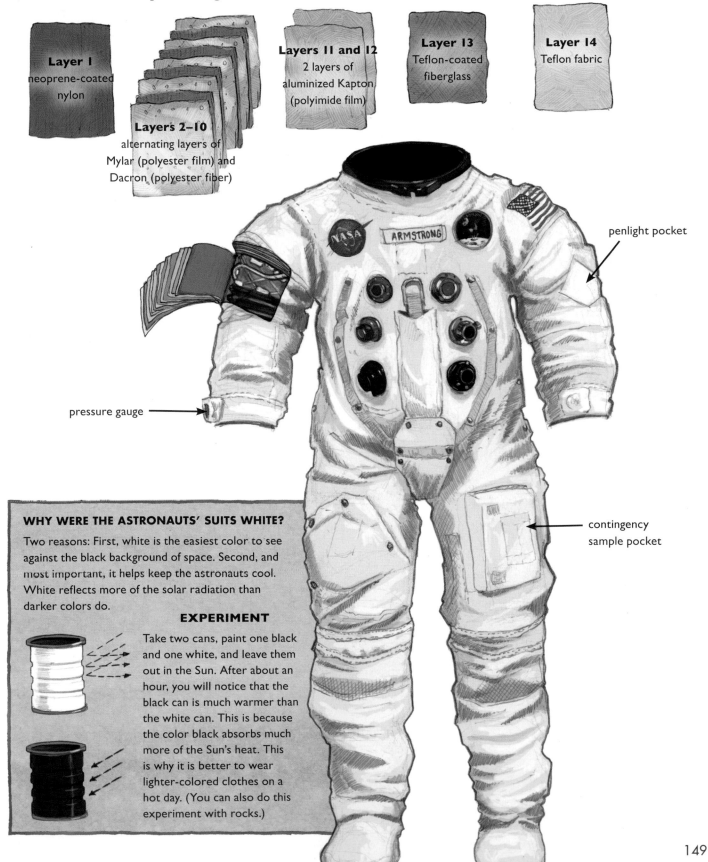

Layer 1
neoprene-coated nylon

Layers 2–10
alternating layers of Mylar (polyester film) and Dacron (polyester fiber)

Layers 11 and 12
2 layers of aluminized Kapton (polyimide film)

Layer 13
Teflon-coated fiberglass

Layer 14
Teflon fabric

penlight pocket

pressure gauge

contingency sample pocket

WHY WERE THE ASTRONAUTS' SUITS WHITE?

Two reasons: First, white is the easiest color to see against the black background of space. Second, and most important, it helps keep the astronauts cool. White reflects more of the solar radiation than darker colors do.

EXPERIMENT

Take two cans, paint one black and one white, and leave them out in the Sun. After about an hour, you will notice that the black can is much warmer than the white can. This is because the color black absorbs much more of the Sun's heat. This is why it is better to wear lighter-colored clothes on a hot day. (You can also do this experiment with rocks.)

149

Helmet Visor Assembly

Fitting over the helmet, the helmet visor assembly provides protection from micrometeoroids, extreme temperatures, and ultraviolet and infrared light rays. It is covered with a coated beta cloth similar to that of the ITMG. It is made up of two main visors. The inner visor's thermal control coating protects against extreme temperatures. The outer visor is coated with several metals, including 24-karat gold to protect against the radiation and unfiltered brightness of the Sun. Two side shades can be pulled down to block out the Sun.

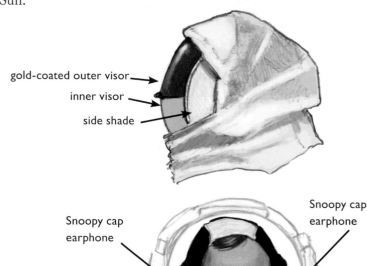

gold-coated outer visor

inner visor

side shade

Communications Carrier Assembly

Also known as the Snoopy cap, nicknamed after the *Peanuts* character whose ears it resembles,* the communications carrier assembly has two earphones and two microphones. (The second microphone is a backup, in case the first one fails.) During Mercury and Gemini, the earphones and microphones were attached to the *inside* of the helmet, which worked because the astronauts didn't need to move much, but for the Apollo missions, the astronauts will need to turn their heads and look up and down. The Snoopy cap allows them to move within the pressurized bubble helmet and still maintain communications.

Snoopy cap earphone

Snoopy cap earphone

microphone

microphone

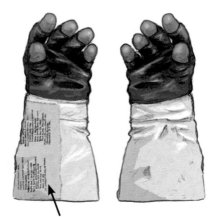

Each pair of gloves has a checklist sewn on the cuff.

Gloves

The coverings that will be worn over the pressurized suit gloves need to be tough and yet allow astronauts enough dexterity to use tools on the Moon. The fingertips are made of silicone rubber to provide touch sensitivity. The outer gray layer is a new cut-resistant fabric called Chromel-R, which is made from woven chromium steel.

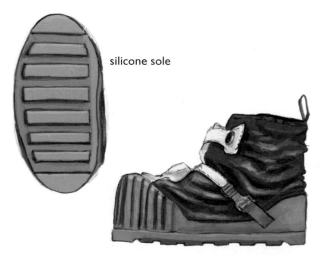

silicone sole

Boots

Lunar boots are essentially overshoes worn over the pressurized boots. They have large, flat soles made from silicone to keep the astronaut from sinking into the lunar dust. The upper part of the boots is made from layers of beta cloth and covered in Chromel-R to protect against extreme temperatures and sharp rocks.

*Snoopy is the unofficial mascot of the Apollo space program.

Portable Life Support System (PLSS) and Oxygen Purge System (OPS)

Built by Hamilton Standard, the Portable Life Support System (PLSS), or life support backpack, is the most important piece of equipment the astronauts will carry. It's what makes each spacesuit function as a "wearable spacecraft," providing all the same life support systems as the LM or CM. The PLSS dispenses oxygen for breathing and pressurization while removing carbon dioxide, moisture, and odors. It also controls temperature and provides a means of communication.

The Oxygen Purge System (OPS) is a safeguard, in case something goes wrong with the backpack. It provides up to 30 minutes of oxygen, which should give the astronauts plenty of time to return to the LM and plug into the life support system on board.

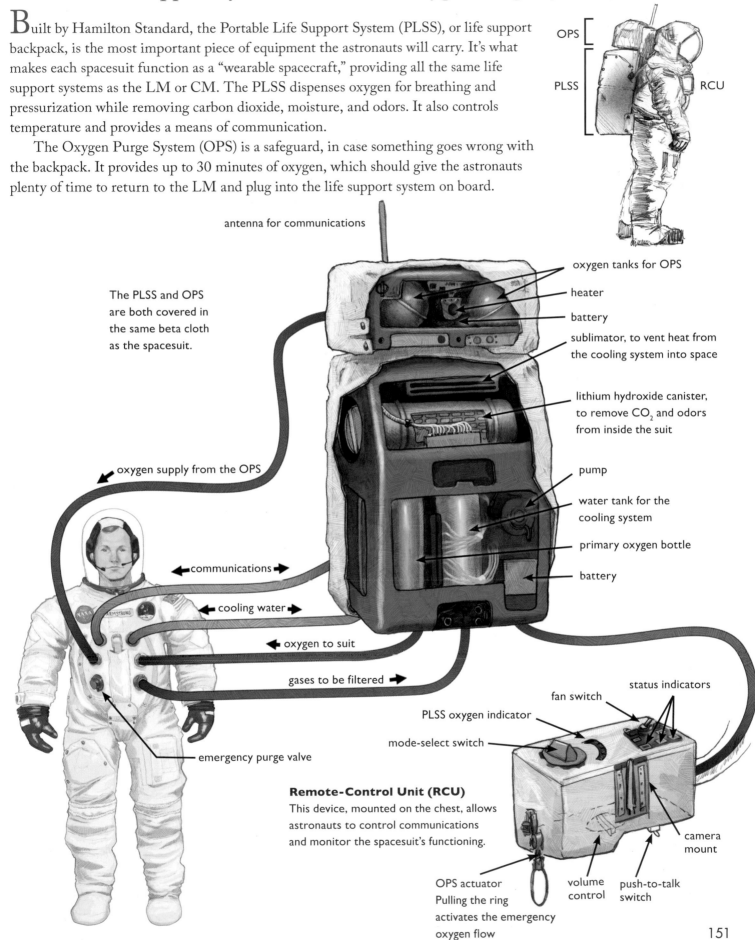

OPS

PLSS

RCU

antenna for communications

oxygen tanks for OPS

heater

battery

The PLSS and OPS are both covered in the same beta cloth as the spacesuit.

sublimator, to vent heat from the cooling system into space

lithium hydroxide canister, to remove CO_2 and odors from inside the suit

oxygen supply from the OPS

pump

water tank for the cooling system

communications

primary oxygen bottle

cooling water

battery

oxygen to suit

gases to be filtered

status indicators

fan switch

PLSS oxygen indicator

mode-select switch

emergency purge valve

Remote-Control Unit (RCU)
This device, mounted on the chest, allows astronauts to control communications and monitor the spacesuit's functioning.

camera mount

OPS actuator
Pulling the ring activates the emergency oxygen flow

volume control

push-to-talk switch

Liquid Cooling Garment (LCG)

Problem! Overheating in the Spacesuit

It's obvious that astronauts wearing heavy multilayered spacesuits are going to get overheated quickly. Hamilton Standard, the company building the PLSS, develops a way to cool the astronauts by pumping cold air from the backpack through the suits. But it's soon discovered that this system doesn't work well. Hamilton Standard engineer Dave Jennings has two weeks to come up with another solution or the company might lose its contract with NASA.

Solution! A Water-Cooled System

Jennings designs the Liquid Cooling Garment (LCG), a spandex-netted tunic similar to long underwear, which is crisscrossed with hundreds of feet of polyvinyl tubing. Water, cooled by a sublimator (see p. 91) on the PLSS backpack, flows through the tubing and carries the heat away from the astronaut through thermal conduction. The astronauts will be able to use the RCUs attached to their chests to adjust the flow of water, which controls the temperature inside their suits. The method works so well that it is still in use today.

water inlet/outlet port that connects to outer layers of spacesuit

Dave Jennings sewing tubing onto the LCG worn by fellow engineer Mark Britanisky

water tubing

Eleanor "Ellie" Foraker (1930–2011)

Seamstress Manager for Apollo Spacesuits

Being a seamstress at Playtex in the early 1960s usually meant that you made bras, girdles, baby clothes, or some other type of undergarment. When NASA chose ILC to make spacesuits for the Moon-bound astronauts, Ellie Foraker was sewing plastic baby pants (used to cover wet cloth diapers).

Only the best seamstresses would do for the Apollo project, and Foraker was one of the best. She understood that the garments they would be creating had to be of the absolute highest quality. If they failed—if even one stitch was wrong or if someone accidentally left a pin in one of the suits—an astronaut could die!

The seamstresses, all women, were suddenly working with unfamiliar materials under guidelines that required them to sew, by hand, 32 stitches for every inch along a seam. There were hundreds of feet of seams in every suit, and every stitch was counted and inspected.

Attached to each suit, from the beginning of its creation to the time it was delivered to NASA, was a small card with an astronaut's picture and autograph, as well as an inscription. This served as a constant reminder of the important work the seamstresses were doing.

The final suits were works of art, and unbeknownst to NASA and the astronauts who wore them, many of the seamstresses signed their names inside the suits, which are now housed at the Smithsonian Institution.

Ellie Foraker worked at ILC for 43 years. During that time, she applied her unique talents to making spacesuits for all the Apollo missions as well as the Space Shuttle missions.

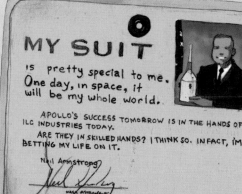

MY SUIT is pretty special to me. One day, in space, it will be my whole world.

APOLLO'S SUCCESS TOMORROW IS IN THE HANDS OF ILC INDUSTRIES TODAY.

ARE THEY IN SKILLED HANDS? I THINK SO. IN FACT, I'M BETTING MY LIFE ON IT.

Neil Armstrong

PART 6

Support on the Ground

"We were experts from the airplane world, but we were novices and naïve about this new world of space travel. This whole business of putting a man into space was getting complicated."

—CHRISTOPHER COLUMBUS KRAFT JR., DIRECTOR OF FLIGHT OPERATIONS

Landing astronauts on the Moon and returning them safely to Earth is going to take a lot more than constructing rocket stages, spacecraft modules, and spacesuits, innovative as they are.

NASA needs people to organize, design, and build a complex for all the different parts to be assembled, tested, and launched. It needs massive machines that can move all the parts into place. It needs buildings for the hundreds of people who will monitor and oversee the launch and the entire mission. And it needs to develop entirely new systems and procedures for training the astronauts.

Each mission will have only three people riding into space, but the massive effort back on Earth will require thousands upon thousands of construction workers, engineers, mechanics, electricians, and other specialists.

Launch Complex 39, Kennedy Space Center

Construction of the different parts of the Saturn V rocket and the Apollo spacecraft are well under way. Now NASA needs to decide where it will build a launch complex. The Mercury and Gemini missions all launched from Cape Canaveral, Florida, but due to the sheer size of the Saturn V, a new complex will be needed. This requires its own set of calculations.

First, there is speed. Because Earth rotates once every 24 hours, the surface at the equator is moving at nearly 1,000 miles an hour. If we want to take advantage of that speed boost, the launch should take place close to the equator in an easterly direction.

Second: transportation. The launch complex needs to be accessible by water so barges can deliver the various stages of the Saturn V. In July 1962, after much research and deliberation, NASA chooses Merritt Island and purchases 140,000 acres of marshy land right on the coast, just north of Cape Canaveral.

Launch Complex 39 will consist of the Vehicle Assembly Building (VAB), where the Saturn V will be put together; the Launch Control Center (LCC), from which the launch will be monitored; and two launchpads.

There is no time to lose. As soon as the land purchase goes through, the construction of Launch Complex 39 moves ahead at full speed. The project will take four years and nearly 7,000 people to complete. Before it is finished, it is renamed Kennedy Space Center (KSC).

a Saturn V S-IC stage heading to the VAB by barge from the Mississippi River

mobile launcher on Crawler

crawlerway: Millions of pounds of Tennessee River rock make up the 3.5-mile road from the VAB to the launchpad.

Putting the launch complex right on the coast is critical. If a rocket fails at launch and falls back to Earth, it will land safely in the water instead of crashing into inhabited areas. This will also ensure that the first two stages fall into the ocean after their jobs are completed.

Merritt Island

Atlantic Ocean

Launch Control Center:
The LCC houses the equipment and people needed to monitor all aspects of the rocket and crew during a launch.

Vehicle Assembly Building:
Unlike earlier rockets, which were assembled horizontally and raised to vertical on the launchpad, the huge Saturn V will be assembled upright.

Barge Canal:
A large canal is dredged from the VAB up the Banana River and out to the Atlantic Ocean to allow barges to deliver the first two stages of the Saturn V.

Mobile Service Structure

crawlerway to Launchpad 39B

Liquid Oxygen Facility and tank

Launch Umbilical Tower

LAUNCHPAD 39A

ramp

flame trench

flame deflector

launch structure

RP-1 holding pond

Liquid Hydrogen Facility and tank

hydrogen burn pond

Bringing It All Together

Many companies spread all over the United States are manufacturing the rocket stages and spacecraft modules needed for up to 20 Apollo/Saturn launches. Each part goes through rigorous testing before it is approved to be sent to the VAB at Kennedy Space Center. As the parts arrive, they are assembled into the world's largest flying machine.

It is, of course, impossible to transport these enormous machines over normal roadways, so they are sent by barges, cargo ships, and a fleet of oversized planes called Super Guppies.

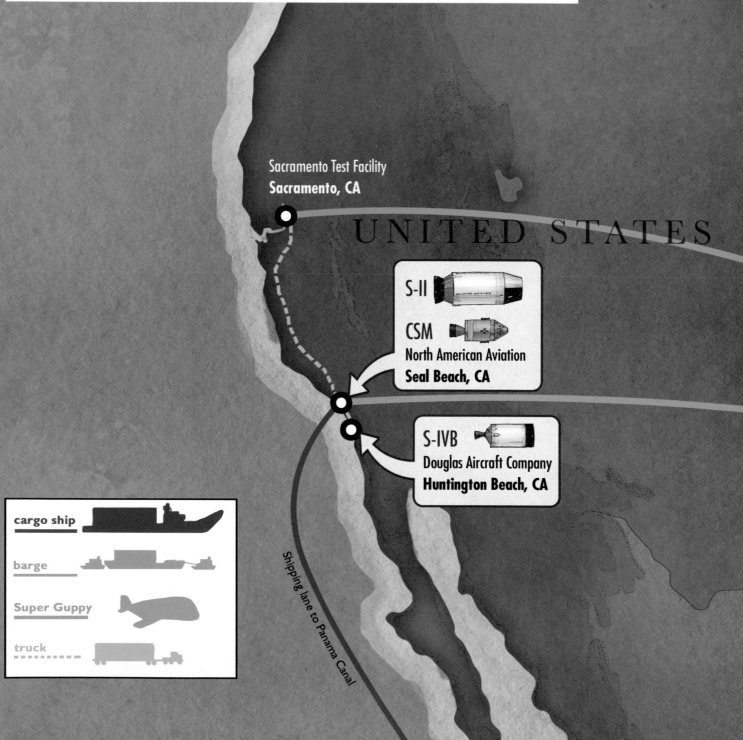

Sacramento Test Facility
Sacramento, CA

UNITED STATES

S-II

CSM

North American Aviation
Seal Beach, CA

S-IVB

Douglas Aircraft Company
Huntington Beach, CA

Shipping lane to Panama Canal

cargo ship

barge

Super Guppy

truck

The first stage **(S-IC)** of the Saturn V is loaded on a waiting barge that will take it to Huntsville, Alabama. After engine testing, it returns via barge to New Orleans for final checking. The S-IC's final trip is by cargo ship to Kennedy Space Center in Florida.

The second stage **(S-II)** is loaded onto a cargo ship in Seal Beach, California, which then journeys thousands of miles to Mississippi via the Panama Canal. Once tested, it travels by cargo ship to KSC.

The third stage **(S-IVB)** is small enough to travel from Huntington Beach, California, to Sacramento by truck. Once testing is complete, it is flown to KSC aboard a Super Guppy.

The **Instrument Unit (IU)**, **Command and Service Module (CSM)**, and **Lunar Module (LM)** are all shipped to KSC aboard a Super Guppy.

of AMERICA

LM
Grumman
Bethpage, NY

IU
IBM
Marshall Space Flight Center
Huntsville, AL

Mississippi Test Facility
Bay Saint Louis, MS

Kennedy Space Center
Merritt Island, FL

S-IC
Boeing
Michoud Assembly Facility
New Orleans, LA

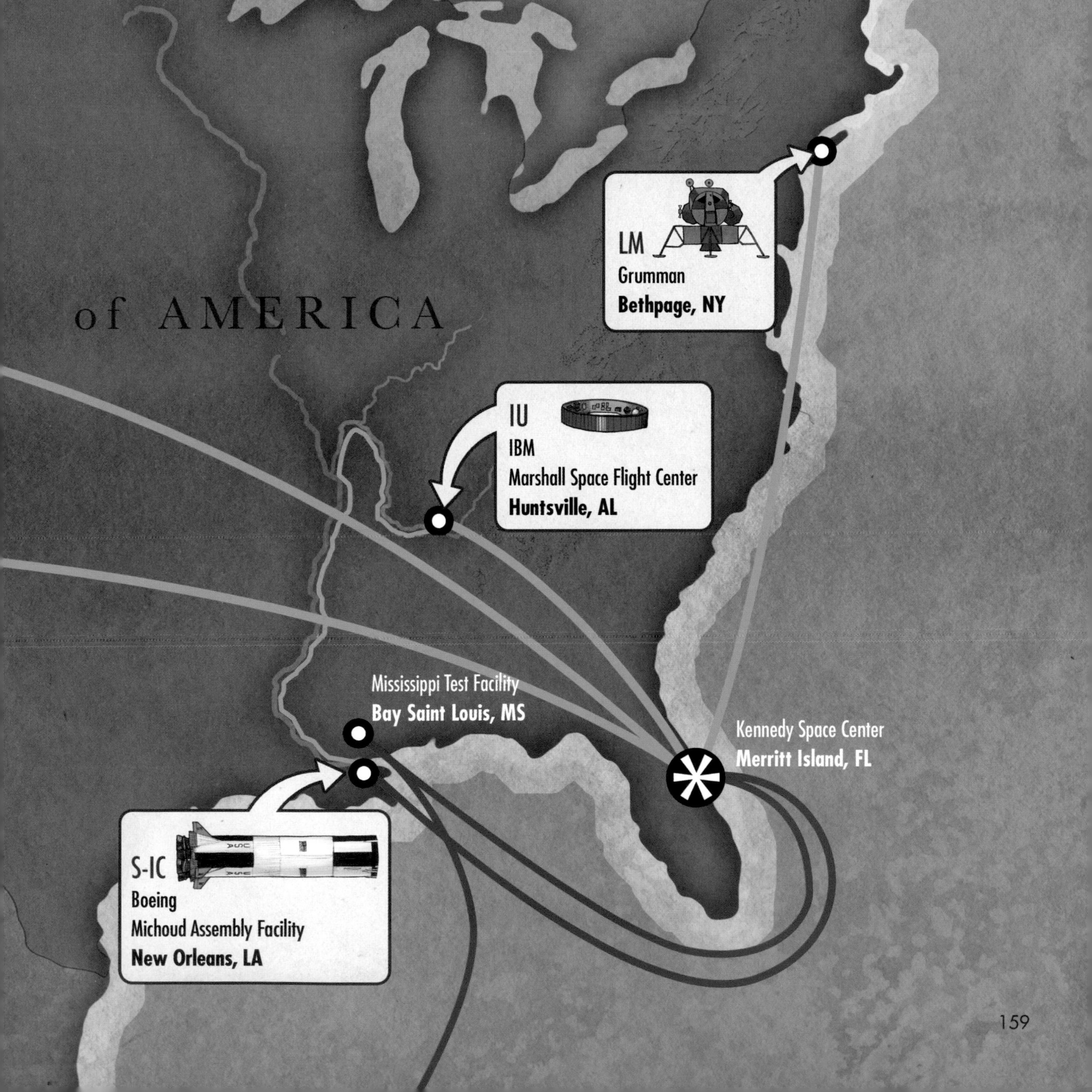

The Pregnant Guppy

Ex–US Air Force pilot Jack Conroy and aircraft salesman Lee Mansdorf are having dinner one night in 1960, discussing NASA's transportation problems. They've been shipping Mercury and Gemini parts to Florida by boat, which is taking weeks. Conroy realizes that if he and Mansdorf could build an oversized aircraft to deliver spacecraft components, they would have a chance at a lucrative NASA contract.

Conroy sells everything he owns and forms Aero Spacelines. He builds the first oversized aircraft, modifying a Boeing 377 he'd bought from Mansdorf. On September 19, 1962, he takes it on its inaugural flight—nearly 2,000 miles from Van Nuys, California, to Marshall Space Flight Center in Huntsville, Alabama, where he'll try to convince Wernher von Braun of his transport plan. One NASA official sees the behemoth plane and says it looks like a "pregnant guppy." The nickname sticks.

Von Braun is so impressed that he immediately climbs aboard for a test flight. While they're in the air, Conroy tells von Braun that NASA doesn't need to spend three weeks getting rocket parts from California to Florida by boat; he can fly them there in a mere 18 hours. Von Braun and NASA know that every minute counts in the race to beat the Russians, and, in 1963, Aero Spacelines receives the contract to deliver rocket parts for the Gemini program via the "Pregnant Guppy."

John M. "Jack" Conroy (1920–1979)

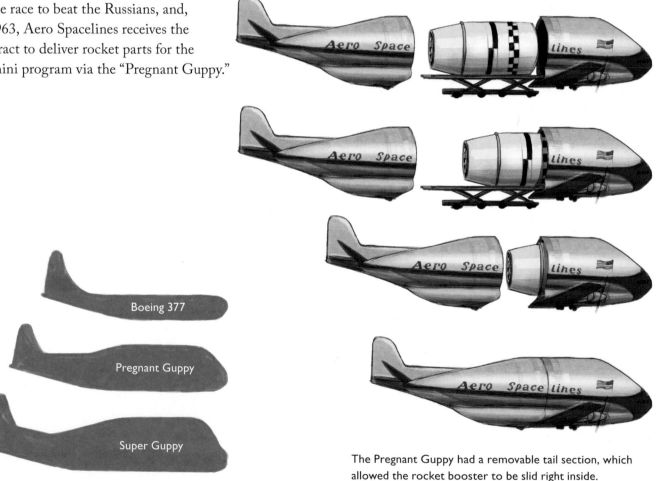

The Pregnant Guppy had a removable tail section, which allowed the rocket booster to be slid right inside.

The Super Guppy

By 1965, with the Apollo program well under way, Conroy builds a bigger plane for Saturn V and Apollo parts. He calls this one the Super Guppy, and it's the largest airplane in the world. Its cargo compartment diameter of 25 feet is just wide enough to house the nearly 22-foot diameter S-IVB stage. The Super Guppy's nose cone can swing out 95 degrees like a door, allowing the more than 58-foot-long S-IVB stage to slide inside.

Super Guppy Facts

Top speed	**300** mph
Length	**141** ft. **2** in.
Empty Weight	**110,000** lb.
Maximum Cargo	**65,000** lb.
Manufacturer	**Aero Spacelines**

The Vehicle Assembly Building (VAB)

Throughout the Mercury and Gemini programs, the rockets were all assembled on the launchpad. Apollo is different. A Saturn V rocket cannot sit for months at a time on the launchpad during all the necessary prelaunch testing, leaving it exposed to Florida's corrosive, salty air and hurricanes. We need to build a home for these gigantic flying machines. It has to be large enough to house several Saturn Vs at a time because of the overlapping launch schedule. It also needs to be at least 3.5 miles away from the launchpad, as that is calculated to be the minimum safe distance in the event that a Saturn V explodes.

In 1963, construction begins on the Vehicle Assembly Building, one of the largest buildings in the world. In order to make sure the VAB is stable, secure, and hurricane-proof, its foundation needs to be strong. Construction crews make pilings out of steel pipe filled with sand, and drive them 164 feet down into the bedrock. In all there are 4,225 pilings, which take 126 miles of steel pipe to create.

In 1966, the VAB is completed, and ready to receive and assemble all the various parts of the Moon rocket. It covers eight acres and can house the equivalent of three and a half Empire State Buildings. It is so massive that under the right conditions, clouds form in the upper levels. Its 465-foot-tall doors take 45 minutes to open or close.

The Big Flag
The American flag and the NASA logo were not painted on the side of the VAB until 1976 and 1998, respectively, but are shown here to provide a sense of scale. This is the largest American flag in the world: 209 feet high and 110 feet wide. An NBA regulation basketball court could fit in the star field, and each stripe is nine feet wide. The NASA logo is the size of a baseball diamond.

Rollout
A fully assembled Saturn V/Apollo spacecraft can be rolled out of one of the VAB's 465-foot doors.

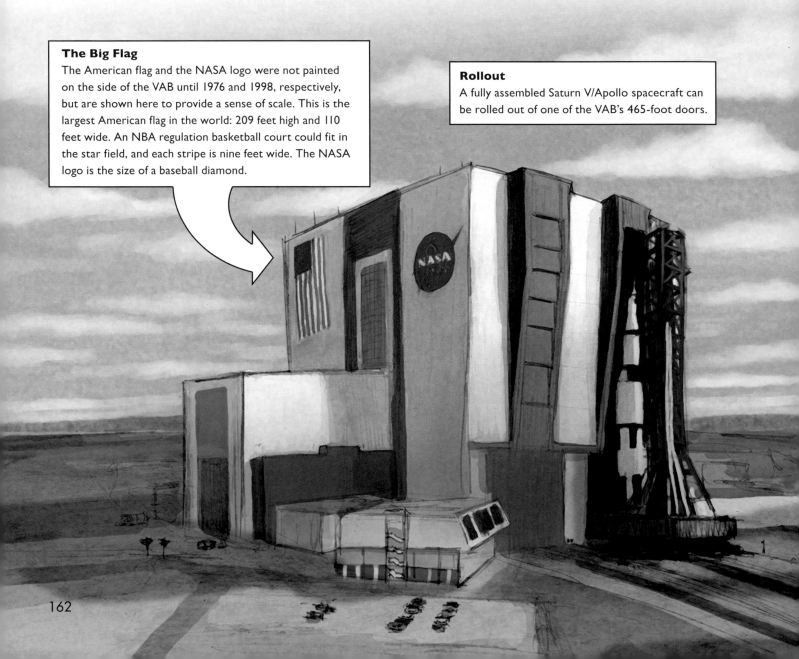

Cranes

The cranes used to lift and assemble all the different parts inside the VAB are some of the biggest and most finely tuned in the world. Seated on tracks, the five overhead bridge cranes can stack the rocket stages carefully, one atop another. The largest crane can lift the equivalent of 50 elephants! The crane operators' skills need to be so expertly honed that they can lower an 88,000-pound second stage onto an egg without cracking it.

Inside the transfer aisle of the VAB, a Saturn first stage (S-IC) is being hoisted off a delivery vehicle by a 250-ton bridge crane.

The Vehicle Assembly Building is more machine than building. It is a giant receiving, testing, and assembly plant for Moon rockets. This is where all the different parts of the Apollo/Saturn vehicle will meet for the very first time. Every plug, bolt, seam, joint, and bit of wiring has to match up perfectly.

The tallest section of the building is called the High Bay. It houses four cells, or bays, where the vehicles are assembled. Each bay is located next to a corresponding door at one of the four corners of the building.

The Low Bay houses eight checkout bays where the different parts are tested prior to integration. Down the middle of the High and Low Bays is the transfer aisle, a cavernous expanse where the huge stages of the Saturn V are moved by crane to their appropriate locations.

a fully assembled rocket on the mobile launcher in High Bay 4

High Bay

Low Bay

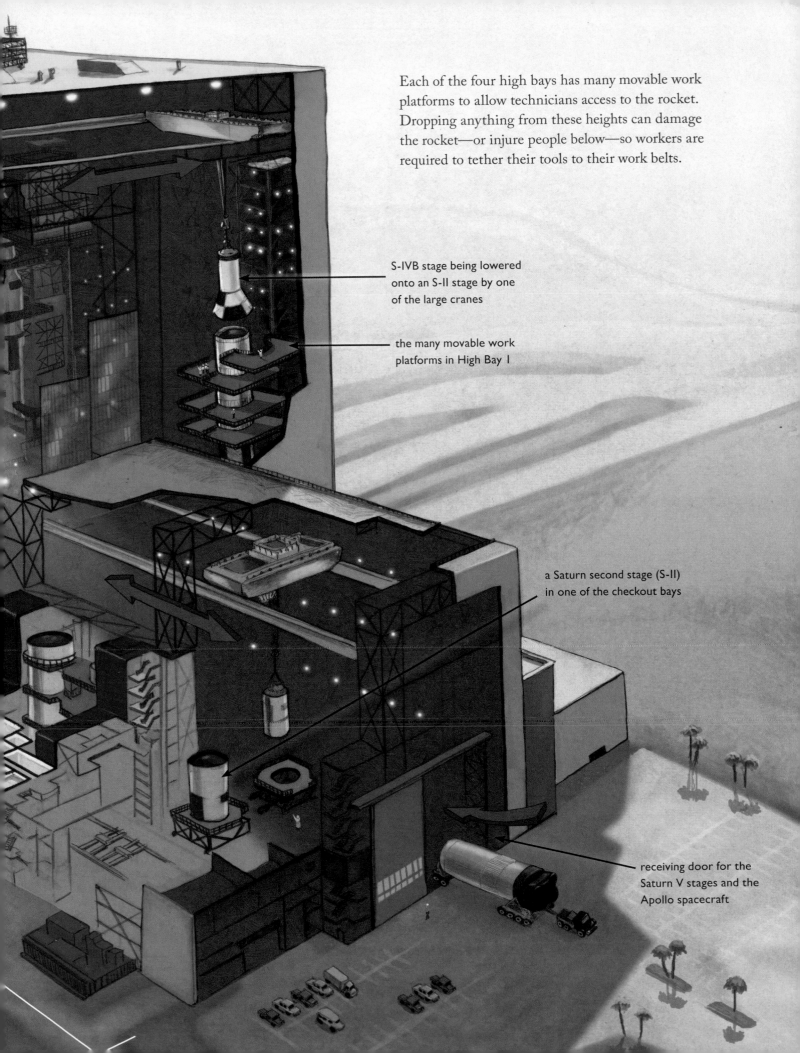

Each of the four high bays has many movable work platforms to allow technicians access to the rocket. Dropping anything from these heights can damage the rocket—or injure people below—so workers are required to tether their tools to their work belts.

S-IVB stage being lowered onto an S-II stage by one of the large cranes

the many movable work platforms in High Bay 1

a Saturn second stage (S-II) in one of the checkout bays

receiving door for the Saturn V stages and the Apollo spacecraft

The Mobile Launch System

Problem! Transporting the Rocket

Now that the Saturn V will be assembled within the safe confines of the VAB, it is up to engineer Don Buchanan to figure out how to transport the rocket to the launchpad three and a half miles away. He first considers digging a channel, building a barge, and floating the rocket to the pad, but tests conclude that a rocket-laden barge will be too top-heavy to work. He also thinks about a possible rail system. All his ideas are either too impractical or too expensive. By February 1963, NASA officials want an answer, and Buchanan is running out of time.

Solution! A Complete Mobile System

On a whim, Buchanan and his team head to Kentucky to look at a strip-mining shovel. It's a huge machine on eight sets of tank treads, able to move tremendous amounts of weight. Buchanan is excited—something like this could plausibly do the job *and* come in on budget.
He and his team do some tests and expand the idea into a two-part mobile launch system made up of a mobile launcher and a Crawler-Transporter.

Here's the winning idea: The rocket will be assembled on a platform that already has a launch tower in place. Underneath the platform, a tracked vehicle called a Crawler-Transporter will slowly move the entire system out to the launchpad. Since the entire launch complex is built on what is basically marshland—and the mobile launch system is a multimillion-pound machine—the road it uses will have to be carefully engineered to support it all.

Pad 39B

crawlerway to Pad 39B (4.2 miles from the VAB)

Pad 39A

Mobile Service Structure (MSS)

crawlerway to Pad 39A (3.5 miles from the VAB)

Crawler-Transporter taking the mobile launcher to Pad 39A

Launch Control Center

Vehicle Assembly Building

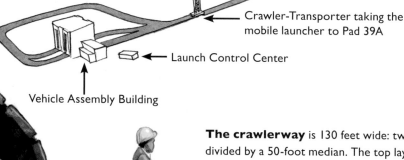

The crawlerway is 130 feet wide: two 40-foot-wide lanes divided by a 50-foot median. The top layer consists of four to eight inches of Tennessee River rock. This type of rock won't spark when crushed, avoiding the possibility of fire, and it also acts like a layer of ball bearings, allowing the Crawler to easily glide around corners. Underneath the river rock is almost eight feet of stone and compacted soil to keep the Crawler from sinking into the marshland.

4–8 in. Tennessee River rock

4 ft. graded crushed stone

2.5 ft. small gravel

1 ft. compacted soil

The Mobile Launcher

The two main parts of the mobile launcher are the Launch Umbilical Tower (LUT) and the launch platform. The Launch Umbilical Tower is a 380-foot-tall open steel structure with 18 levels and two high-speed elevators. It also has eight service arms, which provide propellants, environmental controls, electricity, and venting for the different stages of the rocket. The highest arm is the access arm, or gantry, which provides access to the Command Module for the astronauts and technicians. At its end is an environmentally controlled room (known as the White Room), that rests against the CM.

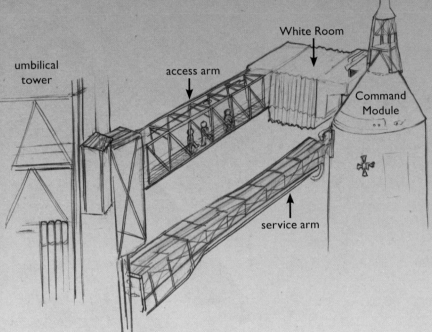

umbilical tower

access arm

White Room

Command Module

service arm

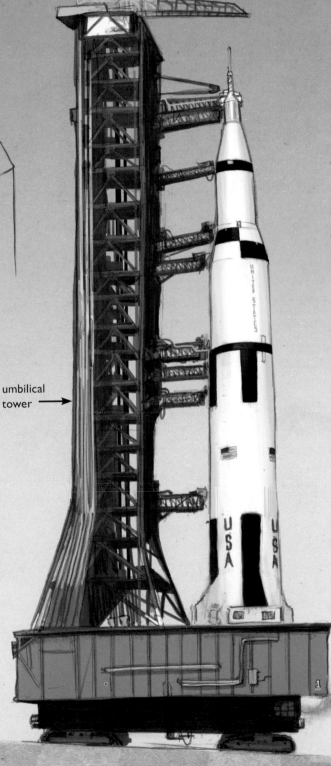

hammerhead crane

umbilical tower

launch platform

Crawler-Transporter

The service arms are also referred to as swing arms because of their ability to disconnect and quickly swing away from the launching rocket. To prevent high winds from making the arms sway, they are built as open-girder structures with steel mesh floors. Walking across the swing arm to the White Room can be a dizzying, frightening experience, because you can look down through the floor and see the launchpad 400 feet below.

The launch platform is a two-story steel structure that provides a base for the umbilical tower and the rocket. Directly below the rocket is a 40-foot-by-40-foot square hole that allows clearance for the five F-1 engines and their exhaust flames to blast into the flame trench of the launchpad. Three launch platforms are built for Apollo, and inside each is a maze of plumbing and electrical cabling, offices, machinery, and bathrooms.

tail service mast

hold-down arm

Hold-Down Arms

The four hold-down arms attached to the launch platform are responsible for keeping the 6.5-million-pound Saturn V rocket firmly in place from assembly until liftoff. Each hold-down arm weighs about 40,000 pounds and produces 770,000 pounds of force at the point of contact, locking the vehicle in place. Once the five F-1 engines reach 95 percent thrust, the arms will release the Saturn V, and liftoff begins.

Tail Service Masts

Three tail service masts are also mounted on the launch platform to provide support for electrical cables and propellant loading for the first stage of the Saturn V. They will retract at liftoff, up and away from the rocket. A visor hood covers the umbilical extensions to prevent damage from the exhaust.

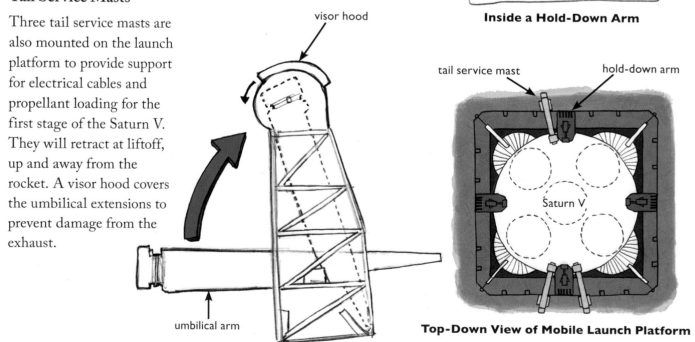

launch vehicle

blast hood
(closes after liftoff)

pneumatic release

point of contact

Inside a Hold-Down Arm

visor hood

umbilical arm

tail service mast

hold-down arm

Saturn V

Top-Down View of Mobile Launch Platform

The Mobile Service Structure (MSS)

Similar to scaffolding on a building, a Mobile Service Structure (MSS) is designed to provide technicians with access to the launch vehicle and spacecraft while it is on the launchpad. Once the MSS is positioned against the Saturn V, several work platforms will completely surround the spacecraft and the section above the S-IVB stage, where the LM is housed.

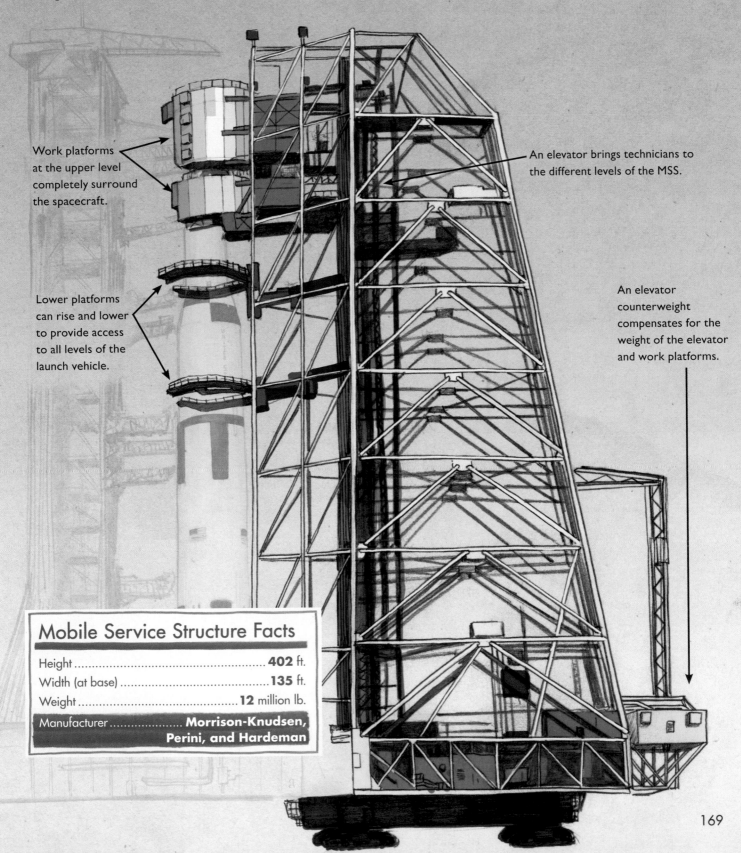

Work platforms at the upper level completely surround the spacecraft.

Lower platforms can rise and lower to provide access to all levels of the launch vehicle.

An elevator brings technicians to the different levels of the MSS.

An elevator counterweight compensates for the weight of the elevator and work platforms.

Mobile Service Structure Facts

Height	**402** ft.
Width (at base)	**135** ft.
Weight	**12** million lb.
Manufacturer	**Morrison-Knudsen, Perini, and Hardeman**

The Crawler-Transporter

Made by the Marion Power Shovel Company in Marion, Ohio, whose steam shovels and giant excavators helped build the Panama Canal, the Crawler-Transporter is the largest self-propelled land-based vehicle in the world. It will move on eight tanklike tracks to bring the LUT and the Saturn V to and from the launchpad. It will also move the MSS into place. Each track has 57 plates, called shoes, that weigh more than 2,000 pounds each! It will take a team of 30 engineers, technicians, and drivers to operate the vehicle.

131 ft.

90 ft.

driver crew cab

single shoe

The 3.5-mile trip from the VAB to Pad 39A takes five hours and uses about 500 gallons of fuel.

Crawler-Transporter Facts

Weight	**6.3** million lb.
Top Speed (loaded)	**1** mph
Top Speed (unloaded)	**2** mph
Lifting Capacity	**12** million lb.
Manufacturer	**Marion Power Shovel Company**

114 ft.

20 ft.

track

Two Crawlers were
built for NASA and
are still in use today.

Each corner of the Crawler-Transporter
can be lowered or raised independently.
A self-leveling system keeps the rocket
completely vertical as it climbs the
5 percent grade at the launchpad.

launchpad

The Launchpad (39A)

While the VAB is being erected, another team of workers is building two launchpads.

When construction first began in 1961, NASA was still considering the Earth Orbit Rendezvous (EOR) approach, which would have required four launchpads to accommodate the different launches for each mission. A year later, Lunar Orbit Rendezvous (LOR) was chosen, so now only two launchpads are necessary.

Pad 39A will be used for almost all the Apollo missions, but there will also be a second, identical launchpad: Pad 39B. Because preparations for Apollo 11 will start early, Apollo 10 is the only Apollo mission planned to launch from Pad 39B.

The layout of the launchpad itself is mostly determined by the design of the flame deflector. Similar to the flame bucket at the test facilities, the flame deflector at the launchpad protects the lower section of the vehicle and the launch stand from the high pressure and flames during ignition and liftoff. It does this by redirecting the exhaust gases outward along a flame trench. Because the launchpad is being built on wet marshland, NASA engineers want the floor of the flame trench at ground level to keep it from flooding like a basement. This means the top of the launchpad will have to be over four stories high to give the flame deflector the clearance it needs.

The vehicle sits over a 40-foot-by-40-foot square hole in the launch platform to allow for flames and exhaust to release into the flame trench.

flame trench

flame deflector

escape tube

blast room

rubber room

Tracks are used to move the flame deflector in place.

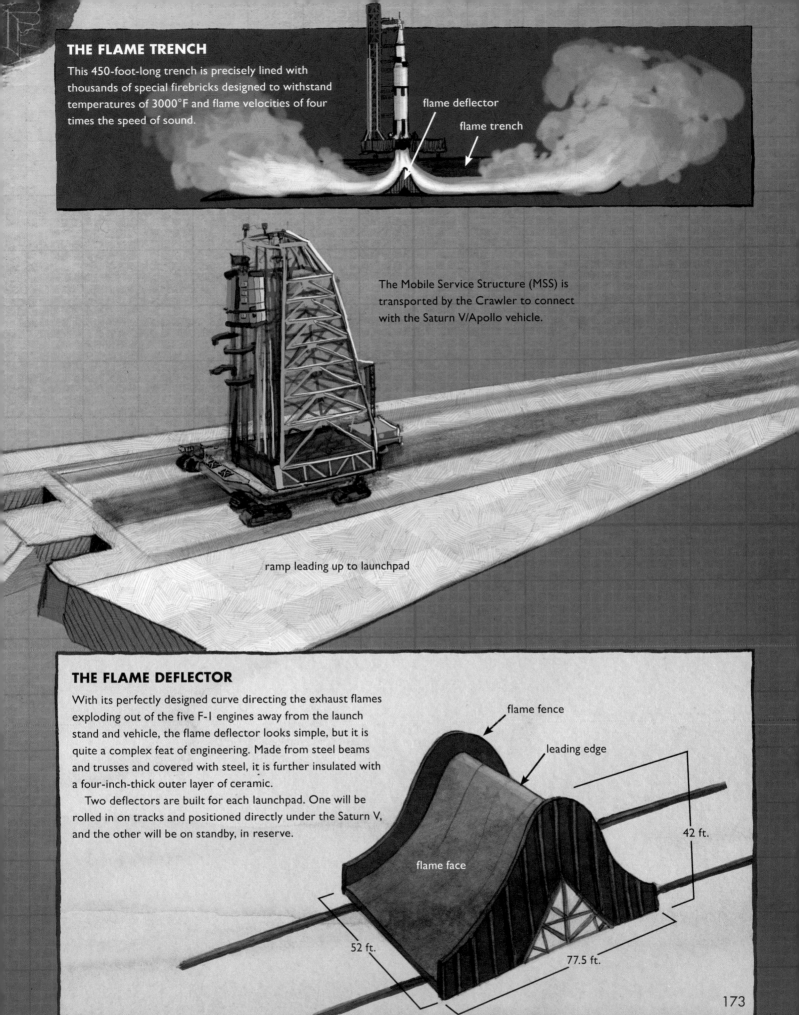

THE FLAME TRENCH

This 450-foot-long trench is precisely lined with thousands of special firebricks designed to withstand temperatures of 3000°F and flame velocities of four times the speed of sound.

flame deflector

flame trench

The Mobile Service Structure (MSS) is transported by the Crawler to connect with the Saturn V/Apollo vehicle.

ramp leading up to launchpad

THE FLAME DEFLECTOR

With its perfectly designed curve directing the exhaust flames exploding out of the five F-1 engines away from the launch stand and vehicle, the flame deflector looks simple, but it is quite a complex feat of engineering. Made from steel beams and trusses and covered with steel, it is further insulated with a four-inch-thick outer layer of ceramic.

Two deflectors are built for each launchpad. One will be rolled in on tracks and positioned directly under the Saturn V, and the other will be on standby, in reserve.

flame fence

leading edge

42 ft.

flame face

52 ft.

77.5 ft.

173

Safety on the Launchpad

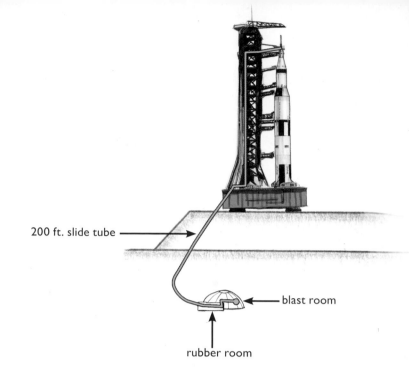

200 ft. slide tube

blast room

rubber room

The Saturn V rocket has enough propellants to make an explosion equivalent to a half-kiloton atomic bomb. Everyone working at Kennedy Space Center knows how important it is to design an emergency escape system for the astronauts and any crew working at the launchpads.

They decide to build an underground blast room 40 feet below the pad. If there were to be an emergency, the crew could take the high-speed elevator on a 30-second journey to the base of the launch tower. From there, they would leap into a tube, slide down into a room called a rubber room, and race through a thick steel door to the blast room, where they'd be safe from the exploding rocket above.

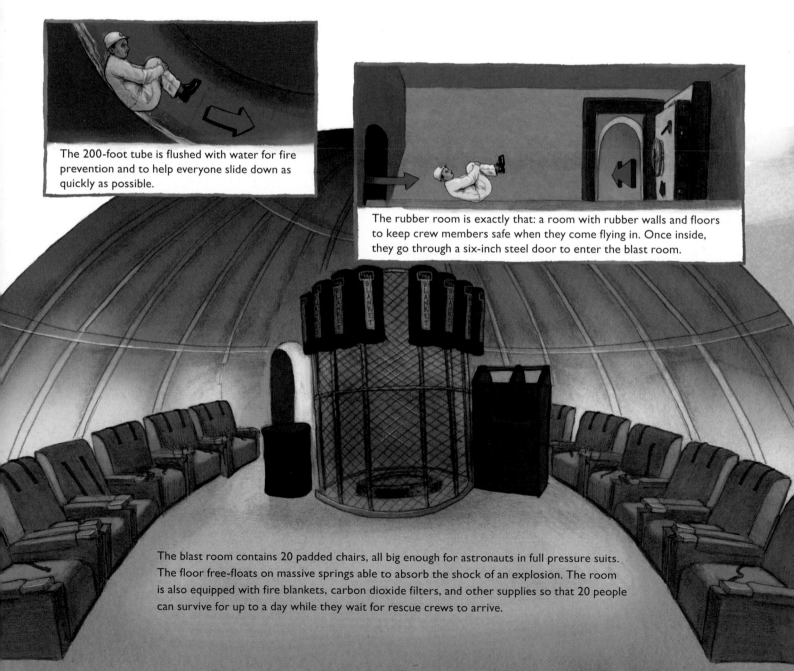

The 200-foot tube is flushed with water for fire prevention and to help everyone slide down as quickly as possible.

The rubber room is exactly that: a room with rubber walls and floors to keep crew members safe when they come flying in. Once inside, they go through a six-inch steel door to enter the blast room.

The blast room contains 20 padded chairs, all big enough for astronauts in full pressure suits. The floor free-floats on massive springs able to absorb the shock of an explosion. The room is also equipped with fire blankets, carbon dioxide filters, and other supplies so that 20 people can survive for up to a day while they wait for rescue crews to arrive.

 **Rockets Explode from the Bottom Up**

The high-speed elevators are only 25 feet away from the 363-foot-tall rocket. If that rocket is about to explode, propellant spills or fires are more likely to be at the base, and the crew would descend right into the inferno.

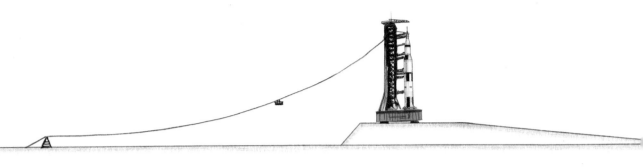

Solution! Emergency Egress System

KSC engineers develop a slide-wire system with a gondola, like at a ski area, for nine people. The gondola sits 480 feet off the ground, just outside the top access arm, and allows the astronauts and up to six others to climb in and strap themselves to a bar inside. They will then pull a release ring and slide down the 1⅛-inch steel cable to a spot 2,200 feet from the tower. The gondola will only be tested once—the engineers are terrified of it!

Launch Control Center (LCC)

The larger the rocket, the larger the potential explosion, so it's determined that launch operations for the Saturn V need to be a minimum of three miles from the launchpad.

Before Apollo, those responsible for the launch operations of a rocket worked in a blockhouse, designed to protect the personnel inside from exploding rockets. Blockhouses have thick walls and few or no windows.

Instead of a blockhouse, the Launch Control Center (LCC) being built at KSC for the Apollo missions is a four-story building with a wall of windows that look out over the launch site. The windows are two inches thick, with metal shutters that can close in the event of an explosion.

The LCC has three firing rooms that house all the consoles and personnel to handle the testing and launching of the Saturn V. Each firing room has over 450 separate consoles to monitor each individual system. Controllers can communicate through a phone line called "the net."

JoAnn H. Morgan (b. 1940)

Instrumentation Controller

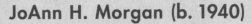

Thirty minutes before any launch, the doors of the firing room are locked, and no one is allowed to enter or leave. For the launch of Apollo 11, there was only one woman among the 450 men in the room. Her name was JoAnn Morgan.

Born in Huntsville, Alabama, to a pilot in the Army Air Corps and a statistician in the Army Corps of Engineers, it's no surprise that Morgan would go on to pursue math and science herself. Her parents placed an equal importance on reading and the arts, starting with having her read the newspaper to them at the age of three!

At 17 years old, after her family moved to Titusville, Florida, Morgan witnessed Explorer 1 launch into orbit. She suddenly realized that the knowledge of the universe was now accessible—and she had to be a part of it.

The next day, at the post office, she discovered a summer job posting for students to work as junior engineers with the Army Ballistic Missile Agency. She got the job and started three days after graduating from high school, working on her first launch that very week. After earning her mathematics degree from Jacksonville State University in Alabama in 1963, she became the first female engineer hired at Kennedy Space Center.

Morgan started working with the site activation team, testing everything from the Crawler to the launchpad. Some of her work, in an office near the very top of the VAB, required her to walk up 18 flights of stairs lugging all her paperwork, because elevators had not yet been installed.

During a time when sexism was rampant and female engineers were almost unheard of, Morgan paved the way for future generations of women and continued to rise up the ranks. Throughout her expansive 45-year career with NASA, Morgan held several executive positions, including acting deputy director of Kennedy Space Center.

Mission Operations Control Room (MOCR)

Johnson Space Center, Houston, Texas

About a thousand miles away from Pad 39A, in a plain-looking building in Houston, Texas, there is a room called the Mission Operations Control Room (MOCR), also known as Mission Control.

In this room, engineers and specialists will watch over and troubleshoot every aspect of every Apollo mission, starting at the moment the rocket leaves the launchpad. Their task will not be complete until the astronauts are recovered upon splashdown.

Their work begins years before each launch. They plan and practice every detail—from the exact second the astronauts need to fire the engine to head to the Moon, to what they will eat for breakfast on their third day in space. It is all scripted and rehearsed until it is second nature.

During a mission, the controllers will monitor their consoles and notify their flight director if anything deviates in the slightest from what they are expecting to happen. Each controller has a team of experts on hand in another room, waiting to help solve any problems that might arise.

1. BOOSTER (booster systems engineer): monitors the Saturn V during prelaunch and ascent

2. RETRO (retrofire officer): responsible for abort procedures and the firing of the engine to bring the spacecraft back to Earth

5. SURGEON (flight surgeon): monitors the crew's health

6. CAPCOM (capsule communicator): communicates directly with the astronauts

7. EECOM (electrical, environmental, and communications): oversees life support systems and electrical systems on the spacecraft

11. INCO (instrumentation and communications officer): responsible for all voice, data, and video communications systems

12. O&P or PROCEDURES (organization and procedures): enforces mission policies and rules

13. AFLIGHT (assistant flight director): monitors the mission and backs up FLIGHT

17. PAO (public affairs officer): relays information to the news media and the public

18. DFO (director of flight operations): intermediary between Mission Control and KSC management. This seat was most often occupied by Chris Kraft (p. 180).

The MOCR is divided into 20 stations, or consoles. Each console displays information about a specific part of the spacecraft or part of the mission. During a mission, four teams of controllers work these consoles in shifts around the clock. Displays in the front of the room show maps, data, and television feeds from the spacecraft.

3. FIDO (flight dynamics officer): responsible for the flight path of the space vehicle

4. GUIDO (guidance officer): monitors the navigation systems and guidance computer on the spacecraft

8. GNC (guidance, navigation, and control): responsible for the reaction control system and the main engine on the CSM

9. TELMU (telemetry, electrical, and extravehicular mobility unit): monitors the LM's electrical and environmental systems, as well as the spacesuits during moonwalks

10. CONTROL (LM guidance and navigation): monitors the LM during flight

14. FLIGHT (flight director): makes all final decisions about the mission during the flight. Responsible for crew safety and mission success—and absolutely no one, including the president of the United States, can override his final decision.

15. FAO (flight activities officer): plans and supports crew activities, checklists, attitude maneuvers, and the timelines the astronauts will follow

16. NETWORK (network controller): supervises ground station communications

19. HQ (NASA headquarters): intermediary between Mission Control and NASA management

20. DOD (Department of Defense): in charge of military involvement in recovery efforts

Flight Teams

Because the missions can last up to two weeks, several teams of controllers work in shifts around the clock from launch to splashdown. Each team is assigned a color and a flight director. The flight directors are ultimately responsible for the safety of the crew and the success of the mission.

White Team	Eugene F. "Gene" Kranz
Black Team	Glynn S. Lunney
Gold Team	Gerald D. "Gerry" Griffin
Maroon Team	Milton L. "Milt" Windler
Green Team	Clifford E. "Cliff" Charlesworth
Orange Team	M. P. "Pete" Frank

Christopher C. "Chris" Kraft Jr. (1924–2019)

Father of Mission Control

Born in Phoebus, Virginia, Christopher Columbus Kraft was given a name that seemed to shape his destiny.

He studied aeronautical engineering at Virginia Tech, completing his bachelor's degree during World War II. He wanted to join the navy, but he was rejected because of a badly burned hand from a childhood accident. In 1945, he went to work at the National Advisory Committee for Aeronautics (NACA). By the time NASA was formed in 1958, 34-year-old Kraft was in charge of mission planning for manned spaceflight. His ideas developed into the rules, procedures, consoles, and everything else that made up Mission Control. His importance to Apollo cannot be understated. Kraft died on July 22, 2019, during the 50th anniversary of the Apollo 11 mission.

The Mission Evaluation Room (MER)

In addition to the back-room experts supporting the individual mission controllers at the MOCR, there's another team in a room housed in a building next door. The Mission Evaluation Room (MER) is full of systems engineers from each of the many contractors working on Apollo. They are the ones who know the hardware and, at a moment's notice, can scramble through piles of blueprints and diagrams to come up with answers and solutions. Unlike the MOCR, where each controller has consoles with computer screens, the MER is a low-tech operation with long gray metal tables, telephones, a bank of television monitors, and uncomfortable chairs. Using basic headsets, the "MER-men" can listen in on the mission while they wait for the phone calls that send them springing into action.

At the back of the room, in a chair on a raised platform sits a lightning-fast engineer named Don Arabian, the man who runs the MER. He's not connected to the audio network, so when he needs to communicate with the engineers, he shouts above the noise in the headsets. His booming voice and his commanding presence earn him the nickname Mad Don.

Communicating with the Astronauts: Go/No-Go

There are thousands of steps and procedures the astronauts have to follow during a mission. It will be up to each controller to let a flight director know that the functions they are monitoring are in good shape before they can go ahead with the next step. There is no way that the controllers can speak directly to the crew—the astronauts wouldn't recognize all the voices, and they wouldn't know what to do if two controllers were to disagree.

So Chris Kraft develops a system of communication that is one of the foundations of Mission Control.

Astronaut Crew

"Let's go around the room. . . . Go/No-Go for powered descent?"

"Go, Flight!"

"GO."

"GO."

"Go, Flight."

Controllers

"CAPCOM, we are Go for powered descent."

Flight Director

"Eagle, you are Go for powered descent."

CAPCOM

Communication Rules

A. The controllers can speak only to each other and their flight director. Before any significant step, the flight director will go around the room (known as "going around the horn") asking controllers whether their systems are "Go" or "No-Go."

B. The flight director will make a final decision on what to communicate to the astronauts and will let the capsule communicator (CAPCOM) know what to tell them.

C. The CAPCOM will be the only one who speaks directly to the crew. The CAPCOM is always another astronaut—one of their own, a colleague who's had the same training and experiences. Plus, it's comforting to hear a familiar voice when you're 240,000 miles from home.

Communicating with the Spacecraft

The spacecraft itself also carries on a running dialogue with Mission Control through three different systems:

1. **telemetry:** data from the spacecraft's systems and subsystems
2. **tracking:** measurements of the precise location and speed of the spacecraft
3. **command:** instructions sent to the spacecraft's computer

Antennas on the spacecraft and large deep-dish antennas on Earth will communicate this information back and forth using radio waves traveling through the vacuum of space. These can be converted into sounds, data, or even pictures.

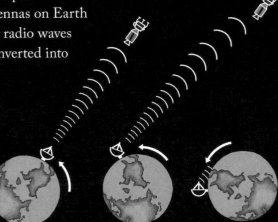

As Earth rotates, a single ground antenna would lose contact with the spacecraft.

Problem! Loss of Contact

Radio waves need a direct "line of sight" from the ground to the spacecraft in order to work. Earth is in constant rotation, so a single antenna on the ground would be able to "see" the Moon-bound spacecraft for only about eight hours a day.

Solution! A Network of Antennas

Placing large antennas in different locations around Earth will make sure that there will be at least one antenna "visible" to the spacecraft at any given time. Then all voice, telemetry, tracking, and command data can be sent through that antenna.

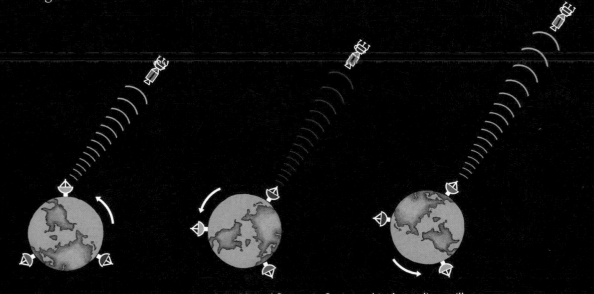

Three large antennas—on the West Coast of the United States, in Spain, and in Australia—will ensure constant contact.

Manned Space Flight Network (MSFN)

Three large "deep-space" antennas located in Canberra (Australia), Goldstone (California), and Madrid (Spain) will handle all communications with the spacecraft for most of the mission. As you can see from this diagram, signals from these deep-space antennas overlap only at around 18,000 miles from Earth, even though they each cover a wide territory.

During the times when the spacecraft is closer—when it is in Earth orbit and when it nears Earth during its return—Mission Control relies upon a network of smaller antennas placed strategically around the globe on land, ships, and planes.

Because of this network, known as the Manned Space Flight Network (MSFN), the spacecraft will be out of contact only when it slips behind the Moon during lunar orbit and when it is reentering Earth's atmosphere.

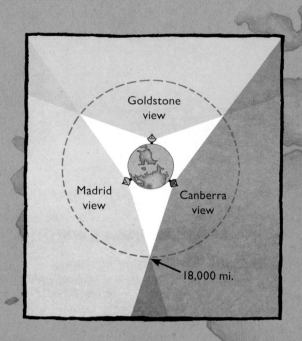

Goldstone view

Madrid view

Canberra view

18,000 mi.

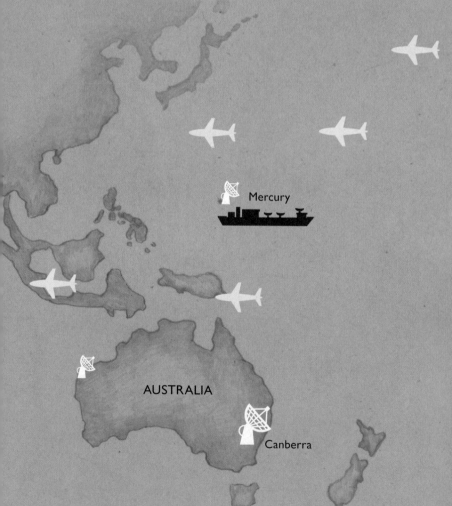

Goldstone, California

Huntsville

Hawaii

Redstone

Mercury

AUSTRALIA

Canberra

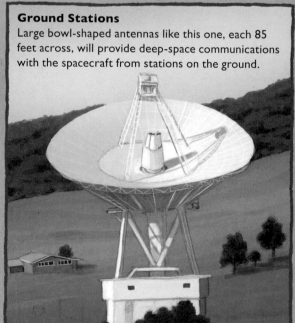

Ground Stations
Large bowl-shaped antennas like this one, each 85 feet across, will provide deep-space communications with the spacecraft from stations on the ground.

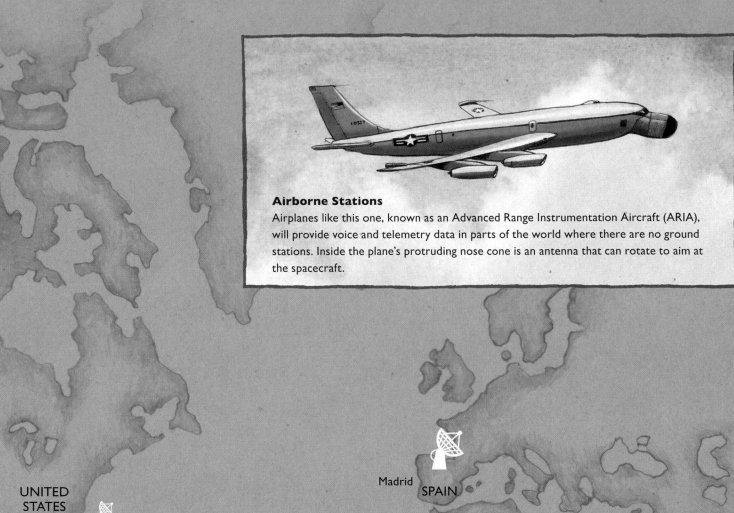

Airborne Stations

Airplanes like this one, known as an Advanced Range Instrumentation Aircraft (ARIA), will provide voice and telemetry data in parts of the world where there are no ground stations. Inside the plane's protruding nose cone is an antenna that can rotate to aim at the spacecraft.

Madrid SPAIN

UNITED
STATES

Vanguard

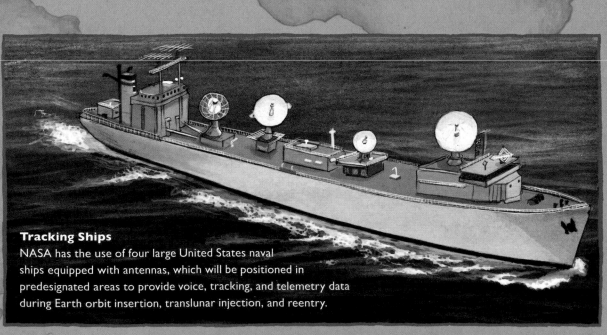

Tracking Ships

NASA has the use of four large United States naval ships equipped with antennas, which will be positioned in predesignated areas to provide voice, tracking, and telemetry data during Earth orbit insertion, translunar injection, and reentry.

The machines have been built, the launch complex has been constructed, and the script has been written. Every last detail of the mission, from launch through splashdown, has been thought through.

Now it is time to practice it—over and over again.

The mission controllers, the launch crew, the astronauts, and all the other people involved in this dangerous enterprise have individual roles to play, and they rehearse their parts with total dedication and true intensity—as if the real mission were unfolding, with astronaut lives on the line.

Simulators

What do you do when you can't practice a space mission in space? You come up with workarounds.

Under the leadership of visionary engineer Hewitt Phillips, NASA builds training simulators for the astronauts to practice rendezvous, docking, lunar landings, and other aspects of the mission. The crew will log thousands of hours in these boxy-looking contraptions, which house perfect replicas of the interiors of the Lunar Module and the Command Module.

To make things even more realistic, the spacecraft windows are replaced with movie screens that show star fields, Earth, or the surface of the Moon, depending on what part of the mission the astronauts are working on.

Cameras mounted on tracks below a model of the lunar surface follow the commands coming from the LM computer. The video is then projected onto the windows of the LM simulator so that the crew can use it to practice landing on the Moon.

Every Apollo mission will have a main crew and a backup crew that will practice the simulations. They are subjected to countless glitches, malfunctions, and computer errors that they will have to figure out on the fly. It is the job of the simulator operators to imagine every possible scenario or potential problem, and the job of the crews to quickly find solutions. The astronauts will "die" many times over during the simulations, but it will be this practice that may save their lives when they actually fly into space.

Astronauts Neil Armstrong (left) and Buzz Aldrin (right) practice lunar landings in the LM simulator.

Mission controllers also practice their skills during these simulated missions.

Robert "Bob" Pearson (b. 1932)

Lunar Module Simulator Lead Instructor

"I've landed on the Moon more times than anybody in the world."

His nickname was "Mr. LMS." Nobody spent more time in the LM simulator than Bob Pearson. It was Pearson who spent countless hours teaching Neil Armstrong, and all the other Apollo astronauts, how to land on the Moon. He taught others, too, including President Lyndon Johnson's wife, Lady Bird. When the chancellor of Germany tried landing on the Moon, Pearson and his team put a tiny model of a Volkswagen Beetle on the plaster-of-paris Moon for him. When he saw it through the window of the LM simulator, he was certainly surprised!

Training to Work in Zero-G

As soon as the spacecraft goes into Earth orbit, the astronauts will be experiencing zero gravity all the way to the Moon and back. To train for this, they fly in a special US Air Force plane, a C-135, where they can experience weightlessness in 25-second bursts. The aircraft makes steep climbs and then dives through the atmosphere. As the plane pulls out of its dive, the astronauts will be subjected to two times the amount of Earth's gravity. This constant flip-flopping from zero-g to 2 g's wreaks havoc on your stomach, and so the plane is nicknamed the Vomit Comet.

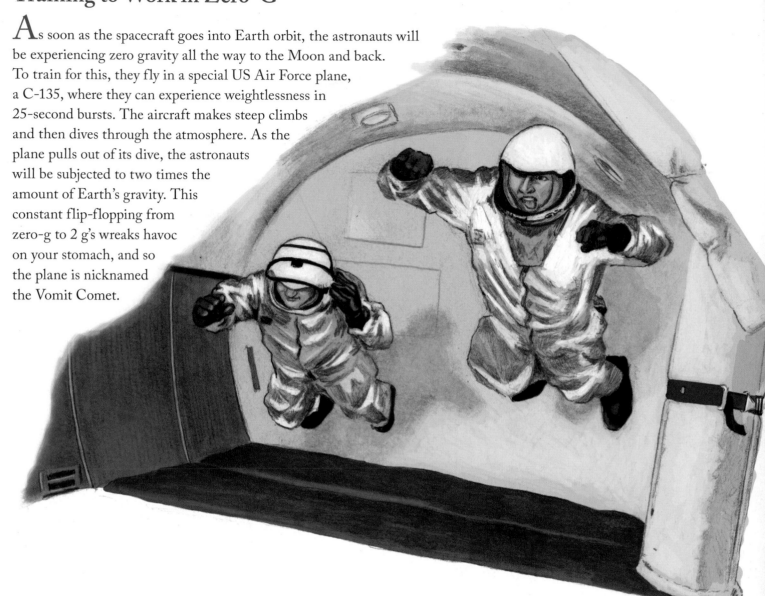

PARABOLIC FLIGHT

The pilot flies the C-135 plane in a series of symmetrical arcs, also known as parabolas. There is a zero-g experience beginning at the top of each arc, much like the feeling you would get driving quickly over a small hill or riding a roller coaster. Because you're inside and falling with the plane, you experience the sensation of weightlessness.

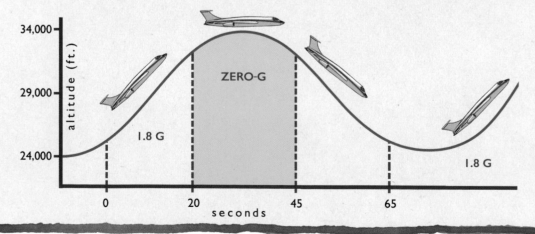

Problem! Not Enough Time

The zero-g experience in the Vomit Comet lasts for only 25 seconds at a time. The astronauts need to train in weightlessness for longer periods.

Solution! Neutral Buoyancy

Scuba divers can be weighted in such a way that they are neither sinking to the bottom nor floating back up to the surface. This is called neutral buoyancy, and it's similar to a zero-g environment. NASA builds large water tanks where the crews can spend long periods of time training for extravehicular activities. There is even a mock-up of the spacecraft at the bottom of each tank. The astronauts can also be weighted to simulate the one-sixth gravity of the Moon so they can practice the work they will do there.

An astronaut practices moving through an underwater replica of a docking tunnel as a safety diver looks on.

The Lunar Landing Training Vehicle (LLTV)

Landing on the lunar surface is considered one of the most difficult and dangerous aspects of an Apollo mission to the Moon. It is made even more dangerous by the fact that the LM is a true *space*craft—there is no way to physically practice flying it on Earth. The mission commanders have to make do with an ungainly contraption called the Lunar Landing Training Vehicle (LLTV). Built by Bell Aerosystems of Buffalo, New York, the astronauts call it the "flying bedstead" because it looks like a big iron bed frame. It has several thrusters and a single engine that allows the vehicle to hover above the ground like a helicopter. The astronauts practice flying, maneuvering, and landing the LLTV safely. These vehicles are extremely difficult to fly, and several of them crash, but luckily each astronaut has an ejection seat and a parachute.

A Dangerous Flight

On May 6, 1968, just two and a half months before the Moon mission, Neil Armstrong lost control of the LLTV thrusters while training. Two seconds before his LLTV crashed and exploded into a fireball, Armstrong ejected and parachuted to the ground. He bit his tongue during the ejection, but otherwise was mostly unharmed—and he was back in his office less than an hour later.

Geology Training

Although President John F. Kennedy set the goal of "landing a man on the Moon and returning him safely to the Earth," it's important for the advancement of science to bring back pieces of the Moon to study.

Geologists, who examine rocks and soil and everything that acts upon them in order to uncover how an area is formed, are especially eager to learn more about the Moon. With the right samples of rocks and lunar dust, who knows what they can find out?

To help the astronauts understand what to look for on the Moon, they are trained in the basics of geology in Hawaii and the deserts of the Southwest.

Survival Training

If all goes well, the astronauts coming back from the Moon will splash down in the ocean, where they will be picked up by a waiting rescue ship. But what if they don't land where they are supposed to? What if they land in a jungle or a desert, only to perish while waiting for rescue crews to find them?

NASA decides survival training is necessary for every astronaut. In the deserts of Nevada and the jungles of Panama, astronauts learn how to find water, hunt and eat snakes, and make clothes and shelter out of their parachutes.

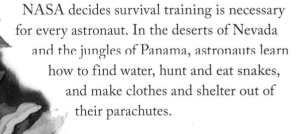

The astronauts and the people who will support them have trained for every possibility they could think of. They've come as close as they can to flying the actual mission. They are as ready as they can be. It is now time to put the plans, the training, the machines, and these people to the test.

On December 24, 1968, as the Apollo 8 spacecraft is completing its fourth orbit of the Moon, astronaut Bill Anders looks out the CM window to see Earth rising above the lunar surface. He takes a photo known as *Earthrise*, which becomes one of the most famous photographs of the 20th century. People all over the world are so affected by it that a new environmental movement begins, focusing on protecting our planet.

PART 7

We Choose to Go to the Moon

"That's one small step for [a] man, one giant leap for mankind."

—NEIL ARMSTRONG, ASTRONAUT

Von Braun's plan for the Apollo program is to have as many as ten unpiloted test flights of the Saturn V before taking the risk of launching a human crew. It would be a step-by-step process.

The first step would be to launch the Saturn V with just one working stage and two "dummy" upper stages. If that went well, a working second stage would be added on the next launch and a working third stage on the next.

Unfortunately, time is not on our side. We are still racing stride for stride with the Russians, and this conservative step-by-step method will mean that we miss President Kennedy's end-of-the-decade deadline.

The Apollo manager, Dr. George Mueller, has a bold idea called the all-up test, which would save time and hardware by launching the entire Saturn V all at once. It's risky because if any part doesn't work, the entire rocket could explode.

At 7:00 a.m. on November 9, 1967, the very first Saturn V takes off from Pad 39A. The sound it makes is so loud that the shock waves cause windows to bend and flex in the media building miles away. Stunned reporters try to hold them in place.

The flight is called Apollo 4, and it is a spectacular success. Everything works perfectly. It is quickly followed by two more un-crewed flight tests with the Saturn V, which also include the Apollo spacecraft. The first crewed flight using the Apollo spacecraft, called Apollo 7, uses a slightly smaller launch vehicle called the Saturn IB.

The next daring move comes just over two months later.

Called Apollo 8, it will send humans into orbit around the Moon. Originally, it is supposed to be a low-Earth orbit flight so the crew can test out both the CM and the LM, but Grumman is running behind schedule. Add to that the fact that the Russians recently sent some tortoises around the Moon—rumor is, they will be sending men next—and the decision is quickly made to turn Apollo 8 into a lunar orbital mission.

On December 21, 1968, for the first time in history, human beings break free of Earth's gravity and fly to the Moon. Astronauts Frank Borman, Jim Lovell, and Bill Anders return to Earth and become *Time* magazine's "Men of the Year" after orbiting the Moon ten times during their mission.

The next big step is a landing on the Moon. This mission is called Apollo 11.*

*In all, there will be 11 piloted Apollo missions (see p. 242).

The Rollout

May 20, 1969

At 12:30 p.m. on May 20, the 363-foot-tall rocket known as Apollo 11 slowly rolls out into the sunlight. Over the past three months, it has been assembled and exhaustively tested inside the cavernous VAB. In less than two months, it will send three men a quarter of a million miles through space to intercept the Moon. If all goes well, two of them, Buzz Aldrin and Neil Armstrong, will fly the LM, which they call Eagle, down to its surface. The third astronaut, Mike Collins, will continue to orbit the Moon in the CSM, called Columbia, knowing that if his colleagues cannot return, he will be going home alone.

Neil A. Armstrong (1930–2012)
Apollo 11 Commander (CDR)

Michael Collins (b. 1930)
Apollo 11 Command Module Pilot (CMP)

Edwin E. "Buzz" Aldrin Jr. (b. 1930)
Apollo 11 Lunar Module Pilot (LMP)

Inch by inch, the powerful Crawler-Transporter carries the mobile launcher and the Saturn V down the crawlerway, pulverizing stones under its heavy burden. The three-and-a-half-mile journey to Pad 39A takes more than five hours.

As it makes its way up the 5 percent–incline ramp at the launchpad, the Crawler continually adjusts to keep the Saturn V level. It is so accurate that the tip of the Launch Escape Tower (LET), almost 400 feet above, moves less than six inches off-center.

The Crawler, as wide as 13 school buses, has to be parked within one inch of dead center of the pad. Once it is in position, workers connect the base of the mobile launcher to each one of the launchpad pedestals.

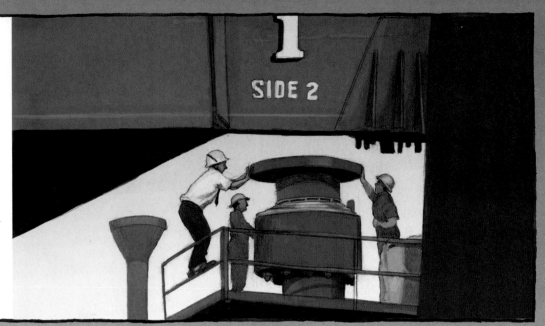

May 22, 1969

The Crawler brings the Mobile Service Structure (MSS) to the launchpad. Once connected to the Saturn V, its platforms give technicians access to the spacecraft and parts of the rocket for further preparations. The next several weeks will be dedicated to loading fuels, explosives, and batteries, and doing even more tests. The MSS will stay out at the pad until 11 hours before launch.

Launch Day

July 16, 1969

TIME UNTIL LAUNCH   005:17:00
                     HR MIN SEC

In the crew quarters of the Manned Spacecraft Operations Building (MSOB), flight crew director Deke Slayton knocks on Armstrong's, Aldrin's, and Collins's doors at 4:15 a.m. They shower, dress, and sit down to a traditional launch day breakfast of steak and eggs, made by the much-adored NASA chef Lew Hartzell. Hartzell, a former marine who worked as a tugboat cook, has been feeding hungry astronauts since the Mercury program.

An hour later, in the suit lab, they're helped into their spacesuits layer by layer, clicking and locking helmets and gloves into place. All the while, the mighty Saturn V is getting loaded with propellants. The astronauts will breathe the pure oxygen inside their suits for the next few hours before the launch. This will purge the nitrogen from their bloodstreams and prevent nitrogen bubbles from forming as the pressure decreases during the launch.

Judy Sullivan, lead engineer for Apollo 11's biomedical system, monitors the data returning from the biomedical sensors that have been attached to the astronauts. The former math and science teacher is the first and only female engineer working in the suit lab. It's her job to communicate with the technicians at the launchpad regarding the astronauts' physical readiness for flight.

TIME UNTIL LAUNCH   003:07:00
                     HR MIN SEC

At 6:25 a.m., Slayton escorts the three Apollo 11 astronauts—each carrying a portable oxygen supply—to the van that will take them the eight miles out to the launchpad.

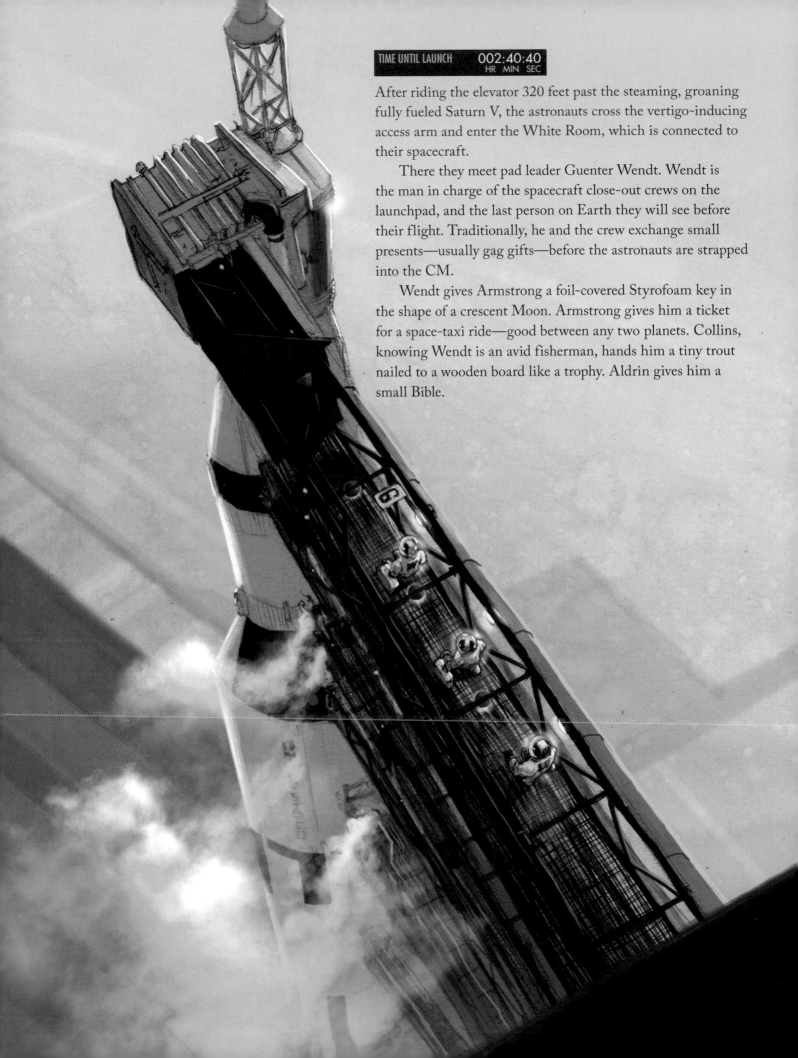

After riding the elevator 320 feet past the steaming, groaning fully fueled Saturn V, the astronauts cross the vertigo-inducing access arm and enter the White Room, which is connected to their spacecraft.

There they meet pad leader Guenter Wendt. Wendt is the man in charge of the spacecraft close-out crews on the launchpad, and the last person on Earth they will see before their flight. Traditionally, he and the crew exchange small presents—usually gag gifts—before the astronauts are strapped into the CM.

Wendt gives Armstrong a foil-covered Styrofoam key in the shape of a crescent Moon. Armstrong gives him a ticket for a space-taxi ride—good between any two planets. Collins, knowing Wendt is an avid fisherman, hands him a tiny trout nailed to a wooden board like a trophy. Aldrin gives him a small Bible.

TIME UNTIL LAUNCH 002:23:46
HR MIN SEC

The director of launch operations, Rocco Petrone, stares intently at the Saturn V from Firing Room 1. The controllers monitor all aspects of the space vehicle from their consoles. It's discovered that there is a leak in the valve that supplies liquid hydrogen to the S-IVB stage, and mechanics are dispatched to the 200-foot level of the rocket to repair it. If they cannot fix it, the launch will be delayed or scrubbed for the day.

TIME UNTIL LAUNCH 001:30:55
HR MIN SEC

Mechanics Wayne Gray and Red Davis manage to isolate and bypass the leaky valve, allowing controllers Jack Kramer and Stephen Coester to continue loading the liquid hydrogen to maintain a full tank level. The launch is still a Go.

TIME UNTIL LAUNCH 000:06:00
HR MIN SEC

Inside the Mission Operations Control Room (MOCR) in Houston, Green Team flight director Cliff Charlesworth goes through the Go/No-Go procedure with his controllers. All are Go.

Along the roads, on the beaches, and by the motels around Kennedy Space Center (KSC), over one million people sit in the sweltering heat, anticipating the historic liftoff. At the space center itself, in the VIP stands, and at the Press Site there are celebrities, politicians, and over 2,000 journalists from 56 nations on the bleachers three and a half miles from the launchpad, watching and waiting.

One special guest, Charles Lindbergh, was not quite two years old when the Wright brothers lifted 12 feet off the ground in the first powered airplane. Less than 24 years later, Lindbergh made the first solo flight across the Atlantic. Now, at the age of 67, he is about to watch human beings fly to the Moon. The pace of technological change is staggering.

At a designated launch abort area in the Pacific Ocean, rescue teams aboard the USS Hornet practice and prepare for their role in recovering the astronauts and the spacecraft. They are all acutely aware that theirs is the last important step of the mission. Once the spacecraft is on its way to the Moon, the Hornet will sail toward the prime recovery area, where the astronauts will splash down after returning to Earth.

NASA communications specialist Hugh Brown scans the horizon from the top of the VAB. Two weeks earlier, he and his team discovered that Russian trawlers and submarines were sitting in the waters off KSC, using radio signals to jam communications between the astronauts and the LCC. Today, Brown's team is ready to intercept those signals.

At KSC, television newscasters like Walter Cronkite prepare to give in-depth explanations of the events as they unfold. Their broadcasts will reach millions of people watching on TV all around the world.

201

Liftoff

Inside the LCC, Jack King, also known as the Voice of Apollo, announces the details of the launch through loudspeakers to the public and the news media outside.

King: *"Astronauts report it feels good. T minus 25 seconds. . . . T minus 15 seconds. Guidance is internal. . . . Twelve, eleven, ten, nine. . . . Ignition sequence starts. . . ."*

TIME UNTIL LAUNCH **000:00:09** HR MIN SEC Nine seconds before liftoff, the engines ignite, spewing fire and smoke until the 6.5-million-pound rocket builds enough thrust to overcome gravity's hold. For a brief moment, it weighs nothing—you could balance it on your finger.

King: *"Six, five, four, three, two, one, zero. All engines running."*

TIME UNTIL LAUNCH **000:00:00** HR MIN SEC At T-minus zero seconds, all five F-1 engines are running at 95 percent capacity. The roar of the engines is the loudest manmade sound ever known besides the explosion of a nuclear bomb. The four hold-down arms release the rocket, and the three tail service masts disconnect and swing up into their protective hoods. The Saturn V rises slowly, engines gimbaling to keep the rocket balanced.

King: *"Liftoff! We have a liftoff! Thirty-two minutes past the hour. Liftoff on Apollo 11!"*

The five service masts still attached to the rocket simultaneously disconnect and swing out of the way. The Saturn V sheds huge sheets of ice that have accumulated on the liquid oxygen and liquid hydrogen tanks as it rides the controlled yet violent flame into the sky. Thousands of gallons of water that pour over the mobile launch platform to cool it instantly turn to steam.

The mission clock now changes from Time Until Launch to Ground Elapsed Time, representing the amount of time passed on Earth since liftoff of Apollo 11.

GROUND ELAPSED TIME   000:00:04
HR   MIN   SEC

Crowds cheer as they watch the rocket silently lift into the sky on a tail of fire and smoke. The rocket leans precariously away from the tower so as not to bump into it. It moves slowly, a mere 14 feet per second, almost imperceptible from the viewing areas three and a half miles away.

Now the sound comes! A thousand thunderclaps in a row, rattling your bones and hammering at your chest, taking your breath away as you watch three human beings head off to the Moon.

GROUND ELAPSED TIME   000:00:10
HR   MIN   SEC

King: *"Tower cleared!"*

The Saturn V passes the LUT, and the controllers in the LCC breathe a sigh of relief. Their job is complete. The five F-1 engines are burning nearly 30,000 pounds of propellant per second, making the vehicle lighter and faster as it rises into the air. The launch is a success!

Eight hundred miles away, in Houston, flight director
Cliff Charlesworth and his Green Team take over
monitoring the flight of Apollo 11.

It will be the responsibility of Mission Control to
oversee every detail of the journey from now until the
astronauts are safely aboard the USS Hornet recovery
ship in eight days.

They are supported by hundreds of engineers in the
back rooms of the MOCR, as well as those throughout
the world in the Manned Space Flight Network.
Thousands more at companies all over the United
States are ready to help—while hoping and
praying that the parts they built, the stitches
they sewed, and the programs they wrote
and wove will all work perfectly.

Capsule communicator Bruce McCandless, in Mission Control, is now the one voice the astronauts will hear.

McCandless: *"Apollo 11, this is Houston. You are Go for staging."*

The propellants in the first stage are nearly gone, and all five F-1 engines shut off. The astronauts are thrown forward in their seats as the acceleration of the rocket abruptly stops. An explosive wire separates the dead weight of the first stage from the second stage. It drops away, and the five J-2 engines on the second stage ignite. Once again the spacecraft builds speed.

Thirty seconds later, another explosive wire does its job, separating the interstage ring, and two seconds after that, the LET and the cover that protected the CM during launch are jettisoned. The discarded parts will fall into the Atlantic Ocean about 357 miles from the launch site.

McCandless: *"11, Houston. Thrust is Go, all engines. You're looking good."*

GROUND ELAPSED TIME	000:09:15
	HR MIN SEC
DISTANCE FROM EARTH	115 MILES
VELOCITY	14,400 MPH

The second stage is emptied of propellants, and explosive charges separate it from the third stage. The spent S-II plummets toward the Atlantic, about 2,371 miles from the launch site. The single J-2 engine on the S-IVB ignites to accelerate the spacecraft to the 17,400 miles per hour it needs to achieve orbit.

Two minutes and 20 seconds later, the engine shuts down. The crew is weightless—silently orbiting Earth.

For the next 180 minutes, as the spacecraft completes one and a half revolutions, the astronauts make sure everything is in good working order. Collins uses star sightings to realign the inertial platform. On the ground, engineers track the spacecraft's orbit and calculate the best trajectory for its flight to the Moon.

GROUND ELAPSED TIME	002:44:15
	HR MIN SEC
DISTANCE FROM EARTH	115 MILES
VELOCITY	17,400 MPH

McCandless: *"Apollo 11, this is Houston. You are Go for TLI."*

At the go-ahead from Mission Control, the translunar injection starts, a nearly six-minute engine burn. The S-IVB engine accelerates the spacecraft to 24,500 miles per hour, on course to intercept the Moon.

This is it. Armstrong, Aldrin, and Collins are on their way.

Transposition and Docking

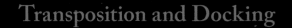

McCandless: *"Apollo 11, this is Houston. You're Go for separation."*

GROUND ELAPSED TIME	003:17:00
	HR MIN SEC
DISTANCE FROM EARTH	3,973 MILES
VELOCITY	17,941 MPH

Mike Collins, the Command Module pilot (CMP), takes control of the Command and Service Module (CSM) as it separates from the third stage. Four petal-like panels open and detach from the S-IVB to reveal the Lunar Module tucked inside.

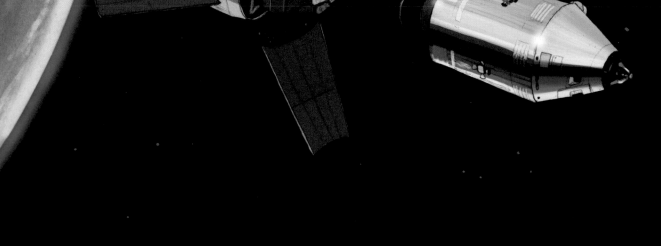

Transposition and Docking Procedure

1. Separate.   2. Pitch CSM 180 degrees.   3. Dock with LM.   4. Extract LM.

Collins pitches the CSM around to face the exposed LM. Using the CSM's thrusters, he lines up the probe jutting out of the CM with the drogue on top of the LM and slowly and carefully flies forward to dock the two spacecraft. This is one of the first critical moments of the mission.

Aldrin: *"How far out are you, Mike?"*

Collins: *"Stand by; we're closing."*

Collins achieves a soft dock with the LM. The probe assembly pulls the LM up tight against the CM, and 12 latches slam into place, creating an airtight seal between the two spacecraft. Hard dock is now complete. Collins spent hundreds of hours in the CM simulator to practice docking, which took only about eight minutes in space.

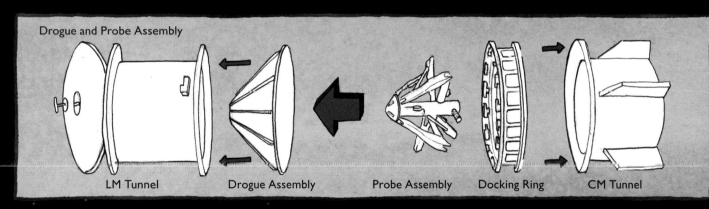

Drogue and Probe Assembly

| LM Tunnel | Drogue Assembly | Probe Assembly | Docking Ring | CM Tunnel |

GROUND ELAPSED TIME	004:16:38 HR MIN SEC
DISTANCE FROM EARTH	15,000 MILES
VELOCITY	10,900 MPH

Armstrong: *"Houston, we're ready for LM ejection."*

McCandless: *"Roger. You're Go for LM ejection."*

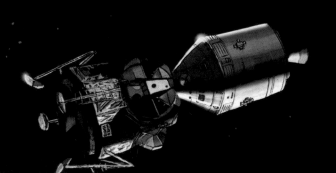

An hour later, the astronauts pull the LM from the top of the third stage as they continue on their journey toward the Moon. The S-IVB will eventually fall into orbit around the Sun.

Journey to the Moon

GROUND ELAPSED TIME	005:28:00
	HR MIN SEC
DISTANCE FROM EARTH	26,400 MILES
VELOCITY	8,640 MPH

Midcourse Correction

Similar to the way the early explorers used sextants on a ship, Collins takes star sightings with a navigation system to determine the spacecraft's position. Using Program 52 on the Apollo Guidance Computer (AGC), he discovers that the measurements are slightly off, and recalibrates the inertial platform by punching new values into the DSKY.

Collins: *"Old star number 30 looks like it's right dab smack in the middle of the sextant."*

McCandless: *"Houston. Roger. Out."*

NAVIGATION

The AGC is programmed with the exact locations of 37 different stars prior to the flight. Using the sextant in the CM, astronauts can measure the angle between a star and the horizon of Earth or the Moon, giving them an accurate measurement of where they are in space. This is done several times during the mission, because the friction in the inertial platform's bearings causes it to drift slightly.

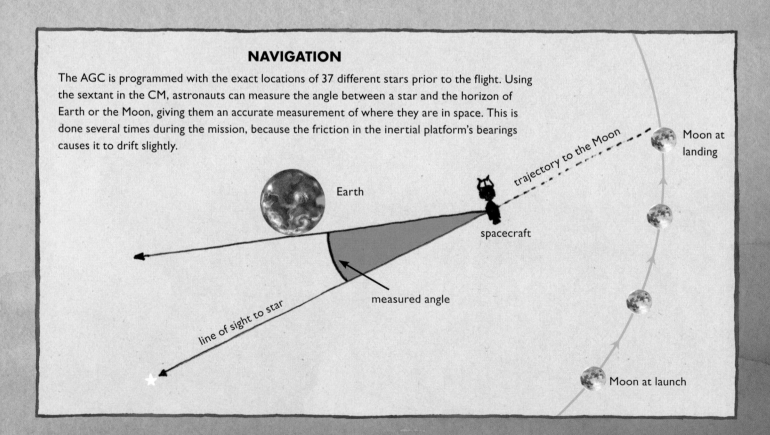

Earth

trajectory to the Moon

Moon at landing

spacecraft

measured angle

line of sight to star

Moon at launch

GROUND ELAPSED TIME	011:20:00
	HR MIN SEC
DISTANCE FROM EARTH	64,000 MILES
VELOCITY	5,400 MPH

After several more hours of "housekeeping"—checking systems, working with Mission Control to resolve equipment issues, and eating dinner—the crew settles in for some well-deserved rest. Collins falls asleep first, and an hour later all three are asleep, according to the data from their biomedical sensors.

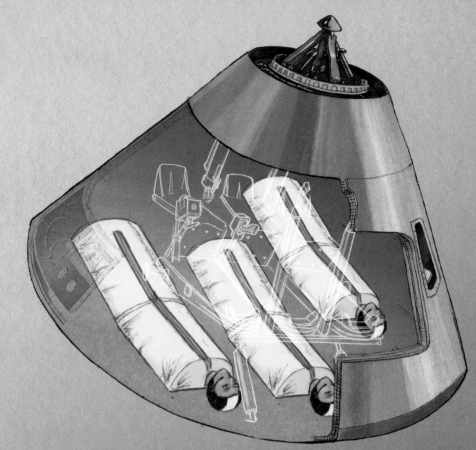

July 17, 1969

GROUND ELAPSED TIME	027:17:09
	HR MIN SEC
DISTANCE FROM EARTH	122,300 MILES
VELOCITY	3,500 MPH

Aldrin watches Earth shrink as it goes by the window of the CM. Over the next two days, the crew will continue to coast toward the Moon, and Earth will be so small they can cover it with their thumb.

213

Lunar Orbit Insertion

July 19, 1969

GROUND ELAPSED TIME	075:30:46	HR MIN SEC
DISTANCE FROM MOON	966	MILES
VELOCITY	4,439	MPH

> **McCandless:** *"11, this is Houston. You are Go for LOI. Over."*

As Apollo 11 comes in close to the Moon, the astronauts know that they are on the verge of one of the more precarious steps of the mission: Lunar Orbit Insertion (LOI).

The Moon's gravity will soon pull the spacecraft around its far side, where communication with Mission Control will no longer be possible. There, the crew will have to perform an engine burn, which should slow them down enough to be drawn into orbit around the Moon.

The procedure has to be perfect. Too long a burn will cause them to crash into the Moon. And if the engine doesn't fire, they'll whip around the Moon and start falling back to Earth.

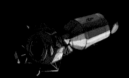

Mission Control will not know if the burn is successful until the spacecraft comes around the other side of the Moon and it can reestablish communications.

It is an agonizing wait.

GROUND ELAPSED TIME	075:59:11	HR MIN SEC

NASA has calculated that the first LOI burn will put the spacecraft into an elliptical orbit of 169.2 nautical miles by 61 nautical miles above the Moon. After the burn, Aldrin checks the data and sees that they are within a few hundred yards of their targeted orbit.

> **Aldrin:** *"Look at that! Look at that! 169.6 by 60.9."*

> **Collins:** *"Beautiful, beautiful, beautiful, beautiful!"*

GROUND ELAPSED TIME	076:15:00	HR MIN SEC
LUNAR ORBITAL VELOCITY	3,736	MPH

Houston reestablishes communications with the crew.

> **McCandless:** *"Apollo 11, Apollo 11, this is Houston. Do you read? Over."*

> **Aldrin:** *"Yes, we sure do, Houston. The LOI-1 burn just nominal as all get-out, and everything's looking good."*

> **Collins:** *"It was like—it was like perfect!"*

> **McCandless:** *"Roger. We copy your burn status report. And the spacecraft is looking good to us on telemetry."*

> **Armstrong:** *"Roger. Everything looks good up here."*

It takes two burns to get into a circular orbit around the Moon. The first burn, called LOI-1, will put the spacecraft into an elliptical orbit. A second burn, called LOI-2, two orbits later, will make the orbit circular about 65 miles above the lunar surface.

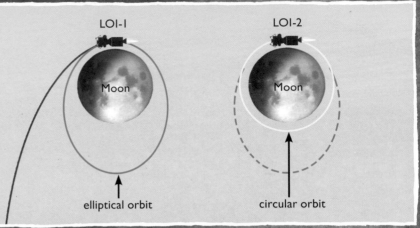

LOI-1

Moon

elliptical orbit

LOI-2

Moon

circular orbit

GROUND ELAPSED TIME 081:24:00
HR MIN SEC

Over the last three days, each team of controllers has worked several shifts in Mission Control. Gene Kranz and the White Team are now at the controls. Astronaut Charlie Duke is the CAPCOM.

Duke: *"Hello, Apollo 11. Houston. We're wondering if you've started into the LM yet. Over."*

Armstrong: *"We have the CSM hatch out, the drogue and probe removed and stowed, and we're just about ready to open the LM hatch now."*

Aldrin and Armstrong float through the tunnel from the Command Module into the Lunar Module. They spend the next few hours making sure everything inside the LM is ready for their trip to the Moon's surface.

Although Aldrin's title is Lunar Module pilot, Armstrong (the commander) will be responsible for flying the Eagle. Aldrin will call out critical data—altitude, fuel levels, and rate of descent.

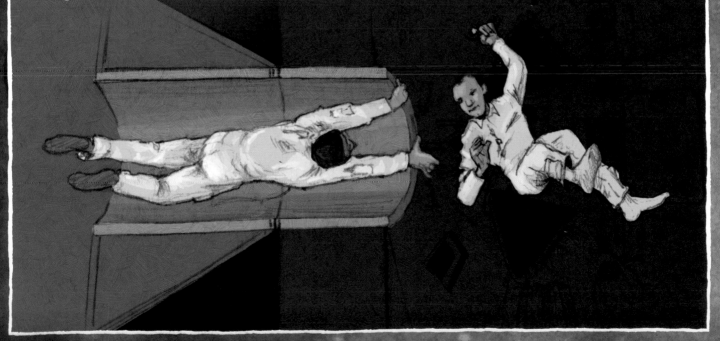

Descent to the Moon

July 20, 1969

GROUND ELAPSED TIME 100:12:00
HR MIN SEC

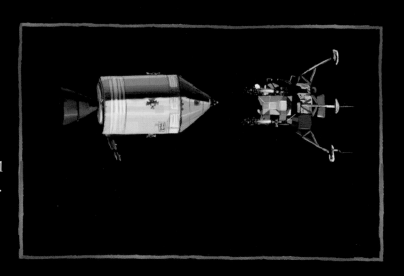

Eagle (LM) undocks from Columbia (CM), and Armstrong and Aldrin do a final check of all systems before committing to the lunar landing.

The landing, which has never been done before, will be the most complex and dangerous part of the mission.

Collins, now alone in Columbia, will continue to orbit the Moon as his crewmates descend to the surface.

Two hours and twenty-one minutes later, Gene Kranz goes around the room at Mission Control, polling his controllers for powered descent. Everyone responds with "Go!"

Kranz: *"CAPCOM, we're Go for powered descent."*

Duke: *"Eagle, Houston. If you read, you're a Go for powered descent."*

Mission Control has just given Armstrong and Aldrin the go-ahead to burn Eagle's untested descent engine to begin the controlled "fall" to the lunar surface. Everyone knows that in the next 12 minutes, they'll either land, abort, or crash.

GROUND ELAPSED TIME 102:33:11
HR MIN SEC

Armstrong: *"Ignition."*

GOUND ELAPSED TIME 102:38:26
HR MIN SEC

1202 ALARM

Less than six minutes into the powered descent, a program alarm starts beeping in the astronauts' headsets. Aldrin checks the DSKY, and it reads *1202*. Neither Aldrin nor Armstrong knows what is wrong.

Armstrong: *"Give us a reading on the 1202 Program Alarm."*

Back in Mission Control, 26-year-old controller Steve Bales is in charge of monitoring the LM guidance computer. It is now up to Bales—a former summer intern—to make the call to abort or to proceed. The lives of two astronauts and the success of the mission are suddenly in his hands.

In Massachusetts, at MIT, Don Eyles, who wrote the programs that are guiding the LM during the lunar landing, holds his breath as he monitors the mission. He knows that a 1202 alarm means that the computer is overloaded, but he does not know why. It has never happened in any of the simulations he used to make sure his programs work. Luckily, Eyles and others designed the system so that it will prioritize what is most important—making sure the LM is on the proper flight path—and ignore everything else.

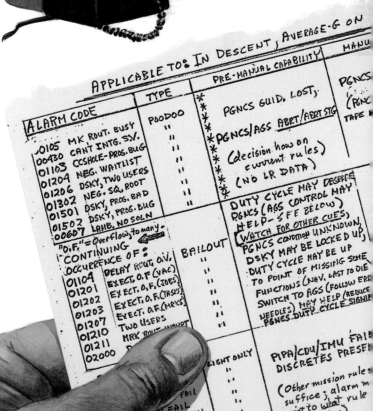

Two weeks earlier, during a lunar landing simulation with a different team of astronauts, a similar alarm came up: a 1201. Bales ordered the crew to abort. Afterward, he and his team wrote down a list of all the possible alarms and their meanings.

GROUND ELAPSED TIME   102:38:42
HR MIN SEC

One of Bales's back-room controllers, 24-year-old Jack Garman, grabs the list—there's a copy on his desk. Garman scans it.

Garman (to Bales): *"It's the executive overflow. If it does not occur again, we're fine."*

| GROUND ELAPSED TIME | 102:38:53 |
| | HR MIN SEC |

Hearing Garman's words, Bales makes the call.

Bales: *"We are a Go on that alarm, Flight."*

The decision is passed on to Armstrong and Aldrin, and they continue their descent to the Moon. The whole process takes less than 30 seconds—which may have seemed like forever for the crew, but is actually lightning-fast, due to years of practice and testing and commitment.*

GROUND ELAPSED TIME	102:41:10
	HR MIN SEC
ALTITUDE	7,000 FT

For most of the descent, Eagle's windows face upward so that the radar system can point down at the lunar surface. At about 7,000 feet above the lunar surface, the computer pitches Eagle forward. Armstrong can now see the landing area ahead in the distance.

| GROUND ELAPSED TIME | 102:42:06 |
| | HR MIN SEC |

Gene Kranz polls Mission Control for landing status. All controllers call out, "Go!"

Duke: *"Eagle, Houston. You're Go for landing. Over."*

*After the mission, Jack Garman and Steve Bales receive awards for their roles in the landing.

GROUND ELAPSED TIME	102:43:10
	HR MIN SEC
ALTITUDE	600 FT

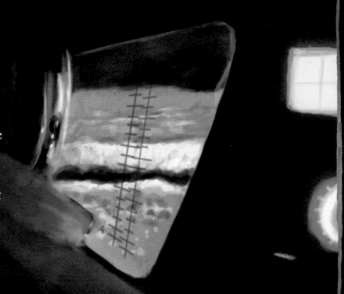

Armstrong: *"Pretty rocky area."*

Looking out the window, Armstrong realizes that the computer is going to land them in a boulder field near the edge of a crater the size of a football stadium. Aldrin is the only other person who can see what Armstrong sees. Armstrong has to make a quick decision: try to stop short and land in an area he can't see below him, or use more fuel and try to fly over it.

Armstrong: *"I'm going to . . ."*

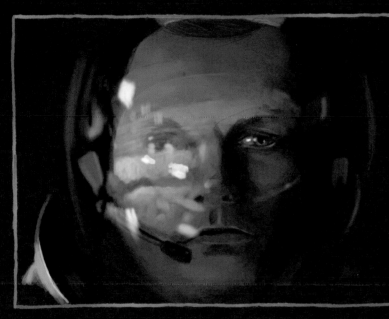

GROUND ELAPSED TIME	102:43:17
	HR MIN SEC
ALTITUDE	500 FT
FUEL REMAINING	167 SEC

Armstrong uses his joystick to control the LM's altitude and fly over the boulder field and crater, pitching Eagle to nearly vertical to maintain forward velocity.

Aldrin continues to call out altitude, rate of descent, and forward motion. Armstrong scans the lunar surface for a smooth place to land.

Back in Mission Control, Gene Kranz and the rest of the team hold their breath.

Altitude of LM not to scale

GROUND ELAPSED TIME	102:44:02
	HR MIN SEC
ALTITUDE	220 FT
FUEL REMAINING	120 SEC

Armstrong: *"Okay. Here's a . . . Looks like a good area here."*

Aldrin: *"I got the shadow out there."*

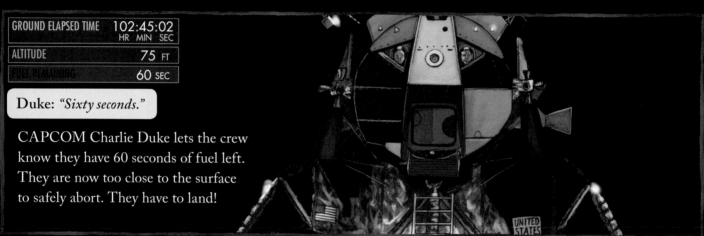

GROUND ELAPSED TIME	102:45:02
	HR MIN SEC
ALTITUDE	75 FT
FUEL REMAINING	60 SEC

Duke: *"Sixty seconds."*

CAPCOM Charlie Duke lets the crew know they have 60 seconds of fuel left. They are now too close to the surface to safely abort. They have to land!

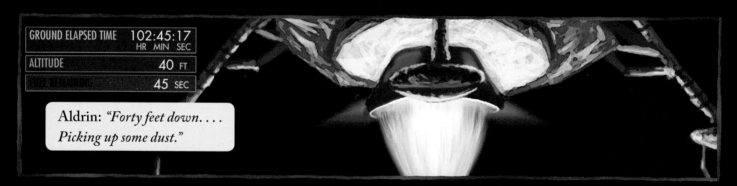

GROUND ELAPSED TIME	102:45:17
	HR MIN SEC
ALTITUDE	40 FT
FUEL REMAINING	45 SEC

Aldrin: *"Forty feet down. . . . Picking up some dust."*

GROUND ELAPSED TIME	102:45:40
	HR MIN SEC
ALTITUDE	5 FT
FUEL REMAINING	22 SEC

One of the footpad probes
touches the surface and triggers
a light on the instrument panel.

Aldrin: *"Contact light."*

| GROUND ELAPSED TIME | 102:45:43 |
| | HR MIN SEC |

Armstrong: *"Shutdown."*

Dust particles shoot out from Eagle and disappear over the
horizon. Everything is profoundly still and thoroughly silent.

Armstrong: *"Houston, Tranquility Base here.
The Eagle has landed."*

Duke: *"Roger, Twan—Tranquility. We copy you on
the ground. You got a bunch of guys about to turn blue.
We're breathing again. Thanks a lot."*

Orbiting overhead in Columbia, Mike Collins smiles to himself.

Man Walks on the Moon

July 20, 1969

GROUND ELAPSED TIME	109:24:12
	HR MIN SEC

After putting on their life support backpacks, special visors, and Moon boots and depressurizing the LM, Armstrong and Aldrin open the hatch, and Armstrong crawls out onto the porch. He pulls a handle, releasing the Modularized Equipment Stowage Assembly, called the MESA, which swings down, exposing their lunar tools and a television camera.

From inside the LM, Aldrin hits the switch to turn on the camera. Now the entire world can watch this historic moment.

> **Armstrong:** *"Okay. I'm going to step off the LM now."*

This is it.

This is the first time that a human being from planet Earth will set foot on another world. It's been just over eight years since President John F. Kennedy made the decision that the country should go to the Moon. Eight years of hard work. Eight years of designing and building and testing. Four hundred thousand engineers, seamstresses, carpenters, doctors, scientists, mathematicians, and technicians worked around the clock, each doing their part to make this moment happen.

> **Armstrong:** *"That's one small step for [a] man, one giant leap for mankind."*

223

Apollo Lunar Television Camera

Television broadcast cameras are enormous 400-pound contraptions in 1964, when NASA contracts Westinghouse Electric Corporation, in Baltimore, Maryland, to build a special camera for the astronauts to use on the lunar surface. It has to be small, lightweight, and able to withstand the extreme environment of space.

Westinghouse engineer Stanley "Stan" Lebar is put in charge of the project. It takes Lebar and his team of engineers four years, and the final product, called the Apollo Lunar Television Camera, weighs a mere 7.25 pounds.

At first, both the astronauts and most of NASA management feel that the added burden of bringing a TV camera to the Moon is too troublesome, but Chris Kraft and Max Faget argue that the American people, who are paying for this historic mission with their hard-earned tax dollars, have a right to witness it. Neil Armstrong agrees, and with that, Stan Lebar's lunar television camera goes to the Moon.

Stan Lebar holds the Apollo Lunar Television Camera.

Getting TV from the Moon

It would now be up to 26-year-old NASA engineer Richard Nafzger to figure out how to get the TV signal from the Moon back down to Earth and out to everyone's television sets. His biggest challenge: the TV signal from the Moon is only 10 frames per second, and in order to broadcast it on TV it will have to be converted to just under 30 frames per second. Nafzger arranges to have a special machine built to convert the images, but doesn't know if the system will work, because there's no way to test it with a signal from the Moon. With the whole world watching, it will be either a terrible failure or a spectacular success.

On July 20, 1969, people around the world are glued to their television sets, waiting to see Neil Armstrong climb down the ladder. Nafzger sits in Mission Control, anxiously watching the display screen at the front of the room.

A mere three seconds after Aldrin flips the switch to turn on the camera, everyone on Earth is able to watch live TV from the Moon.

THE THREE-SECOND JOURNEY OF THE APOLLO TV SIGNAL

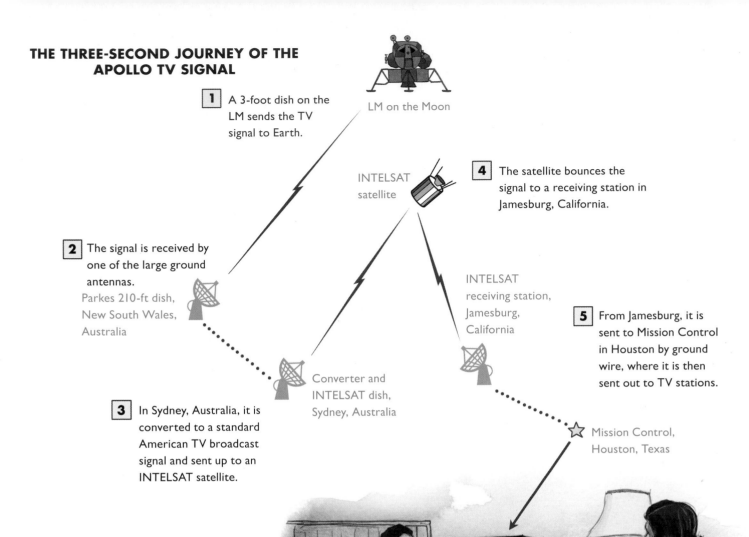

1 A 3-foot dish on the LM sends the TV signal to Earth.

LM on the Moon

INTELSAT satellite

4 The satellite bounces the signal to a receiving station in Jamesburg, California.

2 The signal is received by one of the large ground antennas.
Parkes 210-ft dish, New South Wales, Australia

INTELSAT receiving station, Jamesburg, California

5 From Jamesburg, it is sent to Mission Control in Houston by ground wire, where it is then sent out to TV stations.

Converter and INTELSAT dish, Sydney, Australia

3 In Sydney, Australia, it is converted to a standard American TV broadcast signal and sent up to an INTELSAT satellite.

Mission Control, Houston, Texas

"Live from the Moon"

Two hundred forty thousand miles away, on planet Earth, an estimated 530 million people watch the event unfold—live on television.

Nearly every American watches Neil Armstrong take his first step on the Moon.

A Japanese family watches from their home in Tokyo.

A giant TV screen in Trafalgar Square, London, projects the moonwalk.

Pope Paul VI watches from the Vatican in Rome.

Moonwalk

Back on the Moon, Armstrong and Aldrin have work to do.

They aren't going to travel all that way and not bring back something for scientific study. Americans want to learn more about the Moon: Where did it come from? How old is it? Is there life on the Moon? (Given the Moon's incredibly harsh conditions, scientists think that's extremely unlikely. But they will check anyway.)

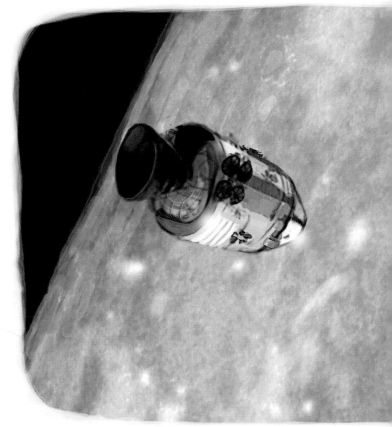

GROUND ELAPSED TIME	109:34:09
	HR MIN SEC

One of the first things on Armstrong's checklist is to get a sample of rocks and soil and put it in a special pocket strapped to his thigh. This is called the contingency sample. In case he has to end the moonwalk quickly, at least he will have gotten a small piece of the lunar surface. He takes several photos and relays to Mission Control what he is seeing.

GROUND ELAPSED TIME	109:43:10
	HR MIN SEC

Aldrin now comes down the ladder to join Armstrong.

Aldrin: *"Beautiful view!"*

Armstrong: *"Isn't that something! Magnificent sight out here."*

Aldrin: *"Magnificent desolation."*

GROUND ELAPSED TIME	110:03:20
	HR MIN SEC

One of the first experiments Aldrin sets up is a solar wind collector—a thin sheet of aluminum foil that collects electrically charged particles emitted by the Sun. At the conclusion of the moonwalk, Aldrin will pack it up to bring home so that scientists can learn more about the composition of solar wind—an impossible task on Earth because the solar wind is deflected by Earth's magnetic field.

GROUND ELAPSED TIME 110:07:38
HR MIN SEC

Together, Armstrong and Aldrin plant an American flag and, soon after, take a phone call from President Richard M. Nixon.

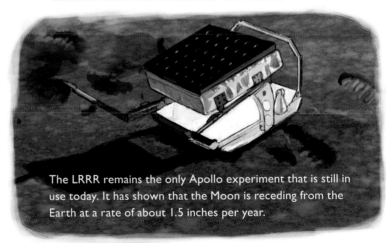

GROUND ELAPSED TIME 110:08:53
HR MIN SEC

Alone in the CM, which is still orbiting the Moon, Mike Collins calls Mission Control to get an update on the EVA.

Collins: *". . . How's it going?"*

McCandless: *"Roger. The EVA is progressing beautifully. I believe they are setting up the flag now."*

Collins: *"Great!"*

McCandless: *"I guess you're about the only person around that doesn't have TV coverage of the scene."*

Collins: *"That's all right. I don't mind a bit."*

Aldrin and Armstrong set up other experiments on the Moon, too. One uses a seismometer, an instrument that will detect "moonquakes" and will help scientists learn about the internal structure of the Moon. It is so sensitive that it picks up the astronauts' footsteps as they walk away.

Another experiment uses a Laser Ranging Retroreflector (LRRR), a sophisticated mirror meant to reflect back a powerful laser beam sent from Earth. Ninety minutes after Aldrin sets it up, astronomers at the Lick Observatory in Mount Hamilton, California, point a laser at the precise location where NASA tells them the retroreflector is. The beam bounces back, and, for the first time in history, we have a way to precisely measure the distance between Earth and the Moon.

The LRRR remains the only Apollo experiment that is still in use today. It has shown that the Moon is receding from the Earth at a rate of about 1.5 inches per year.

GROUND ELAPSED TIME 111:25:04
HR MIN SEC

After less than two hours on the Moon, the astronauts have finished all the tasks on their checklists. Aldrin heads back up the ladder; Armstrong follows 10 minutes later. They have collected almost 50 pounds of rocks and dust to bring back to Earth.

July 21, 1969

`GROUND ELAPSED TIME    114:10:37`
`                       HR  MIN  SEC`

It is now time for Armstrong and Aldrin to rest, if they can. Before they do, they need to get rid of all unnecessary gear to lose weight for the trip back up into lunar orbit. Bags of trash, lunar boots, life support backpacks, cameras, lunar tools, and anything else they don't need gets thrown out the hatch to be left behind forever.

They will leave behind other things, too. A plaque on one of the legs of the Descent Stage will remain there. A small package containing four items: a patch commemorating astronauts Grissom, White, and Chaffee, who died in the Apollo 1 fire; and two medals honoring Russian cosmonauts Vladimir Komarov (who was killed when the parachutes of his spacecraft failed) and Yuri Gagarin (the first human in space, who later lost his life in an aircraft accident). Finally, a small gold olive branch, identical to the ones the crew brought to give to their wives upon their return from the Moon.

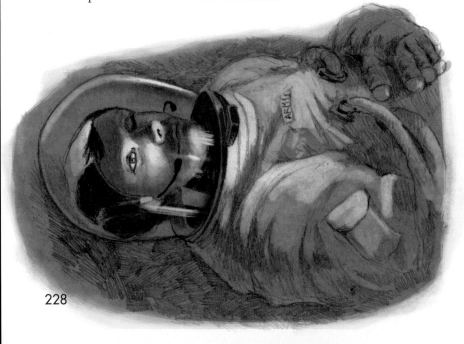

Inside the LM, it is cold and noisy and bright, and the astronauts are too excited about the day's events to sleep soundly. Armstrong lies on top of the ascent engine cover, using a makeshift hammock for his legs, while Aldrin curls up on the floor. At first, they both keep their helmets on to avoid breathing in the moondust they dragged into the LM, but they decide it is much too uncomfortable to keep them on.

Twenty-one hours and thirty-seven minutes after the astronauts landed on the Moon, they ignite the never-tested ascent engine. Simultaneously, pyrotechnics fire to sever the connections between the Ascent and Descent Stages, and Aldrin and Armstrong and their precious cargo are lifted from the lunar surface.

Eagle and Columbia Reunite

The three-and-a-half-hour Lunar Orbit Rendezvous process is how Eagle will reunite with the orbiting Columbia. Armstrong, Aldrin, and Collins all practiced this in Earth orbit during the Gemini program and in simulators, but now they have to do it in lunar orbit for the first time.

As Eagle launches from the Moon's surface, it goes into an 11-by-54-mile elliptical orbit around the Moon. As it gets halfway around the Moon, at its highest point, Armstrong and Aldrin fire the engine again, which puts them into a circular orbit of 54 miles. They will now be flying in an orbit similar to Collins's, only 15 miles apart.

On their next orbit, Armstrong and Aldrin execute several smaller engine burns, raising their orbit up to the height of Collins's in Columbia.

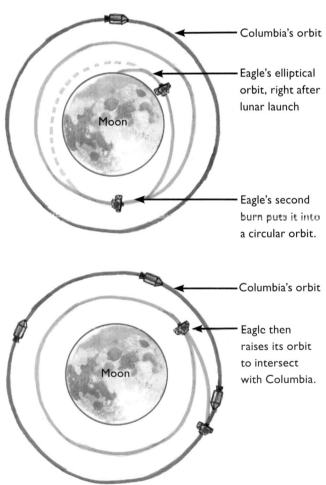

Columbia's orbit

Eagle's elliptical orbit, right after lunar launch

Eagle's second burn puts it into a circular orbit.

Columbia's orbit

Eagle then raises its orbit to intersect with Columbia.

229

GROUND ELAPSED TIME 128:03:00
HR MIN SEC

Orbiting together now, with Eagle just ahead of Columbia, Collins makes the final moves to dock the two spacecraft and reunite with his crewmates.

GROUND ELAPSED TIME 129:05:27
HR MIN SEC

After checking to make sure they have a good seal, Collins removes the drogue and probe assembly, creating a tunnel between the two spacecraft. The two dusty astronauts are a welcome sight to him as they start handing over the bounty of their adventure: boxes of priceless Moon rocks and soil, photographic film, and assorted equipment.

Aldrin (to Collins): *"Get ready for those million-dollar boxes."*

GROUND ELAPSED TIME 130:11:05
HR MIN SEC

Once they are all back inside Columbia and everything has been transferred, they say goodbye to Eagle and jettison it. The Lunar Module will eventually crash back into the Moon.

Collins: *"There she goes. It was a good one."*

Now it's time to go home.

After receiving all the necessary data from Mission Control, the spacecraft once again slips into radio silence around the far side of the Moon. The astronauts fire the Service Propulsion System engine to put them on course to fall back to Earth. If everything goes right, the journey home will take just under three days.

July 23, 1969

GROUND ELAPSED TIME | 177:34:44
HR MIN SEC

DISTANCE FROM EARTH | 91,000 MILES

Forty-two hours have passed. Earth is growing larger through the window. The Apollo 11 astronauts are almost home. During their final television broadcast from space, Mike Collins takes a moment to acknowledge everyone involved in making their flight a success.

Collins: *"This operation is somewhat like the periscope of a submarine. All you see is the three of us, but beneath the surface are thousands and thousands of others, and to all those, I would like to say 'Thank you very much.'"*

Reentry

July 24, 1969

GROUND ELAPSED TIME	194:49:12
	HR MIN SEC
DISTANCE FROM EARTH	2,000 MILES
VELOCITY	21,000 MPH

The crew gets rid of the Service Module. The SM has served the astronauts well over the last eight days, providing Columbia with fuel, power, oxygen, and water, but for a safe reentry the weight has to go. The task of protecting the crew for the final 30 minutes of the journey will fall solely on the Command Module and its carefully designed heat shield.

GROUND ELAPSED TIME	195:03:01
	HR MIN SEC
DISTANCE FROM EARTH	920 MILES
VELOCITY	22,500 MPH

Collins maneuvers the CM so that its blunt end will smash into the atmosphere first. This will create the drag necessary to slow them down from a blistering 25,000 miles per hour to 320 miles per hour. CAPCOM Ronald E. "Ron" Evans gives the Apollo 11 crew some encouraging words.

Evans: *"You're going over the hill there shortly. You're looking mighty fine to us."*

Armstrong: *"See you later."*

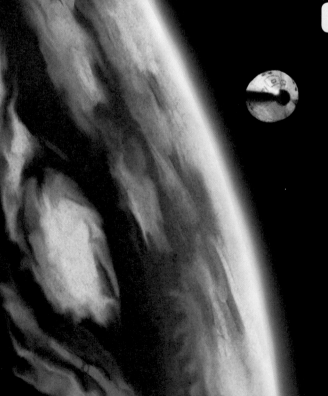

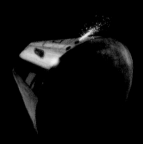

GROUND ELAPSED TIME | 195:03:34
HR MIN SEC
DISTANCE FROM EARTH | 75 MILES
VELOCITY | 25,000 MPH

As the CM enters the atmosphere at around 400,000 feet, the heat of reentry causes a total loss of radio communication with the ground.

All Mission Control can do now is wait and hope the heat shield holds during the blackout of over four minutes.

The three astronauts ride the tip of a 200-mile flame. The heat builds in a shock wave of compressed air below them. Sparks whip past their windows, but the heat shield works.

The buildup of g-force pushes the astronauts deep into their couches as the CM decelerates in the thickening atmosphere.

Evans: *"Apollo 11, Houston through ARIA."*

No answer.

Evans: *"Apollo 11, Houston through ARIA. Standing by. Over."*

No answer.

Evans: *"Apollo 11, Houston. Standing by for your DSKY reading. Over."*

No answer.

Recovery Ship: *"Apollo 11, Apollo 11. This is Hornet. Hornet. Over."*

Silence.

Splashdown and Rescue

GROUND ELAPSED TIME | **195:15:07**
HR MIN SEC

Armstrong: *"Hello, Hornet. This is Apollo 11 reading you loud and clear. Our position 13, 30; 169, 15."*

Drogue parachutes, pilot chutes, and main chutes open in sequence.

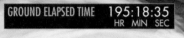

GROUND ELAPSED TIME | **195:18:35**
HR MIN SEC

After traveling almost a million miles through space, Apollo 11 splashes down into the warm waters of the South Pacific. The three astronauts are home.

Once it hits the water, the CM is pulled upside down, into what is known as the stable 2 position. Collins pushes a button deploying three uprighting bags, which inflate, causing the CM to flip over, into the stable 1 position.

Navy SEAL John Wolfram jumps from a rescue chopper at the recovery spot as the CM bobs in the six-foot ocean swells. He swims up to the CM and peers through the window. Armstrong gives him a thumbs-up, which Wolfram relays to the chopper overhead. Next he attaches a sea anchor, which is like an underwater parachute that helps stabilize the craft. Two more swimmers jump from the chopper and help Wolfram secure a flotation collar around the base of the CM to prevent it from sinking once the hatch is opened.

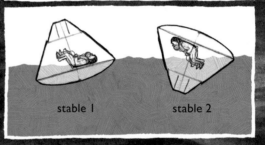

stable 1   stable 2

Moon Bugs

Even though the chances were thought to be infinitesimal, some people worried the astronauts would return to Earth with germs from the Moon that could infect the planet, so NASA takes many precautions with the Apollo 11 crew.

Before exiting the capsule, Armstrong, Aldrin, and Collins all put on Biological Isolation Garments (BIGs). Once they are on the raft, they scrub each other's suits down with a strong disinfectant. A special net, called a Billy Pugh net after its inventor, lifts the astronauts, one by one, into the waiting rescue chopper.

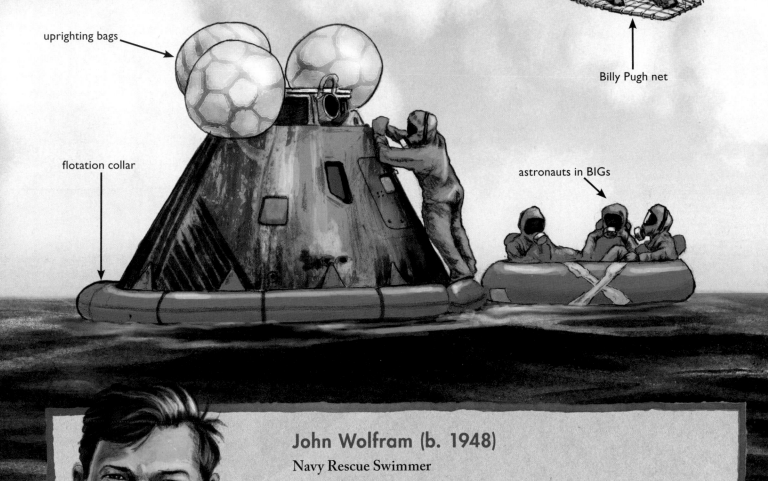

uprighting bags

flotation collar

Billy Pugh net

astronauts in BIGs

John Wolfram (b. 1948)
Navy Rescue Swimmer

When 20-year-old John Wolfram woke up in his bunk aboard the USS Hornet on July 24 at 2:00 a.m., he was not thinking about his place in history—that his face would be the first one that the returning astronauts would see. He was more concerned about his mother recognizing him in his wet suit on TV. To make sure she would, he applied large flower decals to the legs of his wet suit and to the life vest on his chest.

Born in Fort Atkinson, Wisconsin, Wolfram took to swimming at an early age. He joined the navy upon graduating from high school, became an Underwater Demolition Team (UDT) frogman, and served in Vietnam. Upon his return, Wolfram volunteered for the rescue team that would assist NASA with the recovery of the returning Apollo astronauts. He was the fastest swimmer in the group and knew he would be first in the water at splashdown.

In Mission Control, people smoke cigars, wave American flags, and congratulate each other as they watch the crew make it safely to the USS Hornet.

The astronauts disembark from the chopper and walk directly into a trailer called a Mobile Quarantine Facility (MQF). The MQF may be small, but it seems like a palace compared to the CM. It's a relief for the astronauts to take off the hot and uncomfortable BIGs.

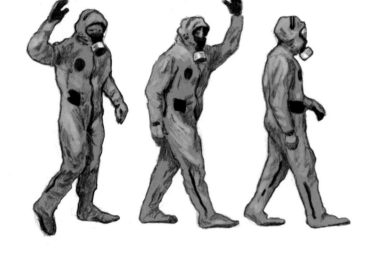

President Nixon greets Armstrong, Aldrin, and Collins, and thanks them for letting the world be one with them during their courageous adventure.

The astronauts will call the trailer home for the next three days, but they are not alone. With them are NASA engineer John Hirasaki and flight surgeon William Carpentier.

While Carpentier looks after the health of the crew, Hirasaki is the MQF technician. He is also responsible for transporting the Moon rocks and decontaminating the CM, which he can access from a plastic tunnel leading out of the trailer. The vacuum-sealed rock boxes are sent through a transfer lock, then transported to the Lunar Receiving Laboratory (LRL) in Houston. The only lunar samples left in the MQF are in the small bag of dust and pebble-sized rocks that Armstrong collected during his first minutes on the surface, now stored in a white Beta cloth pouch. When Hirasaki briefly opened the pouch to peek at the contingency sample bag, he became the first person on Earth to look at bits of the Moon.

Hirasaki (left) and Carpentier (right) in the crew lounge of the MQF

The Mobile Quarantine Facility (MQF)

Built by Melpar, a subsidiary of American Standard, the MQF is an Airstream travel trailer modified to prevent the escape of any germs.

Pumps and fans keep the air pressure inside lower than the pressure outside so that potentially contaminated air will not escape. Its transfer lock allows the crew to receive supplies like food and medicine, and to send out the rock boxes. The transfer lock has doors on either side, and a space between for whatever is being passed through. Once something is inside, the space is filled with a liquid decontaminant and then drained, ensuring that no germs will get out. There is also a plastic transfer tunnel so that Hirasaki and the crew can access the CM.

The MQF will stay aboard the USS Hornet until it reaches port in Honolulu. It will then be loaded into the cargo hold of a C-141 aircraft and flown, with Hirasaki, Carpentier, and the astronauts still on board, to the Lunar Receiving Laboratory.

MQF Facts	
Height	**8** ft. **7** in.
Length	**35** ft.
Weight (empty)	**12,500** lb.
Manufacturer	**Melpar**

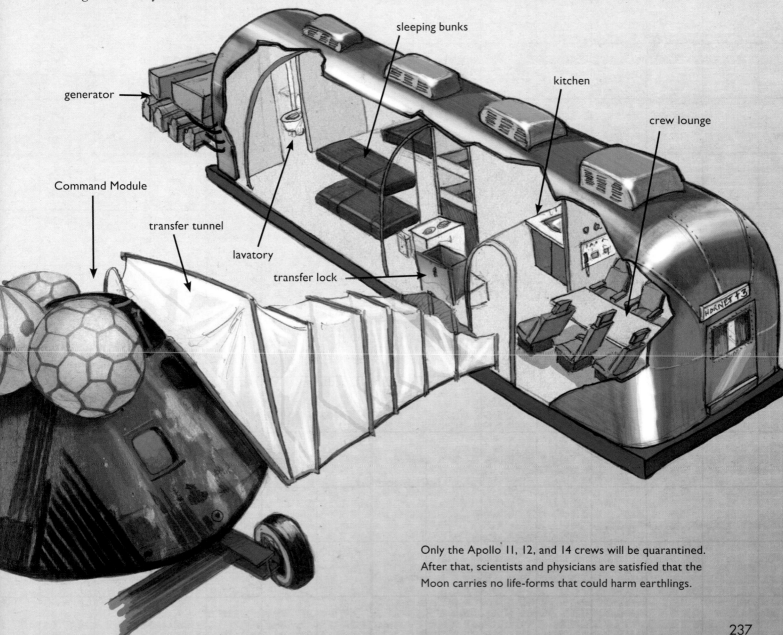

generator

sleeping bunks

kitchen

crew lounge

Command Module

transfer tunnel

lavatory

transfer lock

Only the Apollo 11, 12, and 14 crews will be quarantined. After that, scientists and physicians are satisfied that the Moon carries no life-forms that could harm earthlings.

The Lunar Receiving Laboratory

July 27, 1969

After living inside the MQF for three days, Armstrong, Aldrin, and Collins are relieved to enter the crew reception area of the LRL. Here they will spend another two weeks quarantined, albeit in a much larger facility, for a total of 21 days after the Moon landing.

They will each have their own bedroom as well as access to a gym, offices, a lounge area, a dining room with meals they don't have to rehydrate, and—best of all—real bathrooms.

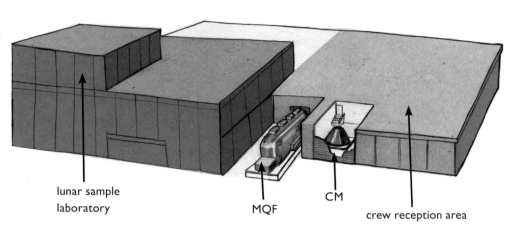

lunar sample laboratory

MQF

CM

crew reception area

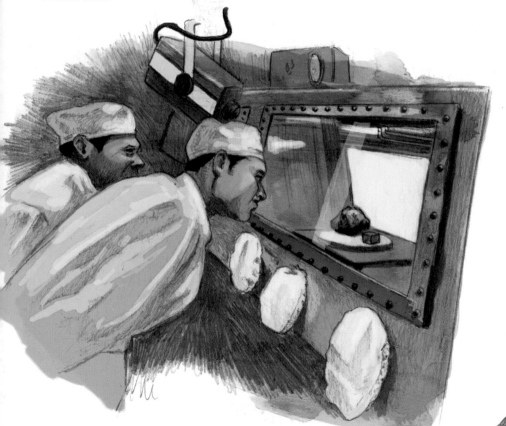

In the lunar sample laboratory, more than 100 excited scientists immediately get to work. The rocks, kept in vacuum chambers so as not to expose them to Earth's atmosphere, are studied, photographed, and tested—for radiation and for possible life-forms.

Fifty days from now, some of these rocks will be distributed to 142 carefully chosen scientists in nine different countries for further experiments. What will they learn about the history of the Moon? What will they learn about our solar system?

World Tour

September 29, 1969

About a month and a half after the Apollo 11 astronauts exit the quarantine facility, they and their wives embark on a global goodwill tour. They visit 24 countries in 37 days and are seen by millions of people.

When they meet people from around the world during their tour, no one says, "You Americans did it!" Instead, they say, "We did it! We went to the Moon!"

It is no longer about a race between the world's two superpowers. It became the human race making a giant leap.

After Apollo 11

Humans had traveled to the Moon and returned safely to Earth. President John F. Kennedy's end-of-the-decade goal had been met.

Suddenly, the Moon seems different. Human beings who have been there can talk about what it was like. They walked around, planted a flag, and even brought pieces of the Moon home.

There are six more piloted Apollo missions to the Moon; five of them are successful in landing on its surface. The missions get longer, and more scientific exploration is accomplished. On the last three missions, the astronauts are equipped with a Lunar Rover, which allows them to cover great distances across the Moon's surface.

However, Americans lose interest in the Moon missions very quickly after Apollo 11. Space travel is no longer news; Apollo is a victim of its own success. NASA's budget is drastically cut, and the final two scheduled missions are canceled.

Astronaut Gene Cernan, commander of Apollo 17, stepped off the surface of the Moon on December 14, 1972. He is the last of the 12 human beings to walk on the lunar surface.

No one has been back since.

Epilogue

Apollo should be remembered not only as the moment that we, as a human race, dared to leave the confines of our home planet to explore another world, but also as a time when we came together to do something that was considered impossible. We sent 24 human beings so far out from Earth that they could look back and see the entire planet with their own eyes. They described it as seemingly fragile, like a Christmas tree ornament floating in the never-ending blackness of space. They couldn't see countries or borders or walls—just a beautiful oasis that contained every person they'd ever known, every place they'd ever been, and every bit of human history ever recorded.

Over 400,000 people worked tirelessly toward the goal of landing a man on the Moon, and the wives, husbands, partners, and families of everyone who participated in the Apollo program made sacrifices on its behalf.

I was two years old when Neil Armstrong and Buzz Aldrin walked on the Moon. My father says I was standing in a playpen near the TV while the rest of my family watched it live. I don't remember the Moon landings, but I think about them often. I look up at the Moon with amazement that we actually went there, and I wonder if we will go back—or where else we might go.

What interests me the most about Apollo is the grit, determination, and hard work it took to achieve the goal—also the problem-solving, the organization, the science, and the sheer cleverness of it all.

Five hundred years from now, will we look back at Apollo as one of humankind's greatest achievements, or as merely the first small step into the unknown?

What new grand idea will bring together hundreds of thousands of individuals to achieve a common goal? And will you, the person reading this right now, be one of those individuals?

APOLLO PILOTED MISSIONS

APOLLO 7

MISSION

Launch: October 11, 1968

Duration: 10 days, 20 hours

Objective: Piloted CSM test flight

CREW

CMD Walter M. "Wally" Schirra Jr.

CMP Donn F. Eisele

LMP R. Walter Cunningham

The first piloted mission after the Apollo 1 fire. Launched into space on a smaller Saturn IB, Apollo 7's goal was to test the newly redesigned Command Module in low-Earth orbit. All systems functioned perfectly. Using an RCA television camera, the Apollo 7 astronauts broadcast a view of their little home in space.

APOLLO 8

MISSION

Launch: December 21, 1968

Duration: 6 days, 3 hours

Objective: Lunar Orbit

CREW

CMD Frank Borman

CMP James A. "Jim" Lovell Jr.

LMP William A. "Bill" Anders

Apollo 8 was originally planned to be an Earth orbital test flight of the Lunar Module. However, the spacecraft was not ready. NASA took a calculated risk and a huge step forward by instead sending the crew on a journey around the Moon. It was not only the first piloted mission using a Saturn V, but also the first time humans had dared to break free of Earth's gravity.

APOLLO 9

MISSION

Launch: March 3, 1969

Duration: 10 days, 1 hour

Objective: LM test flight

CREW

CMD James A. McDivitt

CMP David R. Scott

LMP Russell L. "Rusty" Schweickart

During this 10-day Earth orbital mission, McDivitt and Schweickart tested out all the different systems on board the LM and flew it over 100 miles away from the CSM, where Scott was doing his own tests.

APOLLO 10

MISSION

Launch: May 18, 1969

Duration: 8 days

Objective: Lunar-orbit LM test

CREW

CMD Thomas P. "Tom" Stafford

CMP John W. Young

LMP Eugene A. "Gene" Cernan

Stafford and Cernan flew the LM down to within 50,000 feet of the lunar surface. Apollo 10 was a dress rehearsal for Apollo 11, and the crew did every step of the Moon mission except for actually landing there.

APOLLO 11

MISSION

Launch: July 16, 1969

Duration: 8 days, 3 hours

Objective: Lunar landing

CREW

CMD Neil A. Armstrong

CMP Michael "Mike" Collins

LMP Edwin E. "Buzz" Aldrin Jr.

Apollo 11 was the first time a human being set foot on the Moon. An American flag was planted, rocks were collected, and a mere two and a half hours later, Aldrin and Armstrong were back inside the LM. It was a short visit, designed to touch the finish line of a space race that had started with Sputnik less than 12 years before.

APOLLO 12

MISSION

Launch: November 14, 1969

Duration: 10 days, 4 hours

Objective: Precision lunar landing

CREW

CMD Charles P. "Pete" Conrad Jr.

CMP Richard F. Gordon Jr.

LMP Alan L. Bean

One of Apollo 12's mission goals was to make a pinpoint landing at a specific location. Within the first minute of their launch, lightning struck the rocket not once but twice, knocking the spacecraft's instrumentation off-line. Seconds before aborting the mission, controllers on the ground instructed the crew to switch to a backup power supply. The Instrument Unit, unaffected by the lightning, continued working to put the spacecraft into orbit. Three days later, Conrad and Bean touched down on the Moon, within 600 feet of their target.

APOLLO 13

MISSION	
Launch: April 11, 1970	
Duration: 5 days, 22 hours	
Objective: First science-oriented lunar mission	

CREW	
CMD James A. "Jim" Lovell Jr.	
CMP John L. "Jack" Swigert Jr.	
LMP Fred W. Haise Jr.	

Two days into the flight, when the spacecraft was about 200,000 miles from Earth, an oxygen tank explosion turned this Moon landing mission into a rescue mission. The LM, designed for two men to survive in it for 24 hours, suddenly became a lifeboat for a crew of three. Electricity and life support systems were stretched beyond their limits, and Mission Control tackled every obstacle in order to get the astronauts back alive. Four days later, the crew safely splashed down in the Pacific Ocean. Because of the experience gained in rescuing the crew, Apollo 13 is considered one of NASA's most successful missons.

APOLLO 14

MISSION	
Launch: January 31, 1971	
Duration: 9 days	
Objective: Science-oriented lunar mission	

CREW	
CMD Alan B. Shepard Jr.	
CMP Stuart A. Roosa	
LMP Edgar D. Mitchell	

Apollo 14 was an expanded scientific mission to the Moon. Shepard and Mitchell were just two hours from firing the LM's descent engine when they noticed a circuit malfunction that would cause the spacecraft to abort. Don Eyles at MIT scrambled to write a piece of software that told the computer to ignore the circuit, and it was relayed to the crew by voice so that Mitchell could enter it into the computer by hand. The fix worked, and Shepard and Mitchell touched down in an area of the Moon called the Fra Mauro highlands, the original destination of Apollo 13.

APOLLO 15

MISSION	
Launch: July 26, 1971	
Duration: 12 days, 7 hours	
Objective: First extended science mission	

CREW	
CMD David R. Scott	
CMP Alfred M. "Al" Worden	
LMP James B. "Jim" Irwin	

Scott and Irwin spent over 18 hours on three EVAs, exploring the surface of the Moon in an area called Hadley Rille. As the first astronauts to drive the new Lunar Rovers, they were able to explore much more of the Moon's surface, so they could do more experiments and collect more extensive rock samples. Worden, circling above, spent his time working with a new Scientific Instrument Module (SIM) in the Service Module and taking photographs. His extensive training with geologist Farouk El-Baz paid off when his photographs determined the landing site for Apollo 17.

APOLLO 16

MISSION	
Launch: April 16, 1972	
Duration: 11 days, 1 hour	
Objective: Extended science mission	

CREW	
CMD John W. Young	
CMP Thomas K. "Ken" Mattingly II	
LMP Charles M. "Charlie" Duke Jr.	

Apollo 16's destination was the central lunar area called the Descartes highlands. The crew expanded the amount of scientific research, both on the surface and in orbit around the Moon. As Worden had done on Apollo 15, Mattingly executed a deep-space EVA, 173,000 miles from Earth, to retrieve film canisters from the high-resolution cameras on the SM.

APOLLO 17

MISSION	
Launch: December 7, 1972	
Duration: 12 days, 13 hours	
Objective: Extended science mission	

CREW	
CMD Eugene A. "Gene" Cernan	
CMP Ronald E. "Ron" Evans	
LMP Harrison H. "Jack" Schmitt	

The last Apollo mission was also the longest. Cernan and Schmitt (the first scientist/astronaut) covered over 22 miles of the Taurus-Littrow valley in their rover during their three-day stay on the Moon. The crew returned to Earth with over 240 pounds of soil and rock samples. Cernan was the last person to walk on the Moon.

A Note About Research

The Apollo missions are perhaps the most well-documented event in human history, and for years I have enjoyed reading about the efforts the American workforce made to land a man on the Moon. I gradually began to believe that the story of Apollo is the perfect narrative for demonstrating science and problem-solving to young minds. As the son of a scientist who loves math and problem-solving, I knew this was the kind of book I wanted to make.

As research began, my challenge was to explain how every part of the Apollo/Saturn machine worked and how it was built. I wanted to introduce some of the unsung heroes who helped make the mission happen, and I wanted to show how they went about solving problem after problem using the basic building blocks of science and pure ingenuity.

Luckily, there is an avalanche of information online, and with a little digging you can uncover a plethora of data on just about any part of the Apollo/Saturn, although most of it is written by engineers for engineers. I needed to distill this information in a way that could be understood by all, so I decided to ask the men and women of Apollo for help.

Author with Jim Irwin's Apollo spacesuit

Don Rethke explaining the inner workings of the PLSS

As I was writing and sketching a section about the life support systems aboard the Lunar Module, there were many aspects of it I still didn't understand. I knew that a company in Windsor Locks, Connecticut, had built the system, and I thought if I could find someone who worked there, they could explain it to me. After some searching around the internet, I came across "Dr. Flush," a person who did school talks about the space program. Dr. Flush, also known as Donald Rethke, is an 82-year-old engineer who worked at Hamilton Standard helping to build the Lunar Module life support system. I called Don up out of the blue and told him about the book I was working on. He invited me to come out to the New England Air Museum, where he worked. I said, "When?" and Don said, "How about tomorrow?"

I spent the entire next day with Don, inspecting an actual Apollo spacesuit and looking at one of the original Lunar Module life support systems as he explained every pump and valve and what each did. Afterward, he invited me back to his house where he showed me all kinds of amazing Apollo artifacts. Within minutes, his dining room table was covered in helmets, food pouches, pee pouches, and a liquid cooling garment. Don said, "Come help me with this." And together we dragged an actual life support backpack (PLSS) out of his coat closet.

Author holding an Apollo pressure suit glove

244

Author with Stephen Coester
in front of an F-1 engine

Over the course of the next year we exchanged many phone calls and emails, and his knowledge and expertise gave me a much better understanding than any book, document, or video I could find. I was hooked.

When I wanted to find out more about the parachutes, I tracked down Chuck Lowry, who designed them. When I needed a better understanding of the Apollo Guidance Computer, I was able to talk with Don Eyles—who wrote the software that landed us on the Moon. My list of engineers started to grow, and by the time I started the second draft of my book, I had almost two-dozen experts that I could call upon to answer any question I had about any system, from the F-1 engines to the spacesuits to how the heck they got the TV signal back from the Moon. (For a complete list of Apollo personnel who shared their time and expertise with me, see the Acknowledgments on p. 246.)

I could not have made this book what it is without the men and women of Apollo who unselfishly guided me along the way. Their personal stories enriched this book in so many ways. And I'm proud to preserve these unique and rare moments for the historical record.

A Word About the Artwork

Almost every aspect of the Apollo program has been documented in photographs, drawings, and blueprints, so you may be asking yourself why I bothered to illustrate everything from scratch for this book. My main reason was so that I could make the story and concepts more accessible to the reader. Creating all the visuals allowed me to control and distill the information, leaving in just enough for the reader to understand the concepts without getting overwhelmed by extraneous details. I also felt that there are many different types of information being presented and having it all executed by one hand is more aesthetically pleasing than a hodgepodge of photos, diagrams, and blueprints.

Author with JoAnn Hardin Morgan

Discussing LM training with Bob Pearson

Many of the illustrations are based on historical NASA photographs and diagrams, most of which are in black-and-white, and while my research has uncovered what colors some things are, in several cases I had to make my best guess, or I chose colors that would provide the most clarity to the idea being presented.

In the end, I set out to create a book that I would have loved as a kid and enjoy as an adult. I hope you enjoy it as well.

Acknowledgments

The idea for *How We Got to the Moon* came from my awesome wife, Hayley. Her support and encouragement during the making of this book was the fuel that kept me going.

To everyone at Penguin Random House who supported me in the creation of this book, thank you. To Barbara Marcus, who had faith in this project from the get-go. To my editor, Emily Easton, for her patience and guidance as *How We Got to the Moon* took shape. Her suggestions improved both the content and structure. To my art director, April Ward, whose generous collaboration on the design of this book shows on every page. And thanks to my meticulous copyeditor, Elizabeth Johnson.

To my friends Sharyn November and Brian Floca, who helped with sage advice, expertise, and enthusiasm as I made my own Apollo journey.

Special thanks go to my agent extraordinaire and true friend, Rob Weisbach, for believing in me and my impossibly ambitious ideas.

I received a tremendous amount of help from former Apollo engineers who spent time answering my questions and sharing their stories. Without their input, this book would not have been possible. Stephen Coester, a man with boundless energy, gave my family and me an incredible behind-the-scenes tour of Kennedy Space Center. Thanks to Donald Rethke for providing me with access to Apollo 15 astronaut James Irwin's spacesuit, among many other Apollo-era artifacts. I am eternally grateful to JoAnn Hardin Morgan for including my wife and me in the 50th anniversary celebration for the women of Apollo. Lee Solid and Saverio "Sonny" Morea were invaluable for their patient explanations about the construction and testing of rocket engines. To Don Eyles for his elegant explanations of the inner workings of the Apollo Guidance Computer and for reading early drafts of those sections. For their detailed accounts of splashdown and recovery, I am indebted to Charles H. Lowry and John Wolfram. For answering my questions about the various Apollo systems over email, by phone, and in person, I am humbled and thankful to the following: Fred Warrender, Harvey LeBlanc, Dr. Farouk El-Baz, Don Arabian, Ann D. Montgomery, Ramon L. Alonso, Richard L. Nafzger, James W. McBarron II, Robert Pearson, Eugene F. Kranz, Carl R. Green, Jim Morgan, and Ike Rigell.

Apollo historians Andrew Chaikin and Jonathan H. Ward took time reading early drafts of this book and helped me get the details right. Thank you. Thanks also go to W. David Woods for answering my questions regarding the Saturn V flight trajectories and velocities.

Finally I would like to thank my loving family. Alaya, your love of books always motivates me. I'm sorry your father was so busy for so long—I'll make it up to you. Dad, you've always been an inspiration, and I am proud to be your son. Mom, you kept me laughing through it all. (Don't worry, I won't be going into space.) Hayley, I love you to the Moon and back.

Sources

BOOKS

Bilstein, Roger E. *Stages to Saturn: A Technological History of the Apollo/Saturn Launch Vehicles.* Washington, D.C.: NASA, 2013.

Chaikin, Andrew. *A Man on the Moon: The Voyages of the Apollo Astronauts.* New York: Penguin, 1994.

Cortright, Edgar M. *Apollo: Expeditions to the Moon.* Washington, D.C.: NASA Scientific and Technical Information Office, 1975.

De Monchaux, Nicholas. *Spacesuit: Fashioning Apollo.* Cambridge, MA: The MIT Press, 2011.

Fish, Bob. *Hornet Plus Three: The Story of the Apollo 11 Recovery.* Reno, NV: Creative Minds Press, 2009.

Gray, Mike. *Angle of Attack: Harrison Storms and the Race to the Moon.* New York: Penguin, 1992.

Kluger, Jeffrey. *Apollo 8: The Thrilling Story of the First Mission to the Moon.* New York: Henry Holt, 2017.

Kraft, Chris. *Flight: My Life in Mission Control.* New York: Penguin, 2001.

Lovell, Jim, and Jeffrey Kluger. *Lost Moon: The Perilous Voyage of Apollo 13.* New York: Houghton Mifflin, 1994.

Murray, Charles, and Catherine Bly Cox. *Apollo: The Race to the Moon.* New York: Simon and Schuster, 1989.

Otfinoski, Steven. *Rockets.* New York: Marshall Cavendish Benchmark, 2007.

Paul, Richard, and Steven Moss. *We Could Not Fail: The First African Americans in the Space Program.* Austin, TX: University of Texas Press, 2015.

Riley, Christopher, and Philip Dolling. *NASA Apollo 11: Owners' Workshop Manual.* Somerset, UK: Haynes Publishing, 2009.

Shetterly, Margot Lee. *Hidden Figures.* New York: HarperCollins, 2016.

Ward, Jonathan H. *Rocket Ranch: The Nuts and Bolts of the Apollo Moon Program at Kennedy Space Center.* New York/London: Springer Praxis, 2015.

Watkins, Billy. *Apollo Moon Missions: The Unsung Heroes.* Westport, CT: Praeger, 2005.

Wolfram, John. *Splashdown: The Rescue of a Navy Frogman.* Atlanta, GA: BookLogix, 2012.

Woods, W. David. *How Apollo Flew to the Moon.* New York/London: Springer Praxis, 2008.

Woods, W. David. *NASA Saturn V: Owners' Workshop Manual.* Somerset, UK: Haynes Publishing, 2016.

DOCUMENTARIES

Copp, Duncan, Nick Davidson, and Christopher Riley, dirs. *Moon Machines.* UK: Dox Productions, 2008. bit.ly/2OKxBOu. A six-part documentary series on project Apollo, from the viewpoint of the designers and engineers.

Gray, Mark, prod. *Apollo 11: Men on the Moon.* Atlanta, GA: Spacecraft Films/NASA, 2007. 3-Disc Collector's Edition. Over ten hours of documentary footage from NASA covering the Apollo 11 mission.

Kamecke, Theo, dir. *Moonwalk One.* USA: Francis Thompson, 1970. journeyman.tv/film/6712/moonwalk-one Documentary film giving an in-depth and profound look at the Apollo 11 mission to the Moon.

Miller, Todd Douglas, dir. *Apollo 11.* Atlanta, GA: CNN Films, 2019. Blue-ray Disc 1080p HD. Documentary film featuring rare large-format film footage of the Apollo 11 mission from liftoff to splashdown.

MIT Science Reporter. Boston, MA: MIT/WGBH Boston. infinitehistory.mit.edu/collection/slice-mit-science-reporter Hosted by John Fitch, this series of documentary videos contains several episodes on the Apollo missions with engineers explaining different aspects of what they are building.

WEBSITES

The author consulted these websites numerous times throughout the research process. For this reason, we have not provided specific access dates for these entries.

history.nasa.gov/afj
> Apollo Flight Journal: written transcripts of communications between ground and crew from all the Apollo missions

history.nasa.gov/alsj
> Apollo Lunar Surface Journal: written transcripts of the lunar surface operations conducted by the six pairs of astronauts who landed on the Moon

apolloinrealtime.org
> Apollo in Real Time: a real-time journey through the Apollo missions with thousands of hours of audio from both the spacecraft and mission control, mission control film footage, and all onboard film footage from the spacecrafts

wehackthemoon.com
> Hack the Moon: an extensive website covering the people and the technology that Draper Laboratories developed for the space program, as well as the mission overviews that reveal how all their efforts came together

historycollection.jsc.nasa.gov/JSCHistoryPortal/history/oral_histories/oral_histories.htm
> JSC Oral History Project: interviews with managers, engineers, technicians, doctors, astronauts, and other employees of NASA and aerospace contractors

history.nasa.gov
> NASA history: the main hub for a vast and extensive collection of historical documents, images, and other resources, organized by NASA centers throughout the United States

flickr.com/photos/projectapolloarchive/albums
> Project Apollo Archive: a collection of photos from the Apollo missions

https://3d.si.edu/object/3d/command-module-apollo-11:d8c63e8a-4ebc-11ea-b77f-2e728ce88125
> Smithsonian 3D: an interactive 3D model of the interior of the Apollo 11 Command Module

PLACES VISITED

American Space Museum and Space Walk of Fame. Titusville, FL, July 2019. Met with Apollo engineers Lee Solid, Ike Rigell, Carl R. Green, and Robert Pearson. spacewalkoffame.org

Explorers Club, The. New York, NY, March 2019. Visited space collection and personally met with Apollo astronauts Michael Collins, Fred Haise, Rusty Schweickart, and Walt Cunningham during ECAD 2019. explorers.org

Jet Propulsion Laboratory. La Cañada Flintridge, CA, July 2017 and June 2018. jpl.nasa.gov

JFK Presidential Library and Museum. Boston, MA, May 2019. Visited space race collection. jfklibrary.org

Kennedy Space Center. Merritt Island, FL, May 2017. Guided tour by Apollo engineer Stephen Coester, July 2019. kennedyspacecenter.com

National Air and Space Museum. Washington, D.C., September 2017. airandspace.si.edu

New England Air Museum. Windsor Locks, CT. Guided tour by Apollo engineer Donald Rethke, who provided special access to Jim Irwin's Apollo spacesuit, as well as the rest of their Apollo artifacts, December 2018. neam.org

Pima Air & Space Museum. Tucson, AZ, November 2019. pimaair.org

San Diego Air & Space Museum. San Diego, CA, January 2018. sandiegoairandspace.org

Sotheby's Space Exploration Collection. New York, NY, July 2017. sothebys.com/en/auctions/2017/space-exploration-n09759.html

USS Hornet Sea, Air, & Space Museum. Alameda, CA, March 2019. uss-hornet.org

PERSONAL INTERVIEWS WITH THE MEN AND WOMEN OF APOLLO

Alonso, Ramon L. (Apollo Guidance Computer Designer, Draper Lab at MIT), telephone interview with author, October 2019.

Arabian, Don (Chief, Test Division, Apollo Spacecraft Program, NASA at JSC), telephone and in-person interviews with author, May 2019 and July 2019.

Coester, Stephen (Systems Engineer, Boeing at KSC), in-person interview with author, July 2019.

El-Baz, Farouk (Geologist, Bellcomm, Inc.), telephone interview with author, April 2019.

Eyles, Don (Software Engineer, Draper Lab at MIT), telephone interview with author, May 2019.

LeBlanc, Harvey (Design Engineer, North American Aviation), telephone interviews with author, December 2018.

Lowry, Charles H. (Parachute Systems Design Engineer, North American Aviation at Downey), telephone interview with author, May 2019.

McBarron, James W., II. (Spacesuit Systems Specialist, NASA and ILC), telephone interviews with author, February 2020.

Montgomery, Ann D. (Flight Crew Equipment Engineer, NASA at KSC), telephone interview with author, May 2019.

Morea, Saverio "Sonny" (Project Manager for the F-1 and J-2 Engines, NASA at MSFC), telephone interview with author, March 2019.

Morgan, JoAnn H. (Communications Specialist, NASA at KSC), telephone and in-person interviews with author, April 2019 and July 2019.

Nafzger, Richard L. (Team Lead and Engineer, NASA at Goddard Space Flight Center), telephone interview with author, June 2019.

Rethke, Donald (Life Support Systems Engineer, Hamilton Standard), in-person interview with author, December 2018.

Solid, Lee (Lead Engineer, Rocketdyne at KSC), in-person and telephone interviews with author, July 2019 and August 2019.

Warrender, Fred (Chief Facilities Project Engineer, Boeing), in-person interview with author, August 2018.

Wolfram, John (Navy Seal, Apollo 11 Rescue Team), telephone interview with author, March 2019.

AUTHOR INTERVIEWS

Chaikin, Andrew (author of *A Man on the Moon: The Voyages of the Apollo Astronauts*), in-person interview with author, February 2019. andrewchaikin.com

Ward, Jonathan (author of *Rocket Ranch* and *Countdown to a Moon Launch*), telephone interview with author, January 2019. jonathanhward.com

For Further Reading

Chaikin, Andrew, with Victoria Kohl. *Mission Control, This Is Apollo.* New York: Viking, 2009.

Cruddas, Sarah. *The Space Race: The Journey to the Moon and Beyond.* New York: DK, 2019.

Floca, Brian. *Moonshot: The Flight of Apollo 11.* New York: Atheneum Books for Young Readers, 2009.

Pohlen, Jerome. *The Apollo Missions for Kids: The People and Engineering Behind the Race to the Moon.* Chicago: Chicago Review Press, 2019.

Shetterly, Margot Lee. *Hidden Figures: Young Readers' Edition.* New York: HarperCollins, 2016.

Sparrow, Giles. *Spaceflight: The Complete Story from Sputnik to Curiosity* (2nd edition). New York: DK, 2019.

Thimmesh, Catherine. *Team Moon: How 400,000 People Landed Apollo 11 on the Moon.* New York: Houghton Mifflin Books for Children, 2006.

A more extensive list of websites, places to visit, and further reading can be found at HowWeGotToTheMoon.com

Commonly Used Acronyms During Apollo

AGC: Apollo Guidance Computer

BIGs: Biological Isolation Garments

Caltech: California Institute of
Technology

CAPCOM: Capsule Communicator

CDR: Commander

CM: Command Module

CMP: Command Module Pilot

CO_2: Carbon Dioxide

CSM: Command and Service Module

DSKY: Display and Keyboard

ECS: Environmental Control System

EDS: Emergency Detection System

EOR: Earth Orbit Rendezvous

EVA: Extravehicular Activities

FCS: Fecal Containment System

G or G's: Gravity (also known as
g-force)

H_2O: Water

HR: Hours

IBM: International Business Machines

ILC: International Latex Corporation

INTELSAT: International
Telecommunications Satellite
Organization

ISDD: In-Suit Drinking Device

ITMG: Integrated Thermal
Micrometeoroid Garment

IU: Instrument Unit

JPL: Jet Propulsion Laboratory

KSC: Kennedy Space Center

LCC: Launch Control Center

LCG: Liquid Cooling Garment

LET: Launch Escape Tower

LH_2: Liquid Hydrogen

LiOH: Lithium Hydroxide

LLTV: Lunar Landing Training Vehicle

LM: Lunar Module

LMP: Lunar Module Pilot

LOI: Lunar Orbit Insertion

LOR: Lunar Orbit Rendezvous

LOX: Liquid Oxygen

LRL: Lunar Receiving Laboratory

LRRR: Laser Ranging Retroreflector

LRV: Lunar Roving Vehicle

LUT: Launch Umbilical Tower

LVDC: Launch Vehicle
Digital Computer

MALLAR: Manned Lunar Landing
and Return

MER: Mission Evaluation Room

MESA: Modularized Equipment
Stowage Assembly

MIN: Minutes

MIT: Massachusetts Institute of
Technology

MOCR: Mission Operations
Control Room

MPH: Miles Per Hour

MQF: Mobile Quarantine Facility

MSFN: Manned Space Flight Network

MSOB: Manned Spacecraft Operations
Building

MSS: Mobile Service Structure

NACA: National Advisory Committee
for Aeronautics

NASA: National Aeronautics
and Space Administration

NDEA: National Defense
Education Act

O_2: Oxygen

OPS: Oxygen Purge System

PGA: Pressure Garment Assembly

PLSS: Portable Life Support System

PSI: Pounds Per Square Inch

PTC: Passive Thermal Control

RCA: Radio Corporation of America

RCS: Reaction Control Systems

RCU: Remote-Control Unit

RP-I: Refined Petroleum-1
(alternately Rocket Propellant-1)

SEC: Seconds

S-IC: First Stage of the Saturn Rocket

S-II: Second Stage of the Saturn Rocket

S-IVB: Third Stage of the Saturn Rocket

SIM: Scientific Instrument Module

SM: Service Module

SPS: Service Propulsion System

TLI: Translunar Injection

TRW: Thompson Ramo Wooldridge

UCTA: Urine Collection and Transfer
Assembly

UDT: Underwater Demolition Team

UTS: Urine Transfer System

VAB: Vehicle Assembly Building

VIP: Very Important Person

Index

A

accelerometers, 86, 88–89

accidents, 134, 135, 136–139

Aero Spacelines, 160–161

African Americans, 35–36, 57

Aldrin, Edwin E.

    Apollo 11 mission, 49, 187, 195, 198–199,
        202–203, 209, 213, 214–216, 218–221, 223,
        226–230, 235–236, 238–239, 241–242

    Gemini program, 45

Apollo Guidance Computer (AGC), 56, 96–97,
   108–113, 212

    binary language, 110

    Command Module Control Panel, 96–97

    core rope memory, 112

    core rope weavers, 112

    DSKY Interface, 109

    integrated circuits, 111

    navigation, 212

Apollo program; *see also* Command Module (CM);
   Lunar Module (LM); Saturn V rocket; Service
   Module (SM); *specific astronauts*

    Apollo 1 test accident, 136–139

    Apollo 8 lunar orbital flight, 193

    Apollo 11 descent to the Moon, 216–221

    Apollo 11 journey to the Moon, 212–213

    Apollo 11 launch, 204–207

    Apollo 11 Lunar Orbit Insertion, 41, 81, 214–215

    Apollo 11 Lunar Orbit Rendezvous, 229–230

    Apollo 11 Moon landing, 220–221

    Apollo 11 piloted missions, 242–243

    Apollo 11 pre-launch preparation, 194–203

    Apollo 11 reentry, 232–233

    Apollo 11 return to Earth, 231–232

    Apollo 11 rollout, 194–197

    Apollo 11 splashdown and recovery, 201, 234–235

    Apollo 11 staging, 208–209

    Apollo 11 television, 179, 223–225, 231

    Apollo 11 transposition and docking, 210–211

    Apollo 11 world tour, 239

    Apollo 13 incident, 81, 129, 135

    Apollo-Soyuz mission, 21

    approaches to Moon landing, 46–50

    astronaut communications, 182–185

    computers, 56, 96–97, 108–113, 212

    creation of, 25

    development of spacecraft, 53–54, 92–93

    flight teams, 180

    food, 140–141

    free-return trajectory plan, 81

    human computers, 35, 36, 40, 56

    list of piloted missions, 242–243

    Mission Evaluation Room, 181

    Mission Operations Control Room, 178–179

    modules of, 55

    moonwalks, 222–223, 226–227

    selection of launch site, 156

    selection of Moon landing sites, 43

    spacesuits, 144–153

    Surveyor Program, 42

    training, 186–191

    waste disposal, 20, 142–143

    workforce, 35–36, 56–57, 101, 112, 114, 116, 153,
        155–156

Apollo Spacesuit (EMU), 144–153

    boots, 150

    communications carrier assembly, 150

    development of, 146–147

    gloves, 150

    helmet visor assembly, 150

    Integrated Thermal Micrometeoroid Garment
        (ITMG), 145, 149, 150

    layers of, 145

    Liquid Cooling Garment (LCG), 145, 152

Oxygen Purge System (OPS), 145, 151
Portable Life Support System (PLSS), 145, 151
Pressure Garment Assembly, 148
Armstrong, Neil A., 193
    Apollo 11 mission, 5, 49, 195, 198, 202–203, 209,
        215–216, 218–221, 223–224, 226–230, 232,
        234–236, 238–239, 241–242
    Gemini Program, 45
    simulator training, 187, 190
Ascent Stage, 122–123, 124, 126–127, 229
atmosphere
    beginning of space, 22–23
    carbon dioxide in, 135
    life support systems, 133
    oxygen in, 134–135
    principles of flight, 30, 31
    as radiation protection, 131
    reentry, 9, 18, 21, 50–51, 55, 94, 100–103, 114,
        232–233
    rockets, 32
attitude, 82–83, 87

B
baffles, 70–71
    anti-slosh, 61, 62
batteries, 9, 84, 94, 105, 106, 151, 197
    how they work, 106
binary language, 110
Boeing, 57, 60, 62, 159, 160
boiling point, 75
Borman, Frank, 44, 137, 193, 242

C
Carpenter, M. Scott, 16, 21
Cernan, Eugene A., 240, 242, 243
Chaffee, Roger, 136, 139, 228
Cold War, 7
Collins, Michael, 195, 199, 202–203, 209–214, 216,
    221, 227, 229–230, 232, 234–236, 238–239, 242
Columbia (CM), see Command Module (CM)
Command and Service Module (CSM), 92, 94,
    122, 159, 210–211,
Command Module (CM)
    Apollo 1 test accident, 136, 137
    description of, 55, 94–97
    Environmental Control Systems, 135
    Launch Umbilical Tower, 167

life support systems, 132–133, 135
Lunar Orbit Rendezvous, 50–51
Mobile Quarantine Facility, 237
parachutes, 116–119, 234
as part of Apollo spacecraft, 92
reentry, 100–101, 232–233
software programs, 113
training simulators, 186–187
transposition and docking, 211
computers
    Apollo Guidance Computer (AGC), 108–113, 212
    Command Module Main Control Panel, 96–97
    human, 35, 40, 56, 110
    IBM 7090, 110
Conroy, Jack, 160–161
Cooper, L. Gordon "Gordo," Jr., 16, 21
core rope memory, 112
core rope weavers, 112

D
Descent Stage, 122–123, 125, 128, 229
direct ascent, 46, 48
Dolan, Tom, 48–49
Douglas Aircraft Company, 57, 78, 80, 158
drag, 30–31, 100, 232
Draper, Charles Stark "Doc," 84–87
DSKY Interface, 109, 113, 212, 216
Duke, Charles M., Jr., 215–216, 218, 220–221, 243

E
Eagle (LM), see Lunar Module (LM)
Earth Landing System (ELS), 114–121
    parachutes, 116–119
    reentry, 120–121
Earth-Moon Scale, 39
Earth Orbit Rendezvous (EOR), 47–48, 172
Eisenhower, Dwight D., 14
El-Baz, Farouk, 43
emergency escape systems, 174–175, 196
Evans, Ronald E., 232–233, 243
experiments, 62, 63, 77, 89, 125, 149
Explorer 1, 13
extravehicular activities (EVAs), 142–143
Extravehicular Mobility Unit (EMU), 144–153

F
F-1 rocket engines, 60, 64–68, 70, 168, 204, 206

Faget, Maxime A., 54, 98–100, 102, 224

firework rockets, 33

food, 140–141

Foraker, Eleanor "Ellie," 131, 153

Friden STW-10 calculating machine, 35

fuel cells, 104–106, 133

fuel tanks, 60, 62–63, 72, 73–74, 76–77, 79

G

Gagarin, Yuri, 18–19, 20, 22–23, 24, 228

Geissler, Ernst, 80

Gemini Program, 44–45, 98, 140

geology, 43, 191

Glenn, John H., Jr., 21, 23, 36, 52

Goddard, Robert H., 27, 32

gravity, 37; see also weightlessness
    center of, 62, 100, 101

gravity wells, 41

Grissom, Virgil I., 21, 136, 139, 228

ground support, 176–185
    communication, 182–183
    flight teams, 180
    Launch Control Center (LCC), 176
    Manned Space Flight Network (MSFN), 184–185
    Mission Evaluation Room (MER), 181
    Mission Operations Control Room (MOCR), 178–179

Grumman Corporation, 122–125, 128–129, 159, 193

gyroscopes, 86, 87, 89

H

Haise, Fred W., Jr., 81, 243

Ham (chimpanzee), 16, 17

Hamilton, Margaret, 113

Hamilton Standard, 56, 91, 133, 144, 151, 152

heat
    cooling electronic devices, 90–91
    of reentry, 18, 21, 55, 102–103, 232–233

heat shields, 102–103, 107, 232

heat transfer, 66, 75–77

Hero's reaction engine, 29

Hornet, 201, 233–234, 236–237

Huntington Beach, California, 78, 158, 159

Huntsville, Alabama, 11, 14, 61, 67, 68, 80, 159, 160, 177

I

IBM, 36, 56, 61, 84–85, 90, 110, 159

IBM 7090, 110

Impact Attenuation System, 120–121

Inertial Guidance System, 85, 86–89

inertial platform, 85, 88, 209, 212

Instrument Unit (IU), 84–85, 90–91, 159

insulation, 77, 102–103

Integrated Thermal Micrometeoroid Garment (ITMG), 145, 149, 150

International Space Station (ISS), 22–23, 37

J

J-2 rocket engines, 67, 72, 78–79, 208–209

Johnson, Katherine, 35, 36, 93

K

Kelly, Thomas J. "Tom," 122–123, 128

Kennedy, John F., 24–25, 57, 191, 223, 240

Kennedy Space Center, 56, 61, 156–157, 158, 159, 174, 177, 200
    Launch Complex 39, 156–157
    Launchpad 39A, 156–157, 166, 170, 172, 178, 193, 196–197

King, Jack, 202, 204, 206

Kondratyuk, Yuri V., 48

Kraft, Christopher C., Jr., 155, 180, 224

Kranz, Eugene F. "Gene," 139, 180, 215, 216, 218–219

L

Langley Research Center, 35

Launch Complex 39, 156–157

Launch Control Center (LCC), 156, 157, 176–177

Launch Escape Tower (LET), 98–99, 114, 196, 208

Launch Umbilical Tower (LUT), 167

Launchpad 39A, 156–157, 166, 170, 172, 178, 193, 196–197

LeBlanc, Harvey, 72–73

LeBlanc, Jim, 134

Lee, Dorothy B. "Dottie," 57, 103

life support systems, 132–143; see also spacesuits
    Apollo 1 accident, 136–139
    atmosphere, 134–135
    of Command Module, 132–133, 135
    conditions in space, 131
    electrical power for, 106
    Environmental Control System (ECS), 133
    food, 140–141
    of Lunar Module, 126–127, 128, 133, 135

Service Module, 94

vacuum chamber accident, 134

waste management, 142–143

workforce for, 56

lift, 30–31, 100

Liquid Cooling Garment (LCG), 145, 152

liquid-fueled rockets, 12, 32, 33, 65

liquid hydrogen (LH$_2$), 72–73, 74, 76–79,
 157, 200, 205

liquid oxygen (LOX), 10, 60–61, 63, 64–65,
 70, 72, 74, 76–79, 157, 205

Lovelace, William R. "Randy," II, 15, 17

Lovell, James A., Jr., 44, 45, 81, 113, 193, 242, 243

Lowry, Charles "Chuck," 114–115

Lunar Landing Training Vehicle (LLTV), 190–191

Lunar Module (LM), 122–129; *see also* Lunar Orbit
 Rendezvous

 Apollo 13, 81

 Ascent Stage, 126–127

 descent to the Moon, 215, 216–221

 development of, 55, 92, 95, 122–129

 Environmental Control Systems, 135

 hatch, 128

 life support systems, 126–127, 128, 133, 135

 moonwalks, 223

 shipping to launch site, 159

 sleeping in, 228

 testing of, 128–129

 training simulators, 186–187, 190

 transposition and docking, 210–211

Lunar Orbit Insertion (LOI), 41, 81, 214–215

Lunar Orbit Rendezvous (LOR), 50–51, 52, 122,
 172, 229–230

Lunar Orbiter Program, 43

Lunar Receiving Laboratory (LRL), 236–238

Lunar Roving Vehicle (LRV), 67

M

Manned Space Flight Network (MSFN), 184–185

Marion Power Shovel Company, 170–171

Marshall Space Flight Center, 159

Massachusetts Institute of Technology (MIT), 84,
 86, 108–109, 111–113, 217

 Instrumentation Laboratory, 84, 86,
 108–109, 111

McCandless, Bruce, 208–212, 214, 227

McDivitt, James A., 44

Melpar, 237

Mercury Program

 development of Mercury capsule, 54

 food for, 140

 Launch Escape Tower, 98–99

 list of missions, 21

 rockets used in, 52

 selection of candidates for, 15–17

 stepping-stone to Moon landing, 38–39, 102

Mission Operations Control Room (MOCR),
 178–183, 200, 207

mobile launch Crawler, 156, 166, 170–171, 196–197

mobile launch system, 156–157, 166–171,
 196–197, 205

 Crawler-Transporter, 170–171

 Hold-Down Arms, 168

 Launchpad 39A, 156–157, 166, 170, 172, 178,
 193, 196–197

 Mobile Launcher, 167

 Mobile Service Structure (MSS), 169

 Tail Service Masts, 168

Mobile Quarantine Facility (MQF), 236–238

Mobile Service Structure (MSS), 157, 169, 173, 197

Montgomery, Ann D., 101

Moon

 distance from Earth, 38–39, 227

 gravity on, 37

 lunar orbital velocity, 41

 robotic spacecraft missions to, 42–43

Moon landing, 216–238; *see also* Apollo program;
 Saturn V rocket

 approaches to, 46–50

 Earth orbit as component of, 80

 launch vehicle for, 52–53

moonwalks, 222–223, 226–227

Morea, Saverio F. "Sonny," 64, 67, 70–71

Morgan, JoAnn H., 177

Morrison-Knudsen, Perini, and Hardeman, 169

N

National Advisory Committee for Aeronautics
 (NACA), 36, 54, 99, 103, 180

National Aeronautics and Space Administration
 (NASA); *see also* Moon landing; *specific space
 programs*

 commitment to moon missions, 25, 28, 240

 creation of, 14

human computers for, 35, 36, 40, 56

selection of first astronauts, 15–17

Newton's laws of motion, 28–29, 31, 89

nitrogen, 135, 139, 198

North American Aviation, 57, 61, 72–74, 94, 104, 114, 120, 133, 158

Northrop Ventura, 114–115, 117

O

Oberth, Hermann, 11, 12

Operation Paperclip, 11

orbit, 40, 41, 81

oxygen

Apollo 1 test accident, 136, 138–139

in atmosphere, 134–135

combustion, 31

for spacesuits, 151

vacuum, 144

Oxygen Purge System (OPS), 145, 151

P

parabolic flight, 188

parachutes, 114–119, 234

payload, 52, 54, 74

Pearson, Robert "Bob," 187

pitch, 82–83, 88

Portable Life Support System (PLSS), 145, 151

Pregnant Guppy, 160

Pressure Garment Assembly (PGA), 145, 148

propellants, 33, 59, 60, 62, 64–65, 70–74, 76–79, 81, 83, 104–105, 124, 126, 129, 157, 167, 168, 174–175, 198, 205, 206, 208–209

liquid hydrogen (LH$_2$), 72–73, 74, 76–79, 157, 200, 205

liquid oxygen (LOX), 10, 60–61, 63, 64–65, 70, 72, 74, 76–79, 157, 205

RP-1, 60, 63, 64–65, 66, 70, 73 157

programs

Gemini, 36, 44–45, 46, 52, 95, 98, 102, 114, 137, 139, 140, 150, 156, 160, 162, 229

Lunar Orbiter, 43

Ranger, 42

Surveyor, 42

R

racial equality, and Apollo workforce, 35–36, 57

Ranger Program, 42

Rapp, Rita M., 140

Raytheon, 108, 112

reentry to atmosphere, 9, 18, 21, 50–51, 55, 94, 100–103, 114, 232–233

Rocketdyne, 64, 66, 70–71, 78

rockets; *see also specific rockets*

approaches to Moon landing, 46–47

controlling engine thrust of, 129

engine types for, 32–33

flight principles of, 31

orbital velocities of, 40–41

post-WWII development of, 7

rock samples, 226–227, 236, 238

roll, 82–83, 88, 107

RP-1 fuel, 60, 63–66, 70, 73, 157

S

Saturn V rocket; *see also* Apollo program

F-1 rocket engines, 60, 64–68, 70, 168, 204, 206

Instrument Unit (IU), 84–85, 90–91, 159

Launch Control Center, 156, 157, 176–177

Launch Escape Tower, 98, 114, 196

launch facility for, 156–159, 162–165

Launchpad 39A, 172–173, 193, 196–197

launchpad safety, 174–175

mobile launch system, 156–157, 166–171, 196–197, 205

payload of, 52–53

requirements for, 59

shipping to launch site, 161

Stage One (S-IC), 53, 57, 60–62, 158–159, 208

Stage Two (S-II), 53, 72–74, 158–159, 208–209

Stage Three (S-IVB), 53, 57, 78–79, 81–83, 158–159, 209–211

test stand for, 68–69

uncrewed test flights, 193

V-2 rocket, 10

Werner von Braun, 12, 44, 52–53, 64, 193

Schirra, Walter M., Jr., 21, 44, 142, 242

Scott, David R., 45, 242, 243

Semyorka, 9

service masts, 168, 205

Service Module (SM), 50–51, 55, 92, 94, 104–105, 232

Service Propulsion System (SPS), 104–105, 231

Shepard, Alan B., Jr., 20, 22, 36, 52, 98, 243

Slayton, Donald K. "Deke," 16, 21, 198
slide rules, 34–35
solid-fuel rockets, 33
Soviet Union
    notable space accomplishments of, 18
    post-WWII rocket development, 7, 10–11, 13, 14
    space race with US, 13, 18, 21, 24–25, 28, 44, 193, 239
space race, 13, 18, 21, 24–25, 28, 44, 193, 239
spacesuits, 144–153
splashdown and recovery, 201, 234–235
Sputnik, 8–9, 13, 18, 22–23
Stage One (S-IC), 60–71
    baffles, 61, 62, 70–71
    F-1 Engine, 64–65, 67, 70–71
    injector plate, 70–71
    Saturn V test stand, 68–69
    tanks, 62–63
Stage Two (S-II), 72–77
    bulkhead, 74
    fuel loss, 76
    heat transfer, 75
    insulation, 77
    weight, 72, 74
Stage Three (S-IVB), 78–83
    attitude, 82–83
    auxiliary propulsion, 83
    free return trajectory, 81
    orbit, 80–81
    Saturn V, 78–79
    ullage, 83
Stoner, George H., 60–61
sublimation, 90–91
Super Guppy, 158, 159–161
Surveyor Program, 42

T
Tereshkova, Valentina, 19
thrust, 30–31, 33, 34, 52–53, 60, 65, 66, 68, 70–71, 72, 82–83, 98, 105, 126–127, 129, 168, 204
    chamber, 65, 66, 70–71
thrusters, 45, 100, 122–123, 127, 190, 211
training, 186–191
    geology, 191
    Lunar Landing Training Vehicle (LLTV), 190
    simulators, 186–187
    survival, 191
    zero-g, 188–189
trajectory, 35, 36, 79, 80–81, 93, 104, 110, 209, 212

U
ullage, 83
United States
    post-WWII rocket development, 7, 10–11, 12, 14
    space race with Soviet Union, 13, 18, 21, 24–25, 28, 44, 193, 239

V
V-2 rocket, 10–12
vacuum, 32, 144–145
vacuum chamber tests, 134
Vehicle Assembly Building (VAB), 156, 157, 162–165
velocity, 40–41, 53, 65, 126, 219
von Braun, Wernher, 59
    meeting with Lyndon Johnson, 24
    Moon landing ideas, 27, 47, 49, 52
    NASA, 14
    Saturn V rocket, 12, 44, 52–53, 64, 193
    Super Guppies, 160
    V-2 rocket, 10–12
von Kármán, Theodore, 22, 23
Vostok 1, 19, 22–23

W
waste disposal, 20, 142–143
weight, 30–31, 51, 52, 74, 101, 124–125
weightlessness, 37, 188–189
Wendt, Guenter, 17, 199
White, Edward H., 44, 128, 136, 139, 228
Wolfram, John, 235
Woman in Space Program, 17

Y
yaw, 82–83, 88

JOHN ROCCO is a *New York Times* bestselling author and illustrator of many acclaimed books for children, including *Blackout,* recipient of the Caldecott Honor. Rocco has illustrated the covers for Rick Riordan's internationally bestselling series Percy Jackson and the Olympians, Magnus Chase and the Gods of Asgard, and The Trials of Apollo. He also created the illustrations for the #1 *New York Times* bestsellers *Percy Jackson's Greek Gods* and *Percy Jackson's Greek Heroes.* Before making children's books, Rocco spent many years as creative director for Walt Disney Imagineering. If he couldn't make books, he would like to work as an engineer for NASA. He hopes this book will serve as his application. Rocco lives in Rhode Island with his wife, daughter, and several demanding animals. To find out more, visit roccoart.com.

APOLLO LUNAR LANDINGS

MARE
IMBRIUM
(Sea of Rains)

OCEANUS PROCELLARUM
(Ocean of Storms)

SINUS
AESTUUM
(Seething Bay)

APOLLO 12

Oceanus Procellarum

November 19, 1969

APOLLO 14

Fra Mauro

February 5, 1971

MARE NUBIUM
(Sea of Clouds)

MARE
HUMORUM
(Sea of Moisture)